MW00331122

DUMBARTON OAKS
MEDIEVAL LIBRARY

Jan M. Ziolkowski, General Editor

OLD ENGLISH LIVES OF SAINTS

VOLUME II

ÆLFRIC

DOML 59

Old English
Lives of Saints

VOLUME II

ÆLFRIC

Edited and Translated by

MARY CLAYTON
and
JULIET MULLINS

DUMBARTON OAKS
MEDIEVAL LIBRARY

HARVARD UNIVERSITY PRESS

CAMBRIDGE, MASSACHUSETTS

LONDON, ENGLAND

2019

First Printing

Library of Congress Cataloging-in-Publication Data
Names: Aelfric, Abbot of Eynsham, author. | Clayton, Mary, 1954– editor,
    translator. | Mullins, Juliet, editor, translator. | Aelfric, Abbot of
    Eynsham. Lives of saints. | Aelfric, Abbot of Eynsham. Lives of saints.
    English. (Clayton and Mullins)
Title: Old English lives of saints / Aelfric ; edited and translated by Mary
    Clayton, and Juliet Mullins.
Other titles: Lives of saints | Dumbarton Oaks medieval library ; 58–60.
Description: Cambridge, Massachusetts : Harvard University Press, 2019. |
    Series: Dumbarton Oaks medieval library ; 58–60 | Includes
    bibliographical references and index. | Text in Old English with English
    translation on facing pages; introduction and notes in English.
Identifiers: LCCN 2019015955 | ISBN 9780674425095 (v. 1 ; alk. paper) |
    ISBN 9780674241299 (v. 2 ; alk. paper) | ISBN 9780674241725 (v. 3 ; alk.
    paper)
Subjects: LCSH: Christian saints—Biography—Early works to 1800. |
    Christian women saints—Biography—Early works to 1800. | Christian
    literature, English (Old) | Devotional literature, English—Early works
    to 1800.
Classification: LCC PR1527 .A23 2019 | DDC 270.092/2 [B]—dc23
LC record available at https://lccn.loc.gov/2019015955

Contents

CONTENTS

SHROVE SUNDAY

Shrove Sunday

Þis spel gebyrað seofon niht ær lenctene.

In caput ieiunii

I

On ðysse wucan on Wodnes-dæg, swa swa ge sylfe witon,
is *caput ieiunii,* þæt is on Ænglisc heafod lenctenes fæstenes.
We etað on þam Sunnan-dagum on undern and on æfen,
forðan þe se Sunnan-dæg is swa halig
5 þæt se man bið wyrðe, ðe on þam dæge fæstan wile,
þæt he beo amansumod gif he hit for his an-wylnysse dæð,
ne eac man ne mot cneowian on Sunnan-dagum.
We sculon swaþeah ægðer ge on Sunnon-dagum
ge on oðrum dagum druncennysse and ofer-fylle forbugan,
10 be ðam þe us bec tæcað, and huru swyðost on lencten.
Nu ne beoð na feowertig daga on urum lenctenlicum
                                   fæstene gefyllede
buton we fæsten þær foran to þas feower dagas,
Wodnes-dæg and Þunres-dæg and Frige-dæg and Sæternes-
                                   dæg,
swa swa hit gefyrn geset wæs, þeah ðe we hit eow nu secgan.

Shrove Sunday

This sermon belongs seven days before Lent.

For the Beginning of Fasting

I

In this week on Wednesday, as you yourselves know, is the *beginning of fasting,* that is in English the beginning of the Lenten fast. We eat on Sundays at nine in the morning and in the evening, because Sunday is so holy that the person 5 who wishes to fast on that day deserves to be excommunicated if he does it out of willfulness, nor is one allowed to kneel on Sundays. Nevertheless, both on Sundays and on other days, we must shun drunkenness and overindulgence, as books teach us, and most of all in Lent. Now forty days 10 will not be completed in our Lenten fast unless we fast for these four days beforehand, Wednesday and Thursday and Friday and Saturday, as it was decreed long ago, although we are telling you this only now.

15   On þone Wodnes-dæg, wide geond eorðan,
sacerdas bletsiað, swa swa hit geset is,
clæne axan on cyrcan and þa siððan lecgað
uppan manna heafda, þæt hi habban on gemynde
þæt hi of eorðan comon and eft to duste gewendað,
20   swa swa se ælmihtiga God to Adame cwæð
siððan he agylt hæfde ongean Godes bebod:
"On geswincum þu leofast and on swate þu etst
þinne hlaf on eorðan, oðþæt þu eft gewende
to þære ylcan eorðan þe þu of come,
25   forðan þe þu eart dust, and to duste gewendst."
Nis þis na gesæd be manna sawlum,
ac be manna lic-haman, þe formolsniað to duste,
and eft sceolan on domes-dæg ðurh ures Drihtnes mihte
ealle of eorðan arisan þe æfre cuce wæron,
30   swa swa ealle treowa cuciað æfre on lenctenes timan,
þe ær þurh wyntres cyle wurdon adydde.

2

We rædað on bocum, ægðer ge on ðære ealdan æ ge on þære niwan, þæt þa menn þe heora synna behreowsodon, þæt hi mid axum hi sylfe bestreowodon, and mid hæran hi gescryddon to lice. Nu do we þis lytle on ures lenctenes anginne, þæt we streowiað axan uppan ure heafda to geswutelunge þæt we sculon ure synna behreowsian on ure lenctenlicum fæstene.

2. Sum ungerad mann wæs mid Ælfstane bisceope on Wiltunscire on hirede. Se man nolde gan to ðam axum on þone Wodnes-dæg, swa swa oðre men dydon þe þa mæssan

On the Wednesday, far and wide throughout the earth, 15
priests, as it is decreed, bless clean ashes in church and then
put them on people's heads, so that they may keep in mind
that they came from earth and will return again to dust, as 20
the almighty God said to Adam after he had sinned against
God's command: "In toil shall you live and in sweat shall you
eat your bread on earth, until you return back to that same
earth from which you came, because you are dust and to 25
dust you shall return." This is not said about people's souls,
but about people's bodies, which will crumble to dust, and
on judgment day, through the power of our Lord, all who
were ever alive will have to arise again from the earth, just 30
like all trees that had been killed by the winter's cold always
come to life again in the springtime.

2

We read in books, both in the old law and in the new, that
those people who repented of their sins covered themselves
with ashes, and they clothed their bodies with sackcloth.
Now let us do this little thing at the beginning of our Lent,
that we sprinkle ashes on our heads as a sign that we must
repent of our sins in our Lenten fast.

2. There was a foolish man living in Bishop Ælfstan's
household in Wiltshire. This man refused to receive the
ashes on the Wednesday, as other people did who went to

gesohton. Þa bædon his geferan þæt he eode to þam mæsse-
preoste and underfæncge þa gerynu þe hi underfengon. He
cwæð: "Ic nelle." Hi bædon þa git. He cwæð þæt he nolde
and wealode mid wordum and sæde þæt he wolde his wifes
brucan on þam unalyfedum timan. Hi leton þa swa and hit
gelamp þæt se gedwola rad on ðære wucan ymbe sum
ærende. Þa gestodon hine hundas hetelice swyðe and he
hine werode oþþæt his sceaft ætstod ætforan him and þæt
hors hine bær forð, swa þæt þæt spere him eode þurh ut, and
he feoll cwelende. He wearð ða bebyrged and him læg onuppan fela byrðena eorðan binnon seofon nihton, þæs ðe he
forsoc þa feawa axan.

3. On þære ylcan wucan com sum truð to þæs bisceopes
hirede. Se ne gymde nanes lenctenes fæstenes ac eode him
to kicenan þa hwile ðe se bisceop mæssode and began to
etenne. He feoll þa æt ðære forman snæde underbecc geswogen and spaw blod, ac him gebyrede swaðeah þæt feorh
earfoðlice. Us sæde eac oft Aþelwold, se halga bisceop þe nu
wyrcð wundra ðurh God, þæt he cuðe anne mann mid
Ælfege bisceope, se wolde drincan on lenctene þone hine
lyste. Þa sume dæg bæd he þone bisceop Ælfeh blætsian his
ful. He nolde and se dysiga dranc butan bletsunge and eode
him ut. Man slætte þa ænne fearr feringa þær-ute and se fear
arn him togeanes and hine ðyde þæt he his feorh forlet, and
gebohte swa ðone untiman drenc. Ælc þæra manna þe yt
oððe drincð on untiman on þam halgan lenctene, oððe on
rihtfæsten-dagum, wite he to soðan þæt his sawl sceal sarlice
hit gebicgan, ðeah þe se lic-hama her lybbe gesund.

the Mass. Then his companions begged him to go to the priest and to receive the rites that they had received. He said: "I do not want to." They still begged him. He said that he was not willing and spoke shamelessly and said that he intended to have sexual intercourse with his wife at that forbidden time. They left it like that then, and it happened that the fool rode that week on some errand. Then dogs attacked him very viciously and he defended himself until his spear shaft became fixed in the ground in front of him, and his horse carried him forward, so that the spear went right through him, and he fell dying. Then he was buried and within seven days there lay upon him many loads of earth, because he had refused those few ashes.

3. In that same week a trumpet player came to the bishop's household. He did not observe any Lenten fast but went to the kitchen while the bishop was saying Mass and began to eat. Then at the first morsel he fell backward, unconscious, and spat up blood, but nevertheless his life was preserved with difficulty. Æthelwold, the holy bishop, who now works miracles with the aid of God, also often told us that he knew a man in the house of Bishop Ælfheah, who used to drink in Lent whenever he wished. Then one day he asked Bishop Ælfheah to bless his cup. He refused, and the fool drank without his blessing and went outside. By chance a bull was being baited outside and the bull ran toward him and gored him so that he lost his life, and thus paid for his untimely drink. Let every person who eats or drinks at an improper time in the holy Lent, or on prescribed fast days, truly know that his soul will have to pay sorely for it, although his body may live uninjured here.

4. We sceolan gewilnian symle þæs ecan lifes, forþan þe on þam life syndon gode dagas—na swaþeah manega dagas ac an, se ne geendað næfre. Þeah þe hwa wille her on life habban gode dagas, he ne mæg hi her findan, þeah þe he sy welig, forðan þe he bið oþþe untrum oððe hohfull, oþþe his frynd him ætfeallað oððe his feoh him ætbyrst oððe sum oðer ungelimp on þysum life him becymð, and þær-toecan he him ondræt his deaðes symble. Ne bið nan þyssera yfela on þam ecan life, ac bið se an goda dæg mid Gode sylfum, butan sorge and sare and ealra geswencednyssa, and ungeendod blis betwux eallum halgum. Wel mæg gehwa witan þæt, gif ahwær is myrcð and wuldor, þæt þær is unasecgendlic wuldor þær se wunað þe ealle ðincg gesceop, and God sylf hæfð gehaten eallum þam ðe hine lufiað þæt hi moten wunian on ðam ylcan wuldre mid him sylfum, a butan ende. Wite nu þæt God ne lihð næfre and warna þæt þu him ne leoge. Gif þu him lihst ne bepæcst þu na hine, ac þe sylfne swyþe wraðe.

5. Mænig welig man is on ðyssere worulde þe wolde mycelne scet and ungerim feos syllan wið þam, gif he hit gebicgan mihte, þæt he her for worulde lybban moste butan eallum geswyncum, æfre ungeendod, and him ealle þincg gelumpon swa swa him sylfum gelicode, and he wære orsorh æfre ælces yfeles. Ðeah þe hit swa beon mihte þæt he þas blisse begitan mihte þe ic nu foresæde, nære hit swaðeah þe geliccre þære ecan myrhðe þonne bið þam menn þe sit on cweart-erne wið þam menn þe færð frig geond land. Nu se rica mann ne mæg her habban, þe ma þe ure ænig, þa orsorgan and þa unateorigendlican blysse. Hwi nele he þonne

4. We must always desire eternal life, because in that life there are good days — not many days, however, but one, one that will never end. Though someone may wish to have good days here in this life, he cannot find them here, even if he be wealthy, because he will be either ill or full of care, or his friends will desert him or his money will be lost to him or some other misfortune will befall him in this life, and in addition he will always be afraid of his death. There will be none of these evils in the eternal life, but there will be the one good day with God himself, without sorrow and pain and all affliction, and bliss without end among all the saints. Everyone is capable of knowing that if there is joy and glory anywhere, there is inexpressible glory where he lives who created all things, and God himself has promised all those who love him that they may live in that same glory with him, forever without end. Know now that God never lies and take heed that you do not lie to him. If you lie to him you will not deceive him at all, but you will deceive yourself very badly.

5. There is many a wealthy man in this world who would be willing to give a large payment and incalculable wealth on condition that, if he could purchase it, he would be permitted to live here in this world free from all hardships, eternally without end, and that all things would happen to him as pleased him, and that he would always be unconcerned about any harm. Even if it could so happen that he could obtain that happiness that I have just mentioned, nevertheless it would not be any more like the eternal joy than is the person who sits in prison compared to the person who goes free throughout the land. Now the rich person cannot have here, any more than any of us, that carefree and unceasing

oððe we gebycgan on þysum earmum life þa ecan myrhðe mid godum geearnungum and ælmys-dædum? Git we magan secgan sume bysne be þysum. Gif man læt nu ænne þeof to slege, hu wenst ðu? Nolde he syllan ealle his æhta, þeah þe he welig wære, wið þan þe he libban moste, gif man him þæs geðafian wolde? He ne mihte swaþeah æfre libban, þeah ðe he hine þa ut alysde, ac he hæfde fyrst ane feawa geara.

6. Bið nu micel ræd þam þe his sylfes recð þæt he him ge-bycge þæt ece lif þe we embe spræcað. Nu þencst ðu and cwiðst, hu mæg ic þæt ece lif gebycgan? Ic ðe secge, sele þe sylfne Gode, swa þæt þu lufige þa ðingc þe God lufað and þa ðincg onscunie þe God onscunað. God ascunað leasunga and lufað soðfæstnysse. Ne beo þu na leas-breda oþþe swicol, ac beo soðfæst and symle getrywe, forðan þe se trywleasa ne bið nanum hlaforde to hæbbenne ne eac se soðfæsta God his ne recð.

7. Hit bið swiðe langsum þæt we ealle Godes beboda her nu eow gereccan, ac doð an ðincg: cepe gehwa þæt he his lif on unnyt ne aspende ac leornige Godes beboda æt wisum lareowum and þa healde swa he selost mæge. Gif he hwæt tobrece ongean Godes willan, bete þæt georne—þonne bið he Godes mann and God him sylð to medes þæt ece lif þe we ær embe spræcon.

8. Nu bið ælc mann gefullod on naman þære halgan Þryn-nysse and he ne mot na beon eft gefullod, þæt ne sy forsewen þære halgan Ðrynnysse toclypung. Ac seo soðe behreow-sung and dæd-bot mid geswicennyssum yfeles us aþwyhð eft fram urum synnum, þe we æfter urum fulluhte gefremedon.

happiness. Why then is he (or are we) not willing to purchase that eternal joy in this wretched life, by good actions that deserve reward and by acts of almsgiving? Furthermore, we can relate an example of this. If a thief were now being led to death, what do you think? Would he not be willing to give all his possessions, wealthy though he might be, provided he might live, if this were allowed him? Nevertheless he could not live forever, even if he were to purchase his freedom then, but he would have a respite of only a few years.

6. Now it is very advisable that he who cares about himself should purchase for himself that eternal life of which we speak. Now you think and say, how can I purchase that eternal life? I say to you, give yourself to God, so that you love the things that God loves and reject the things that God rejects. God abhors lies and loves truth. Do not be a deceiver or treacherous, but be true and always faithful, because the faithless man is of no value for any lord to have, nor does the true God care about him.

7. It would take a very long time for us to tell you all of God's commands here now, but do one thing: let each person take heed that he not squander his life in idleness, but let him learn God's commands from wise teachers and observe them as best he can. If he should violate something against God's will, let him eagerly atone for that—then he will be God's man and God will give him, as a reward, that eternal life about which we spoke earlier.

8. Now every person is baptized in the name of the holy Trinity and he may not be baptized again, so that the invocation of the holy Trinity may not be held in contempt. But true repentance and penance along with abstention from evil will cleanse us again from our sins that we committed

Se mild-heorta God cwæð be eallum synfullum mannum twa word swiðe fremfulle: *Declina a malo, et fac bonum.* Þæt is: "Buh fram yfele, and do god." Nis na genoh þæt þu fram yfele buge butan þu symle be þinre mæðe god gefremme. Dæd-bot mid geswicennysse yfeles, and ælmys-dæda, and halige gebedu, and geleafa, and hiht on Gode, and seo soðe lufu Godes and manna, gehælað and gelacniað ure synna, gif we þa læcedomas geornlice begað.

9. God cwæð þæt he nolde þæs synfullan deað, ac he wile swyðor þæt he gecyrre fram his synnum and libbe. Eft cwæð se ælmihtiga God: "Gif se arleasa and se synfulla wyrcð dæd-bote ealra his synna and hylt mine beboda and rihtwysnysse begæð, he lifað and ne swylt na yfelum deaðe, and ic ne gemune nanre his synna þe he gefremode." Nis nan leahter swa healic þæt man ne mæge gebetan, gif he yfeles geswycð and mid soðre behreowsunge his gyltas be lareowa tæcinge behreowsað. Se man þe wile his synna bewepan and wið God gebetan, þone mot he geornlice warnian, þæt he æft þam yfelum dædum ne geedlæce.

10. Se man þe æfter his dæd-bote his manfullan dæda geedniwað se gegremað God and he bið þam hunde gelic þe spywð and eft ytt þæt þæt he ær aspaw. Ne nan man ne sceal elcian þæt he his synna gebete, forðan þe God behet ælcum behreowsigendum his synna forgifnysse, ac he ne behet nanum elciendum gewis lif oþ mergen. Ne sceamige nanum menn þæt he anum lareowe his gyltas cyðe, forðan þe se þe nele his synna on ðissere worulde andettan mid soðre behreowsunge, him sceal sceamian ætforan Gode ælmihtigum, and ætforan his engla werodum, and ætforan eallum mannum, and ætforan eallum deoflum æt ðam micclan dome þær we ealle gegaderode beoð.

after our baptisms. The merciful God uttered two very beneficial commands with respect to all sinful people: *Decline from evil, and do good.* That is: "Turn from evil, and do good." It is not enough that you turn from evil unless you always do good according to your ability. Penance with abstention from evil, and acts of almsgiving, and holy prayers, and faith, and hope in God, and the true love of God and human beings, heal and cure our sins, if we eagerly practice these remedies.

9. God said that he did not desire the death of the sinful person, but he wishes rather that he should turn from his sins and live. The almighty God said another time: "If the wicked and the sinful man does penance for all of his sins and keeps my commandments and practices righteousness, he will live and not die an evil death, and I will remember none of the sins that he committed." There is no sin so great that one cannot atone for it, if one abstains from evil and repents of one's offenses with true repentance, in accordance with scholars' teaching. The person who is willing to weep over his sins and atone to God for them must then eagerly take heed that he not repeat the evil deeds again.

10. The person who resumes his evil deeds after his penance angers God, and he is like the dog who vomits and then eats what he had earlier vomited up. No person ought to procrastinate in atoning for his sins, because God promised every penitent forgiveness for his sins, but he did not promise certain life until the next day to any procrastinator. Let no person be ashamed to reveal his sins to a single teacher, because he who is not willing to confess his sins with true repentance in this world will have to be ashamed before almighty God, and before the hosts of his angels, and before all people, and before all the devils at that great judgment where we will all be gathered.

13

11. Þær beoð cuðe ure ealra dæda eallum þam werodum, and se ðe ne mæg for sceame his gyltas anum menn geandettan, him sceal þone sceamian ætforan heofon-warum and eorð-warum and hel-warum, and seo sceamu him bið endeleas. Witodlice ne begit nan mann hys synna forgifnysse æt Gode, buton he hi sumum Godes menn geandette and be his dome gebete.

12. Eft ne mot nan mann ne ne sceal secgan on hine sylfne þæs ðe he wyrcende næs, swa swa we on bocum rædað be sumum treowfæstum wife, þe wolde hire lif forlætan ærþan þe heo luge. Hieronimus, se halga lareow, awrat on sumere stowe be ðam wife þus:

3

He cwæð þæt sum wer wære þe his wif forsæde,
swa þæt heo sceolde hi sceandlice forlicgan,
and hi wurdon þa gebrohte buta to ðam deman,
þæt unscyldige wif and se fore-sæda cniht.
5   Hi wurdon þa beswungene and swyðlice getintregode,
swa swa þa wæs gewunelic to witnigenne forligr.
Hi man clifrode þa mid isenum clawum,
þæt hi sceoldan secgan hweðer hit soð wære.
    Ða wolde se cniht his wite geendian
10 mid sceortum deaðe and forsæde hi buta.
Þa cwæð þæt an-ræde wif betwux þam anðræcum witum:
"Eala ðu Drihten Crist, þe ealle digle þincg wast,
ðu þe eart modes smeagend and manna heortan,
þu wast þæt ic ne wiðsace þæt ic sylf ne forfare,
15 ac ic nelle secgan unsoð on me sylfe,

11. There all our deeds will be known to all the hosts, and he who for shame cannot confess his sins to one man will then have to be ashamed before the inhabitants of heaven and the inhabitants of earth and the inhabitants of hell, and that shame will be endless for him. Truly no man will obtain forgiveness from God for his sins, unless he confess them to some man of God and atone according to the penance that he imposes.

12. Then again, no one may nor ought to accuse himself of something that he did not do, as we read in books concerning a faithful woman, who was willing to lose her life sooner than lie. Jerome, the holy teacher, wrote in one place about this woman thus:

3

He said that there was a man who falsely accused his wife of having shamefully committed adultery, and they were both then brought to the judge, the innocent wife and the young man already mentioned. They were then beaten and severely 5 tortured, as was customary then in order to punish adultery. Then they were clawed with iron claws, to make them say whether it was true.

The young man then wished to put an end to his torture with a quick death and falsely accused them both. Then the 10 resolute woman said during the terrible tortures: "You Lord Christ, who knows all secret things, you who are the searcher of the minds and hearts of people, you know that I do not deny this in order not to die, but I am not willing to 15

þæt ic wið þe ne syngie gif ic me sylfe forleoge."
Heo cwæð þa to ðam cnihte: "Eala þu forcuðost manna!
Hwi woldest þu forsecgan unc unscildige swa?
Ic wylle eac sweltan, na scyldig swaþeah,

20 and ic ferige mid me forð unsceðþignysse
forðan þe nateshwon ne swylt se þe bið ofslagan to life."

Þa wundrode se dema þæs wifes an-rædnysse,
þæt heo nolde andettan on swa earfoþum witum
þæt se cniht sæde sona for yrhðe,

25 and demde þæt hi man sceolde ofslean buta.
Þa arn þæt folc to ardlice for wafunge
and se cwellere sloh sona þone cniht
þe hine sylfne forleah, þæt he læg heofodleas
mid anum swencge, and hine siððan bewende

30 to þam an-rædan wife: wolde hi ofslean.
Heo let to slege and he sloh þa to
mid eallum mægene, ac þæt swurd ne mihte
buton þa hyde ceorfan, þeah þe he hetelice sloge.
He wearð þa ofsceamod and sloh eft swiðe.

35 Þa ætstod þæt swurd and þone swuran ne hrepode,
ac þam cwellere ætfeoll færlice his gold,
þa þa he swa hetelice his handa cwehte.
Þæt wif him cwæð to: "Cniht, nim þin gold,
þe læs þe hit þe losige þæt ðu lange beswunce."

40 Swa orsorh wæs þæt wif under þam wæl-hreowan cwellere
þæt heo locode his goldes þe hi belifian wolde.
Þa sloh se cwellere git mid þam swurde hire to,
ac seo halige Þrynnys þæt swurd gelette,
þæt hit wundian ne moste þæs wifes swuran.

45 Þa wolde he þurhþyn hi þwyres mid þam swurde,
ac se ord bigde upp to þam hiltum:

tell an untruth against myself, that I may not sin against you if I perjure myself." Then she said to the young man: "You most wicked of men! Why were you willing to accuse us two innocent ones falsely like this? I also wish to die, but yet am not guilty, and I will carry my innocence with me to the next 20 life because he does not die at all who is killed in order to live."

Then the judge marveled at the woman's resolution, that among such painful tortures she refused to confess what the young man had said immediately out of cowardice, and he 25 judged that they should both be killed. Then the people ran there quickly for the spectacle and the executioner immediately struck the young man who had perjured himself, so that he lay headless with one stroke, and afterward he turned to the resolute woman: he intended to kill her. 30

She bent down for the stroke and then he struck with all his might, but the sword could cut only the skin, even though he struck violently. He was ashamed then and struck again powerfully. Then the sword came to a halt and did not 35 touch the neck, but his gold suddenly fell from the executioner's grasp, when he was shaking his hands so violently. The woman said to him: "Young man, take your gold, lest you lose that for which you have worked for a long time." So 40 unconcerned was the woman while submitting to the cruel executioner that she paid attention to the gold belonging to him who wished to deprive her of life. Then the executioner struck at her again with his sword, but the holy Trinity stopped the sword, so that it might not wound the woman's neck. Then he wished to pierce her through with his sword, 45 but the point bent up to the hilt: it did not dare touch her

ne dorste hi hreppan forðan þe heo næs dyrne forligr.
Þa cwæð eall seo meniu þe ðær mid stod ofwundrod
þæt se cwellere ne sceolde swencan hi na leng,
50 and drifan hine aweg, mid wæpne mid ealle.

God wolde þa git his wundra geswutelian
þurh þæt an-ræde wif, and him gewearð þa eallum
þæt man funde niwe swurd and niwne slagan þær-to,
forðan þe Crist wolde hi geedcucian of deaðe.
55 Heo wearð þa ofslagan, ac hire swura næs þurhslagen.
Heo wæs swaþeah dead and sona bebyrged,
ac God hi eft aærde eaðelice of deaðe
on þære ylcan nihte and heo ansund lyfode
on worulde siððan lange, to wuldre þam Ælmihtigan,
60 se þe hyre unscæððignysse swa geswutelode mid wundrum.
Heo nolde seccgan unsoð and hi sylfe fordeman,
forðan þe se leasa muð ofslihð þæs mannes sawle.

Nu ge habbað gehyred þæt ge forhelan ne sceolan
eowre agenne synne ne eac secgan na mare
65 þonne ge wyrcende wæron, þe ma þe þis wif dyde,
forðan þe ælc hiwung is antsæte Gode.
Se cniht leah on hine sylfne and ofslagen wearð sona,
swa eac Dauid cynincg het acwellan þone mann
þe him sæde þæt he ofsloge Saul þone cynincg,
70 and wolde mid þære leasunge licettan wið Dauid.
Dauid clypode þa ða se cniht dead wæs:
"Nu ðu cwæde þæt þu acwealdest þone cynincg Saul,
beo þin blod ofer þe and bufan þinum heafde."

because she was not a secret adulterer. Then all the crowd that stood there, astonished, said that the executioner must not torment her any longer, and they drove him away, 50 weapon and all.

God still intended to reveal his miracles through that resolute woman, and they all agreed that a new sword be found and a new killer besides, because Christ wished to restore her to life again from death. Then she was slain, but her 55 neck was not cut through. Nevertheless she was dead and immediately buried, but God easily raised her again from death on that same night and she lived in good health for a long time afterward in the world, to the glory of the Almighty, who had revealed her innocence in this way with 60 miracles. She refused to tell a lie and damn herself, because the lying mouth kills the person's soul.

Now you have heard that you must not conceal your own sins nor tell any more than you have committed either, any 65 more than this woman did, because every false speech is repugnant to God. The young man lied about himself and was killed immediately, just as king David also commanded the man to be killed who told him that he had killed Saul the king, and with this lie wished to pretend to David. David 70 called out when the young man was dead: "Now that you have said that you killed Saul the king, let your blood be on you and on your head."

4

Se man þe wile his synna andettan and gebetan, he sceal don
þonne forgifnysse eallum þam mannum þe him ær abulgon,
swa swa hit stent on þam *Pater nostre,* and swa swa Crist
cwæð on his god-spelle. He cwæð: "Buton ge forgifan þam
mannum þe wið eow agyltað mid inwerdre heortan, nele se
heofonlica Fæder eow forgifen eowre gyltas." Ælc Cristen
man sceal cunnan his *Pater noster* and his credan. Mid þam
Pater nostre he sceal hine gebiddan and mid þam credan he
sceal his geleafan getrymman. Se lareow sceal secgan þam
læwedum mannum þæt andgyt to þam *Pater nostre* and to
ðam credan, þæt hi witon hwæs hi biddað æt Gode, and hu
hi sceolon on God gelyfan.

5

We sceolan beon þeonde symble on godnysse
and elce dæg geeacnian us þa ecan speda
þa hwile þe we moton, forðan þe we ne magon
æfter ure geendunge aht to gode don,
5   ac þær we habbað edlean þæs ðe we geearnodon her.
Ne sceal nan mann wenan ne on his mode þencan
þæt he hæbbe gefremod fela to gode
and ne þurfe na mare þyllices began,
forðan þe he forlyst þæt lytle þæt he ær dyde,
10 gif he wenð þæt he ne ðurfe þanon forð wyrcan
nan þincg to gode, swylce he to god sy.
Fela halige men, fram frymðe middan-eardes,
wæron beforan us wundorlice geþogene,
þam we nu ende-menn geefenlæcan ne magon,

4

The person who wishes to confess and atone for his sins must then forgive all the people who had offended him previously, as it stands in the *Our Father,* and as Christ said in his gospel. He said: "Unless you forgive those people who sin against you with your innermost heart, the heavenly Father will not be willing to forgive your sins." Every Christian person must know his *Our Father* and his creed. With the *Our Father* he must pray and with the creed he must strengthen his faith. The teacher must tell lay people the meaning of the *Our Father* and the creed, so that they may know what they pray to God for, and how they must believe in God.

5

We ought always to be advancing in goodness, and every day increase eternal riches for ourselves while we may, because we cannot do anything good after our deaths, but then we will have the reward for what we will have earned here. No person ought to believe or think in his heart that he has done much that is good and that he need not engage in any more of that sort, because he will lose the little that he did before, if he believes that he need not from then on do anything good, as if he were too good. Many holy people before us, from the beginning of the world, were wonderfully advanced in spirit, whom we, people of the last age, cannot

15 ne ða þing gefyllan þe hi gefremodon on life —
forði we sceolan habban huru ead-modnysse.
Eft is us to smeagenne hu se ælmihtiga Crist
his ead-modnysse cydde þa ða he to cwale sealde
hine sylfne for us, and swa ure synna ætbræd.

20 Hu mæg nu manna ead-modnys beon mycel geþuht
togeanes his ead-modnysse þe ælmihtig God is?
Sy him a wuldor on ecnysse. Amen.

6

We sædon nu þis spel, forðan þe her bið læs manna on
Wodnes-dæg and eow gebyrað þæt ge beon gescrifene on
ðissere wucan, oððe huru on ðære oðre.

emulate, nor can we carry out the things that they per- 15
formed in their lives—therefore we ought at least to have
humility. Moreover, we must consider how almighty Christ
revealed his humility when he gave himself to death for us,
and so took away our sins. How can people's humility now 20
be considered great compared to his humility, who is almighty God? Glory be to him in eternity. Amen.

6

We have delivered this sermon now, because there will be
fewer people here on Wednesday and it is fitting for you to
be confessed during this week, or at least during the next
one.

ON THE PRAYER
OF MOSES FOR
MID-LENT SUNDAY

On the Prayer of Moses for Mid-Lent Sunday

De oratione Moysi: In medio Quadragesimae

Æfter ðam ðe Moyses se mæra here-toga
of Aegypta lande mid his leode ferde
and ofer ða Readan Sæ siðodon mid fotum
and becomon to ðam westene, þa wan him on swiðe
5 Amalech se cynincg, mid his leode feohtende.
Þa cwæð Moyses to þam cenan Iosue:
"Geceos ðe nu wæras and gewend tomergen
togeanes Amaleh and win him on swyðe.
Ic sylf wille standan on ðisum steapum munte,
10 hæbbende me on handa þa halgan Godes gyrde."
Iosue þa ferde and feaht wið Amalech
and Moyses þa astah to þam sticolan munte
mid Aarone and Hur, þone Ælmihtigan to biddenne.
Þa ahefde Moyses his handa on gebedum
15 and Iosue hæfde sige and sloh þa hæðenan.
Eft ðonne Moyses ne mihte lencg habban
his handa astrehte, þonne hæfde Amalech
sige þa hwile and sloh þæt Godes folc.

On the Prayer of Moses for Mid-Lent Sunday

On the Prayer of Moses: In Mid-Lent

After Moses the great army leader had departed from the land of Egypt with his people and had traveled over the Red Sea on foot and had arrived at the desert, then Amalek the king attacked him fiercely, fighting with his people. Then Moses said to the brave Joshua: "Choose men for yourself now and tomorrow go against Amalek and attack him fiercely. I myself intend to stand on this high mountain, holding the staff of holy God in my hand." Joshua then went and fought against Amalek, and Moses then climbed up the high mountain with Aaron and Hur, to pray to the Almighty. Moses then raised up his hands in prayer, and Joshua was victorious and killed the heathens. Then when Moses could no longer hold his hands outstretched, Amalek had victory for that time and killed God's people. Whenever Moses

Swa oft swa Moyses ahefde his handa on gebedum,

20 swa hæfde Iosue heofonlicne fultum,
and sona swa his earmas for unmihte aslacodon
sona sloh Amalech and sige hæfde on him.
Moyses handa wæron mycclum gehefegode.
Aaron þa alede ænne ormetne stan

25 under Moysen and he sæt þær onuppan
and Aaron ahæfde his hand upp on gebedum
and Hur heold þa oðre oþþæt hit æfnode.
Iosue þa hæfde heofonlicne fultum
and afligde Amalech and his folc mid wæpnum.

30 Be þisum we magon tocnawen þæt we Cristene sceolan
on ælcere earfoðnisse æfre to Gode clypian
and his fultumes biddan mid fullum geleafan.
Gif he ðonne nele his fultum us don
ne ure bene gehyran, þonne bið hit swutol

35 þæt we mid yfelum dædum hine ær gegremedon,
ac we ne sceolon swaðeah geswican þære bene
oðþæt se mild-heorta God us mildelice ahredde.
Moyses hæfde sige and mycelne fultum
þa hwile þe he heold his handa on gebedum

40 and his willa ne ateorode, ac se werige lic-hama.

Nu habbe we gewinn wið þone hetelan deofol
and he winð on us forðan þe he wæl-hreow is.
Hu bið þonne gif we nellað to þam hælende clypian,
þonne Moyses werignyss ne mihte beon beladod?

45 Witodlice bið oferswiðed þurh þone swicolan deofol
se ðe nele clypian Crist him to fultume.
Ælc rihtwis man hæfde, swa swa we rædað on bocum,
fultum and hreddinge, se ðe mid fullum geleafan
on his earfoðnyssum to ðam Ælmihtigan clypode.

raised his hands in prayer, Joshua had heavenly help, and as 20
soon as his arms drooped from weakness then Amalek
struck and was victorious over them. Moses's hands were
terribly heavy. Aaron then placed an enormously large stone
under Moses, and he sat there on it and Aaron raised up one 25
hand in prayer and Hur held the other one until evening
came. Then Joshua had heavenly help and put Amalek and
his people to flight with his weapons.

From this we can understand that we Christians must call 30
to God always in every tribulation and ask for his help with
complete faith. If he is not willing to help us or listen to our
prayer, then it will be clear that we have angered him previ- 35
ously with our evil deeds, but nevertheless we must not
cease from prayer until the merciful God mercifully saves
us. Moses had victory and great help as long as he held up his
hands in prayer, and his will did not weaken, but rather his 40
weary body.

Now we have a battle against the malignant devil, and he
makes war on us because he is cruel. How will it be then if
we are not willing to cry out to the savior, when Moses's
weariness could not be excused? Truly he who is not willing 45
to cry out to Christ to help him will be defeated by the
treacherous devil. Every just person who with perfect faith
has called to the Almighty in his tribulations has had help
and salvation, as we read in books. Nothing is as hateful to 50

50 Nis nan þincg swa lað þam geleafleasum deofle
swa þæt hine man gebidde bealdlice to Gode,
forðan þe se swicola wat þæt his wæpne sceolan
þurh halige gebedu toberstan swiðost,
and he bið oferswiðod simble þurh gebedu.

55 Forþi he cunnað georne, þonne we clypiað to Gode,
hu he mæge tobræcan þa gebedu mid costnungum
and ure mod awendan of þam weorce þurh þæt:
oððe he mid geameleaste huru us gebysgað
oþþe mid smeagungum smealice us hremð.

60 Þonne we us gebiddað mid byle-witum mode,
þonne sprece we soðlice to Gode sylfum swa,
and þonne we bec rædað oððe rædan gehyrað,
þonne sprecð God to us þurh þa gastlican rædincge.
Se man mot hine gebiddan swa swa he mæg and cann,

65 forðan þe se ælmihtiga God cann ælc gereord tocnawan,
and on ælcere stowe man mot mærsian his Drihten
and hine gebiddan, beo þær þær he beo.
Man sceal swaþeah secan cyrcan gelome
and man ne mot spellian ne spræce drifan

70 binnan Godes cyrcan, forðan þe heo is gebed-hus,
Gode gehalgod to þam gastlicum spræcum.
Ne man ne sceal drincan oððe dwollice etan
binnan Godes huse, þe is gehalgod to þam
þæt man Godes lic-haman mid geleafan þær þicge.

75 Nu doð menn swaþeah dyslice foroft,
þæt hi willað wacian and wodlice drincan
binnan Godes huse and bysmorlice plegan
and mid gegaf-spræcum Godes hus gefylan.
Ac ðam wære betere þæt hi on heora bedde lagon

80 ðonne hi gegremedon God on þam gastlican huse.

the faithless devil as that one should pray confidently to God, because the traitor knows that his weapons will be broken by holy prayers above all else, and he will always be defeated by prayers. For this reason he diligently seeks to 55 discover, when we cry out to God, how he may be able to interrupt those prayers with temptations and by that means turn our minds away from that task: either he engages us in negligence at the least, or he cunningly hinders us with questioning.

When we pray with an innocent heart, then we truly 60 speak in this way to God himself, and when we read books or hear them read, then God speaks to us through the spiritual reading. A person may pray in whatever way he is able and knows how to, because the almighty God is able to un- 65 derstand every language, and a person may glorify his Lord in every place and pray, no matter where he may be. Nevertheless one must go to church frequently, and one may not chatter or engage in conversation within God's church, be- 70 cause it is a house of prayer, consecrated to God for spiritual speech. One must not drink or foolishly eat within God's house, which is consecrated in order that one may partake there of God's body with faith. Nevertheless people behave 75 foolishly very often now, in that they are accustomed to keep a vigil and drink insanely within God's house and amuse themselves disgracefully and defile God's house with frivolous talk. But it would be better for them to lie in their beds than to anger God in that sacred house. He who wishes 80

Se þe wylle wacian and wurðian Godes halgan,
wacie mid stilnysse and ne wyrce nan gehlyd,
ac singe his gebedu swa he selost cunne.
And se ðe wile drincan and dwæslice hlydan,
85   drince him æt ham, na on Drihtnes huse,
þæt he God ne unwurðige to wite him sylfum.
Us is neod þæt we clypian to Criste gelome
buton hygeleaste and hiwunge swaðeah.
Swa swa se lic-homa leofað be hlafe and drence
90   swa sceal seo sawl libban be lare and gebedum.
    Fela dyslice dæda deriað man-cynne
oððe for an-wylnysse oððe for ungerade,
swa swa sume menn doð þe dyslice fæstað
ofer heora mihte on gemænelicum lenctene,
95   swa swa we sylfe gesawon, oðþæt hi seoce wurdon.
Sume fæston eac swa, þæt hi forsawon to etanne
buton on ðone oðerne dæg, and æton þonne grædiglice,
ac us secgað bec þæt sume fæston
swa þæt hi geswencton hi sylfe forðearle
100   and nane mede næfdon þæs mycclan geswinces,
ac ðæs þe fyrr wæron fram Godes miltsunge.
Nu gesetton ða halgan fæderas þæt we fæston mid gerade
and ælce dæg eton mid gedafenlicnysse,
swa þæt ure lic-hama alefed ne wurðe
105   ne eft ofermæst to idelum lustum.
Þes eard nis eac ealles swa mægenfæst
her on uteweardan þære eorðan bradnysse,
swa swa heo is tomiddes, on mægenfæstum eardum,
þær man mæg fæstan freolicor ðonne her.
110   Ne nu nis man-cynn swa mihtig swa menn wæron æt
                               fruman.

to keep a vigil and honor God's saints, let him keep vigil in silence and not make any noise, but recite his prayers as best he can. And he who wishes to drink and stupidly make noise, let him drink at home, not in the Lord's house, so that he 85 may not dishonor God and so bring about his own punishment. It is necessary for us to call upon Christ frequently, yet without foolishness and hypocrisy. Just as the body lives by food and drink, so must the soul live by doctrine and 90 prayers.

Many foolish acts harm mankind either because of obstinacy or lack of reason, just like some people do who foolishly fast beyond their strength in the universally observed Lent, as we ourselves have seen, until they became sick. 95 Some people moreover fasted so that they scorned to eat except on every second day and then ate greedily, but books tell us that some people fasted so that they afflicted themselves very severely and had no reward for their great effort, 100 but were the further from God's mercy on account of it. Now the holy fathers decreed that we should fast with discretion and eat appropriately every day, so that our bodies be neither enfeebled nor overfattened, leading to vain de- 105 sires. Also this country is not quite as strong here at the exterior of the earth's extent as it is in the middle, in strong countries, where one can fast more freely than here. Nor is 110 mankind as strong now as people were at the beginning.

Nis nan fæsten swa god ne Gode swa gecweme
swa swa þæt fæsten is þæt man fulnysse onscunige
and leahtras forbuge and forlæte sace
and mid godum biggencgum Gode gecweme
115 and mid gesceade libbe, swa swa we sædon ær.
    Ne sceal se wise mann beon butan godum weorcum,
ne se ealde ne beo buton æwfæstnysse,
ne se iunga ne beo butan gehyrsumnysse,
ne se welega ne beo butan ælmes-dædum,
120 ne wif-men ne beon butan sidefulnysse,
ne se hlaford ne beo leas on wordum,
ne nan Cristen man ne sceal sceandlice flitan.
Eft bið swiðe þwyrlic þæt ðearfa beo modig
and forcuðlic hit bið þæt cyning beo unrihtwis.
125 Eac bið swyþe derigendlic þæt bisceop beo gymeleas
and unfremful bið þæt folc beo butan steora,
oððe butan æ, him eallum to hearme.
    Þissere worulde hæl is þæt heo witan hæbbe,
and swa ma witena beoð on bradnysse middan-eardes,
130 swa hit bet færð æfter ðæs folces þearfa.
Ne bið se na wita þe unwislice leofað,
ac bið open sott, þeah þe him swa ne ðince.
Gif ða gehadodan menn healdað Godes ðeowdom
on gesettan timan and syferlice libbað,
135 and gif ða læwedan menn libbað æfter rihte,
þonne wite we to gewissan þæt God wile foresceawian
ure gesundfulnysse and sibbe mid us,
and ðær-toecan us syllan ða ecan myrhðe mid him.
Gif ðonne þa heafod-menn and ða gehadodan lareowas
140 þyses ne gymað, ac þencað embe woruld-þincg
and Godes beboda ne his biggencga ne gymað,

There is no fasting as good or as pleasing to God as is that fasting that consists of rejecting foulness and shunning vices and abandoning dissension and pleasing God with good practices and living according to reason, as we said before. 115

The wise man must not be without good works, nor the old man be without religion, nor the young man be without obedience, nor the rich man be without almsgiving, nor 120 women be without modesty, nor the lord be false in his words, nor must any Christian be shamefully contentious. Likewise it is very perverse that a poor person should be proud, and it is disgraceful that a king should be unjust. Also 125 it is very harmful that a bishop be negligent, and it is not beneficial that people be without discipline or without law, to the harm of them all.

This world's welfare depends on having wise men, and the more wise men there are on the surface of the earth, the 130 better it goes for the people's needs. He is not a wise man who lives unwisely, but is a public fool, though he may not think so. If those in religious life observe God's service at the set times and live purely, and if the lay people live ac- 135 cording to what is right, then we know for certain that God will be willing to provide for our good fortune and peace among us, and in addition give us eternal happiness with him. Then if the leaders and the teachers in religious life do 140 not care about this, but think about worldly affairs and do not care about God's commandments or his rites, then God

þonne wile God geswutelian his forsewennysse on him,
oððe mid hungre oþþe mid cwealme, þæt hi tocnawan
                                               magon
þæt se ælmihtiga wealdend wrycð his forsewennysse swa,
145 and hi ðær-toecan sceolan on þam oþrum life þrowian
lange oððe æfre for heora lifes gymeleaste.
    Wel we magon geðencan hu wel hit ferde mid us
þa ða þis ig-land wæs wunigende on sibbe
and munuc-lif wæron mid wurðscipe gehealdene
150 and ða woruld-menn wæron wære wið heora fynd,
swa þæt ure word sprang wide geond þas eorðan.
Hu wæs ða siððan ða þa man towearp munuc-lif
and Godes biggengas to bysmore hæfde,
buton þæt us com to cwealm and hunger,
155 and siððan hæðen here us hæfde to bysmre?
    Be swilcum cwæð se ælmihtiga God to Moyse on þam
                                               wæstene:
"Gif ge on minum bebodum farað and mine beboda healdað,
þonne sende ic eow ren-scuras on rihtne timan symble
and seo eorðe spryt hyre wæstmas eow
160 and ic forgife sibbe and gesehtnysse eow,
þæt ge butan ogan eowres eardes brucan,
and ic eac afyrsige ða yfelan deor eow fram.
Gif ge þonne me forseoð and mine gesetnyssa awurpað,
ic eac swyðe hrædlice on eow hit gewrece:
165 ic do þæt seo heofen bið swa heard eow swa isen
and seo eorðe þær-togeanes swylce heo æren sy.
Þonne swince ge on idel gif ge sawað eower land,
ðonne seo eorðe ne spryt eow nænne wæstm.
And gif ge þonne git nellað eow wendan to me,

will wish to demonstrate on them their contempt of him, either by means of famine or plague, so that they may know that this is how the almighty ruler avenges contempt of himself, and in addition to that they will have to suffer in the other life for a long time or forever because of the carelessness of their lives.

We do well to think about how well it turned out for us when this island was living in peace and monasteries were treated with honor and the laity were vigilant against their enemies, so that our fame spread widely throughout this world. How was it then afterward when monasteries were destroyed and God's rites were held in contempt, but that plague and famine came upon us, and then a heathen army held us in contempt?

Almighty God spoke to Moses in the desert concerning this: "If you walk in my commandments and keep my commandments, then I will always send you showers of rain at the right time, and the earth will produce its fruits for you, and I will give you peace and concord, so that you may possess your land without fear, and I shall also take harmful wild animals away from you. But if you hold me in contempt and reject my laws, I will likewise very quickly avenge it on you: I shall cause the heavens to be as hard as iron to you and the earth below it like brass. Then you will toil in vain if you sow your land, since the earth will not produce any crop for you. And if you are not willing to turn to me then, I will send the

170 ic sende eow swurd to and eow sleað eowre fynd
and hi þonne awestað wæl-hreowlice eower land,
and eowre burga beoð tobrocene and aweste.
Ic asende eac yrhðe into eowrum heortum,
þæt eower nan ne dear eowrum feondum wiðstandan."

175 Þus spræc God gefyrn be þam folce Israhel.
Hit is swaðeah swa gedon swyðe neah mid us,
nu on niwum dagum and undigollice.
We sceolan God wurðian mid soðre an-rædnysse,
forðan þe he is ælmihtig and he us to menn gesceop.

180 Nu do we swyðe wolice gif we ne wurðiað hine,
us sylfum to þearfe and urum sawlum to blisse.

God gewræc fram frymðe mid witum his forsewennysse,
ærest on ðam ænglum þe unrædlice modegodon
and siððan on Adame þa þa he gesyngod hæfde,

185 eft on Noes dagum, ða ða menn dysgodon to swyðe
and mid forligre gegremedon God ælmihtigne þearle,
swa þæt he sende flod and besencte hi ealle
butan Noe anum mid his agenum hiwum,
forðan þe he ana wæs of him eallum rihtwis.

190 Eft ða þa God wolde wrecan mid fyre
þa fulan forligeras þæs fracodostan mennisces,
Sodomitiscra ðeoda, þa sæde he hit Abrahame.
Habraham þa bæd þone Ælmihtigan ðus:
"Þu Drihten, þe demst eallum deadlicum flæsce,

195 ne scealt ðu þone rihtwisan ofslean mid þam arleasan.
Gif ðær beoð fiftig wera wunigende on þam earde,
rihtwise ætforan ðe, ara him eallum."
Ða cwæð God him to eft: "Ic arige him eallum
gif ic ðær finde fiftig rihtwisra."

200 Þa began Abraham eft biddan God georne

38

sword to you and your enemies will strike you, and then they will cruelly lay waste your land, and your cities will be ruined and laid waste. I will also send cowardice into your hearts, so that none of you will dare resist your enemies." Thus God 175 spoke of old concerning the people of Israel. It has, however, very nearly happened among us, now in recent days and openly. We must honor God with true constancy, because he is almighty and he created us as human beings. Now we act very wrongly if we do not honor him, for our 180 own need and for our souls' happiness.

From the beginning God avenged contempt of himself by punishments, first on those angels who unadvisedly grew proud and afterward on Adam when he had sinned, again in 185 the days of Noah, when people erred too much and enraged almighty God greatly by their fornication, so that he sent a flood and drowned them all, except for Noah only along with his household, because he alone of them all was just. Likewise when God intended to punish by fire the foul for- 190 nicators of that most wicked people, the people of Sodom, then he told this to Abraham. Abraham then prayed to the Almighty thus: "You Lord, you who judge all mortal flesh, you ought not to kill the just person with the impious per- 195 son. If there are fifty people living in this region, just in your judgment, spare them all." Then God spoke to him again: "I will spare them all if I find fifty just people there." Then Abraham began again to entreat God urgently not to 200

þæt he hi ne fordyde gif ðær feowertig wæron
rihtwisra wera wunigende on ðære leode.

God him ðæs getiþode and he began git biddan
oðþæt he becom to tyn mannum, and him tiðode ða God
205 þæt he nolde hi fordon gif he funde ðær tyn
rihtwisra manna, and he wende ða him fram.

God sende ða sona to ðam sceandlicum mannum
twegen englas on æfen and hi Abrahames broðor sunu,
Loth, mid his hiwum, alæddon of ðære byrig
210 and ðær næs na ma þe manful nære gemet.

God sende ða fyr on merigen and fulne swefel him to
and forbærnde hi ealle and heora burga towende
and ealne þone eard mid egeslicum fyre,
and ðær is nu ful wæter ðær ða fulan wunodon.
215 And Loth se rihtwisa wearð ahred ðurh God.

Be ðysum man mæg tocnawan þæt micclum fremiað
þam læwedum mannum þa gelæredan Godes ðeowas,
þæt hi mid heora ðeowdome him ðingian to Gode,
nu God wolde arian eallum ðam synfullum
220 gif he þær gemette tyn rihtwise menn.

Ealswa Dathan and Abiron ðe dyslice spræcon
and mycelne teonan Moyse gedydon
ongean Godes willan ða ða hi on þam westene wæron,
and forsawon his wisunge and swyðe hine tældon.
225 God him wearð þa yrre and seo eorþe tobærst
þær ðær hi wicodon mid wifum and mid cyldum
on heora geteldum, and hi ealle ða suncon
swa cuce into ðære eorðan, ofrorene mid moldan,
and ðæt oðer folc fleah, afyrht for heora hreame.
230 Manega of ðam folce myslice oft ceorodon
and fandoden Godes and gremedon mid spræcon,

destroy them if there were forty just men living among that people. God granted him that and he began to entreat again until he came to ten people, and God granted him then that 205 he would not destroy them if he found there ten just people, and then he went away from him. God immediately sent two angels in the evening to the shameful people, and they took Abraham's brother's son Lot, with his family, out of the city, and no more were found there who were not evil. Then 210 in the morning God sent fire and foul sulfur to them and burned them all up and destroyed their cities and all that region with a terrifying fire, and now there is foul water where the foul ones lived. And Lot the just man was saved by God. 215 From this it can be known that the learned servants of God greatly benefit lay people, in that they intercede for them with God by their service, since God was willing to spare all the sinful people if he found ten just people there. 220

Likewise with Dathan and Abiram, who spoke foolishly and did great wrong to Moses against God's will, when they were in the desert, and scorned his guidance and reproached him very much. Then God became angry with them and the 225 earth broke in two where they were encamped with their wives and children in their tents, and they all sank into the earth, alive like that, covered by earth, and the other people fled, frightened by their outcry. Many of that people often 230 grumbled in different ways and tried the patience of God and angered him with their speeches, but God immediately

ac God hit gewræc sona þæt hi swultan gehu,
forðan ðe seo ceorung is swyðe lað Gode,
and huru þæt mann gremige hine mid wordum.

235 And Gode is swyðe lað on geleaffullum folce
þæt hi beon ungeðwære and þwyre him betwynan,
and Crist cwæð on his god-spelle þæt nan cyne-rice
ne stent nane hwile ansund, gif hi gesome ne beoð,
and God lufað soðfæstnysse and sibbe on man-cynne.

240 Eft Dauid se cyning, ðeah þe he gecweme were Gode,
agylte swyðe þearle and God him sende ða to
Gad þone witegan, ðas word him secgende:
"Geceos ðe nu an wite, swa swa ðu wyrðe eart,
oþþe ðreo gear hunger oððe þry monðas gewinn,

245 þæt ðu swa lange fleo þine fynd gif ðu mage,
oððe ðry dagas man-cwealm." Þa cwæð Dauid him to:
"Uneaðe me is ðis, ac me is swaðeah leofre
þæt ic on Godes handa befealle þonne ic on mannes handa
                                                      befealle,
forðan þe his mild-heortnyssa syndon mænigfealde."

250 God sende ða sona sumne encgel him to
and se encgel ofsloh hundseofontig ðusenda
on Dauides anwealde, ealle wæp-menn.
Þa com se encgel þær se cynincg sylf wæs
and wolde ða slean þa ceaster-gewaran.

255 Ac Gode ofhreow ða and hraðe cwæð to ðam engle:
"Genoh, genoh hit is nu; heald þine handa."
Þa geseah Dauid sylf hu se encgel sloh þæt folc
and clypode to Gode and cwæð mid angsumnysse:
"Ic eom þe ðær syngode and ic sylf unrihtlice

260 dyde togeanes ðe. Hwæt dydon þas scep?
Ic bidde þæt þu awende wið min þine hand

avenged this in that they died in all sorts of ways, because grumbling is very abhorrent to God, and especially that he should be angered by words. And it is very abhorrent to God in his faithful people that they should be quarrelsome and in a state of discord among themselves, and Christ said in his gospel that no kingdom will stand undamaged for any space of time if they are not united, and God loves truth and peace among mankind.

Likewise David the king, although he may have been pleasing to God, sinned very greatly and God then sent Gad the prophet to him, saying these words to him: "Choose now one punishment for yourself, as you have deserved, either famine for three years, or war for three months, so that you will flee your enemies for that long if you can, or plague for three days." Then David said to him: "This is distressing for me, but nevertheless I prefer to fall into God's hands rather than into the hands of a man, because his mercies are numerous." God then immediately sent an angel to him, and the angel killed seventy thousand in David's realm, all male. Then the angel came to where the king himself was and intended to kill the citizens. But then God felt pity and quickly said to the angel: "Enough, it is enough now; hold back your hand." Then David himself saw how the angel had killed the people and called out to God and said with anguish: "I am the one who sinned there and I myself acted wrongfully against you. What did these sheep do? I beg you to turn your hand against me and your anger against my

and wið minne hired þine hat-heortnysse."
Þa com Gad se witega gangende and cwæð him to:
"Far nu and arær hraðe an weofod Gode
265 and geoffra ðine lac þæt ðes egsa geswice."
Þa dyde Dauid swa and Drihten him gemiltsode
and se encgel ne moste þa menn ofslean leng.
God nolde ofslean þone scyldigan Dauid,
þeah ðe he syngode, forðan þe he swyðe oft dyde
270 ge ær ge siððan swyðe ænlice ðincg,
Gode to gecwemednysse, and God him forði arode.
And ða þe ðær ofslagene wæron heora sawla wæron
                                        gehealdene.

Eft wæs sum leodscipe þe se lifigenda God
wolde gewitnian for heora gewitleasum dædum:
275 þæt wæron ða Niniueiscan þe wodlice færdon.
Þa sende God him to sumne witegan,
Ionas gehaten, and het hi geswican
oððe hi ealle sceoldon endemes forwurðan.
Se cynincg ða gecyrde sona mid his leode
280 to ðam ælmihtigan Gode and hi ealle fæston
ðry dagas on an, and Drihten him gemiltsode.

Ne mæg nan mann awritan ne mid wordum areccan
hu oft se ælmihtiga God egeslice gewræc
his foresewennysse on scyldigum mannum
285 oððe hu oft he gemyltsode man-cynne gehu,
þa ðe mid andetnysse heora yfeles geswicon.
We ne sceolan ceorigan ne sorhlice bemænan,
þeah ðe us ungelimp on æhtum getime,
forðan þe seo ceorung is swyðe mycel pleoh,
290 þæt man wið God ceorige, swa swa us sæde Paulus.
Fela ungelimpa beoð on ende ðissere worulde,

44

household." Then Gad the prophet came and said to him: "Go now and quickly build an altar to God and offer your 265 sacrifice so that the terror may cease." Then David did that, and the Lord had mercy on him and the angel was not allowed to kill people any longer. God did not wish to kill the guilty David, although he had sinned, because he had very often done very excellent things, both before and after that, 270 to God's satisfaction, and God spared him for that reason. And the souls of those who were killed there were saved.

Again there was one people that the living God intended to punish for their foolish deeds: they were the Ninevites 275 who were behaving insanely. Then God sent a prophet to them called Jonah, and commanded them to stop or they would all have to perish together. Then the king immediately turned with his people to the almighty God, and they 280 all fasted for three days continuously, and the Lord had mercy on them.

No one can state in writing or express in words how often the almighty God has terrifyingly avenged on guilty people their contempt of him or how often he has had mercy on 285 mankind in some way, on those who ceased from their evil with confession. We must not grumble or sorrowfully lament, even if misfortune as regards our possessions befall us, because grumbling is a very great danger, that one should 290 grumble against God, as Paul said to us. There will be many misfortunes at the end of this world, but each person must

ac gehwa mot forberan emlice his dæl,
swa þæt he ðurh ceorunge ne syngie wið God
and for ðære woruld-lufe him wite geearnige.

295   Þes tima is ende-next and ende þyssere worulde
and menn beoð geworhte wolice him betwynan,
swa þæt se fæder winð wið his agenne sunu,
and broðor wiþ oþerne, to bealwe him sylfum,
and mid ðam geeacniað yfelnysse him sylfum,
300 ge on ðissere worulde ge on ðære toweardan.
   Þonne ðincð þam arleasum swylce hi æfre motan libban
and ne cunnon ðone cwyde þe God cwæð be swylcum:
Viri sanguinum et dolosi non dimidiabunt dies suos.
"Ða blodigan weras and ða þe willað facn,
305 ne sceolan hi libban heora dagas healfe."
Ða synd blodige weras ðe wyrcað man-slihtas
and ða ðe manna sawla beswicað to forwyrde.
Ða sceolan geendian swyðe yfelum deaðe,
gif hi ær geendunge heora yfel ne gebetað.
310 And ðeah þe hi sume lybbon leng ðonne hi sceoldon,
for Godes geðylde, þæt him ne fremað naht,
ac hi geeacniað heora wita gif hi ær ende ne cyrrað.
   Godes wisdom clypað and cwyð to eallum mannum
mid fæderlicre lufe, þus fægere tihtende:
315 "Min bearn, ne forgit ðu mine beboda and æ,
ac healde ðin heorta hi geornlice.
Hi gelengað þin lif and þu leofast on sibbe
and mild-heortnyss, and soðfæstnys þe soðlice ne forlætað.
Hafa þe truwan on God of ealre ðinre heortan,
320 and ne truwa ðu na swyðe on þinre snoternysse.
Þenc æfre embe God on eallum ðinum wegum
and he sylf gewissað wel þine fare.

endure his lot with equanimity, so that he may not sin against God by grumbling and earn punishment for himself on account of his love of this world.

This time is the last and the end of this world, and people will be evilly disposed among themselves, so that the father will fight with his own son, and brother with brother, to their own destruction, and by that they add to the evil for themselves, both in this world and in the future one. Then it seems to the impious as if they may live forever, and they do not understand the saying that God spoke about such people: *Bloody and deceitful men shall not live out half their days.* "Bloody men and those who intend deceit, they will not live out half their days." Those are bloody men who commit murders and those who betray people's souls to damnation. They shall die with a very evil death, if they do not atone for their evil before their deaths. And even though some of them live longer than they ought to, on account of God's patience, that will not do them any good at all, but they will add to their torments if they do not reform before the end. God's wisdom calls out and says to all people with fatherly love, gently urging them thus: "My child, do not forget my commandments and law, but let your heart guard them diligently. They will lengthen your life and you will live in peace and mercy, and truth truly will not abandon you. Have trust in God with all your heart, and do not trust greatly in your own prudence. Think always about God in all your ways, and he himself will direct your course well. Blessed is the

295

300

305

310

315

320

Eadig bið se man se ðe gemet wisdom
forðan þe se wisdom is selra þone scinende gold,
325 and he ana is deor-wurðra þonne ða dyran maðmas."
Þæt is se wisdom, þæt man wislice libbe,
and his dæda gefadige to his Drihtnes willan,
þæt he edlean underfo on ðam ecan life
mid ðam ælmihtigan Gode, þe on ecnysse rixað. Amen.

man who finds wisdom, because wisdom is better than shining gold, and it alone is more valuable than precious trea- 325
sures." This is that wisdom, that one should live wisely and
order his actions according to his Lord's will, so that he may
receive reward in the eternal life with the almighty God,
who reigns in eternity. Amen.

SAINT GEORGE

13

Saint George

XIX Kalendas Maii: Natale sancti
Georgii martyris

Gedwol-men awriton gedwyld on heora bocum
be ðam halgan were ðe is gehaten Georius.
Nu wille we eow secgan þæt soð is be ðam,
þæt heora gedwyld ne derige digellice ænigum.
5   Se halga Georius wæs on hæþenum dagum
rice ealdor-man under ðam reþan casere
þe wæs Datianus geciged, on ðære scire Cappadocia.
Þa het Datianus ða hæðenan gegaderian
to his deofol-gildum, his Drihtne on teonan,
10 and mid manegum ðeow-racum þæt man-cynn geegsode,
þæt hi heora lac geoffrodon þam leasum godum mid him.
Þa geseah se halga wer þæra hæðenra gedwyld,
hu hi ðam deoflum onsægdon and heora Drihten forsawon,
ða aspende he his feoh unforht on ælmyssum
15 hafenleasum mannum þam hælende to lofe,
and wearð þurh Crist gebyld and cwæð to ðam casere:
"*Omnes dii Gentium demonia, Dominus autem caelos fecit.*
'Ealle þæra hæðenra godas synd gramlice deofla,

13

Saint George

Heretics have written heresy in their books concerning the holy man who is called George. Now we wish to tell you what is true about him, so that their heresy may not secretly harm anyone.

In heathen days the holy George was a wealthy ruler under the cruel emperor who was called Datianus, in the province of Cappadocia. Then Datianus ordered that the heathens be gathered together to worship his idols, as an insult to his Lord, and he terrified that people with many threats, so that they offered their sacrifices to the false gods with him. When the holy man saw the heresy of the heathens, how they sacrificed to the devils and rejected their Lord, then, fearless, he distributed his money in alms to poor people in praise of the savior, and he was emboldened by Christ and said to the emperor: "*All the gods of the Gentiles are devils, but the Lord made the heavens.* 'All the gods of the heathens are

and ure Drihten soðlice geworhte heofonas.'

20 Þine godas, casere, syndon gyldene and sylfrene,
stænene and treowene, getreowleasera manna hand-
geweorc,
and ge him weardas settað þe hi bewaciað wið þeofas."
Hwæt þa Datianus deofollice geyrsode
ongean ðone halgan wer and het hine secgan
25 of hwilcere byrig he wære oððe hwæt his nama wære.
Þa andwyrde Georius ðam arleasan and cwæð:
"Ic eom soðlice Cristen and ic Criste þeowige.
Georius ic eom gehaten and ic hæbbe ealdordom
on minum earde, ðe is gehaten Cappadocia,
30 and me bet licað to forlætenne nu
þisne hwilwendlican wurð-mynt and þæs wuldorfullan
Godes
cynedome gehyrsumian on haligre drohtnunge."
Þa cwæð Datianus: "Ðu dwelast, Geori.
Genealæc nu ærest and geoffra þine lac
35 þam unoferswiðendum Apolline, se ðe soþlice mæg
þinre nytennysse gemiltsian, and to his man-rædene
gebigan."
Georius þa befran þone feondlican casere:
"Hwæðer is to lufigenne, oððe hwam lac to offrigenne,
ðam hælende Criste, ealra worulda alysend,
40 oþþe Apolline, ealra deofla ealdre?"
Hwæt ða Datianus, mid deofollicum graman,
het ðone halgan wer on hencgene ahæbban
and mid isenum clawum clifrian his lima
and ontendan blysan æt bam his sidum.
45 Het hine þa siððan of ðære ceastre alædan
and mid swinglum þreagen and mid sealte gnidan,

cruel devils, and our Lord truly made the heavens.' Your 20
gods, emperor, are made of gold and silver, of stone and of
wood, the handiwork of faithless people, and you set guards
on them who keep watch over them against thieves."

Well then, Datianus became diabolically angry with the
holy man and ordered him to say from what city he was or 25
what his name was. Then George answered the impious man
and said: "I am truly a Christian and I serve Christ. I am
called George and I have authority in my own country,
which is called Cappadocia, and it pleases me better to leave 30
behind now this temporal honor and to obey the supreme
authority of glorious God in a holy way of life." Then Datianus said: "You are wrong, George. First approach now and
offer your sacrifice to the invincible Apollo, he who can 35
truly have mercy on your foolishness, and convert to service
to him." George then asked the fiendish emperor: "Which
one is to be loved, or to whom is sacrifice to be offered,
the savior Christ, redeemer of all ages, or Apollo, lord of all 40
devils?"

Well then, Datianus, with diabolical anger, ordered the
holy man to be hung on a rack and his limbs clawed with
iron claws and torches to be set on fire at both his sides.
Then afterward he ordered that he be led out of the city 45
and tortured by whipping and rubbed with salt, but the

ac se halga wer wunode ungederod.
Þa het se casere hine on cweart-erne don
and het geaxian ofer eall sumne æltæwne dry.

50 Þa geaxode þæt Athanasius se dry
and com to ðam casere and hine caflice befran:
"Hwi hete ðu me feccan þus færlice to þe?"
Datianus andwyrde Athanasie ðus:
"Miht þu adwæscan þæra Cristenra dry-cræft?"

55 Þa andwyrde se dry Datiane ðus:
"Hat cuman to me þone Cristenan mann,
and beo ic scyldig gif ic his scyn-cræft ne mæg
mid ealle adwæscan mid minum dry-cræfte."
Þa fægnode Datianus þæt he funde swylcne dry

60 and het of cweart-erne lædan ðone Godes cempan
and cwæð to ðam halgan, mid hetelicum mode:
"For ðe, Geori, ic begeat þisne dry.
Oferswyð his dry-cræft oððe he þe oferswyðe:
oððe he fordo þe oððe þu fordo hine."

65 Georius ða beheold þone hæðenan dry
and cwæð þæt he gesawe Cristes gife on him.
    Athanasius ða ardlice genam
ænne mycelne bollan mid bealuwe afylled
and deoflum betæhte ðone drenc ealne

70 and sealde him drincan, ac hit him ne derode.
Þa cwæð eft se dry: "Git ic do an þincg
and gif him þæt ne derað, ic buge to Criste."
He genam ða ane cuppan mid cwealm-berum drence
and clypode swyðe to þam sweartum deoflum

75 and to ðam fyrmestum deoflum and to ðam ful strangum
and on heora naman begol þone gramlican drenc;
sealde ða drincan þam Drihtnes halgan,

holy man remained unhurt. The emperor then ordered that he be put in prison and ordered that an excellent sorcerer be sought everywhere. Athanasius the sorcerer then learned of this and came to the emperor and boldly asked him: "Why did you order that I be fetched like this to you without delay?" Datianus answered Athanasius thus: "Can you put an end to the magic of those Christians?" Then the sorcerer answered Datianus thus: "Order the Christian man to come to me, and let me be the guilty one if I cannot completely put an end to his sorcery with my magic." Then Datianus rejoiced that he had found such a sorcerer and ordered God's soldier to be led out of prison, and he said to the saint, in a violent state of mind: "I got this sorcerer for you, George. Defeat his sorcery or he will defeat you: either he will destroy you or you will destroy him." George then looked at the heathen sorcerer and said that he saw Christ's grace in him.

Athanasius then quickly took a large bowl filled with a poisonous drink and dedicated all that drink to the devils and gave it to him to drink, but it did not harm him. After that the sorcerer said then: "I will do one more thing and if it does not harm him, I will convert to Christ." Then he took a cup with the deadly drink and called loudly to the black devils and to the chief devils and to the very strong ones, and in their names he cast a spell over the terrible drink; then he gave it to the Lord's saint to drink, but the

ac him naht ne derode se deofollica wæta.

Ða geseah se dry þæt he him derian ne mihte

80   and feol to his fotum fulluhtes biddende

and se halga Georius hine sona gefullode.

    Hwæt ða Datianus deoflice wearð gram

and het geniman þone dry þe ðær gelyfde on God

and lædan of ðære byrig and beheafdian sona.

85   Eft on þam oþrum dæge het se arleasa casere

gebindan Georium on anum bradum hweowle

and twa scearpe swurd settan him togeanes

and swa up ateon and underbæc sceofan.

Þa gebæd Georius hine bealdlice to Gode:

90   *Deus in adiutorium meum intende; Domine, ad adiuvandum me*

festina.

"God, beseoh ðu on minum fultume; Drihten, efst þu nu me

to fultumigenne."

And he wearð þa gebroht mid þysum gebæde on þam

hweowle.

Þa tyrndon þa hæðenan hetelice þæt hweowl,

ac hit sona tobærst and beah to eorðan

95   and se halga wer wunode ungederod.

Datianus þa dreorig wearð on mode

and swor ðurh ða sunnan and ðurh ealle his godas

þæt he mid mislicum witum hine wolde fordon.

Ða cwæð se eadiga Georius him to:

100 "Þine ðeow-racan synd hwilwendlice,

ac ic ne forhtige for ðinum gebeote.

Þu hæfst minne lic-haman on ðinum anwealde

ac ðu næfst swaþeah mine sawle, ac God."

    Þa het se casere his cwelleras feccan

105 ænne ærene hwer and hine ealne afyllan

diabolical drink did not harm him at all. Then the sorcerer
saw that he could not harm him and fell to his feet asking for   80
baptism, and the holy George baptized him at once.

Well then, Datianus became diabolically angry and ordered that the sorcerer who had believed in God be seized
there and brought out of the city and beheaded immediately. Again on the second day the impious emperor ordered   85
that George be bound on to a large wheel and two sharp
swords be placed against him and that in this position he be
pulled up and pushed backward. Then George prayed confidently to God: *O God, come to my assistance; O Lord, make haste*   90
to help me. "God, look upon me with help; Lord, make haste
now to help me." And then with this prayer he was put on to
the wheel. Then the heathens turned the wheel violently,
but it broke immediately and collapsed to the ground and   95
the holy man remained unharmed. Datianus then became
furious in his mind and swore by the sun and by all his gods
that he intended to kill him with various torments. Then
the blessed George said to him: "Your threats are temporal,   100
but I am not afraid of your vow to harm me. You have my
body in your power, but it is not you, however, who has my
soul, but God has."

Then the emperor ordered his executioners to fetch
a cauldron of bronze and to fill it all with boiling lead and to   105

mid weallendum leade and lecgan Georium
innon ðone hwær þa ða he hattost wæs.
Þa ahof se halga to heofonum his eagan,
his Drihten biddende and bealdlice cweðende:
110 "Ic gange into þe on mines Drihtnes naman
and ic hopige on Drihten, þæt he me ungederodne
of ðisum weallendum hwere wylle nu ahreddan.
Þam is lof and wuldor geond ealle woruld."
And he bletsode þæt lead and læg him onuppan,
115 and þæt lead wearð acolod þurh Cristes mihte
and Georius sæt gesund on ðam hwere.
Ða cwæð se casere to þam Cristes þegene:
"Nast þu, la Geori, þæt ure godas swincað mid þe
and git hi synd geþyldige þæt hi þe miltsion.
120 Nu lære ic ðe, swa swa leofne sunu,
þæt ðu þæra Cristenra lare forlæte mid ealle
and to minum ræde hraðe gebuge,
swa þæt ðu offrige þam ar-wurðan Appolline,
and þu mycelne wurð-mynt miht swa begitan."
125 Þa se halga martyr, mid ðam Halgan Gaste afylled,
smearcode mid muðe and to ðam manfullan cwæð:
"Us gedafenað to offrigenne þam undeadlicum Gode."
Æfter ðisum bebead se ablenda Datianus
þæt mann his deadan godas deor-wurðlice frætewode
130 and þæt deofles templ mid deor-wurðan seolfre
and het þider lædan þone geleaffullan martyr.
Wende þæt he wolde wurðian his godas
and his lac geoffrian ðam lifleasum godum.
        Hwæt ða Georius to eorðan abeah,
135 þus biddende his Drihten gebigedum cneowum:
"Gehyr nu, God ælmihtig, þines ðeowan bene

put George into the cauldron when it was at its hottest. Then the saint raised his eyes to heaven, praying to his Lord and confidently saying: "I enter into you in the name of my 110 Lord, and I hope in the Lord, that he will rescue me now unharmed from this boiling cauldron. To him is praise and glory throughout the whole world." And he blessed the lead and lay down on top of it, and the lead was cooled through 115 the power of Christ, and George sat uninjured in the cauldron. Then the emperor said to Christ's servant: "Do you not know, George, that our gods are working on your side, and they are still patient so that they may pardon you. Now 120 I exhort you, like a dear son, that you completely abandon the teachings of those Christians and immediately accept my advice, so that you make an offering to the worthy Apollo, and you can obtain great honor in this way." Then 125 the holy martyr, filled with the Holy Spirit, smiled with his mouth and said to the evil man: "It is fitting for us to make an offering to the immortal God." After this the deluded Datianus commanded that his dead gods and the devil's temple be splendidly adorned with precious silver, and he 130 ordered that the faithful martyr should be brought there. He thought that he would be willing to honor his gods and offer his sacrifice to the lifeless gods.

Well then, George bowed down to the earth, praying to 135 his Lord on bended knees thus: "Hear now, God almighty,

and þas earman anlicnyssa mid ealle fordo
swa swa wex formylt for hatan fyre,
þæt menn ðe oncnawan and on ðe gelyfan,
140 þæt þu eart ana God, ælmihtig scyppend."
Æfter ðisum gebede bærst ut of heofonum
swyðe færlic fyr and forbernde þæt templ
and ealle ða godas grundlunga suncon
into þære eorðan and ne æteowdon siððan.
145 Eac swylce þa sacerdas suncon forð mid
and sume ða hæðenan þe þær gehende stodon,
and Georius axode þone arleasan casere:
"On hwilcum godum tihst þu us to gelyfenne?
Hu magon hi ahreddan ðe fram frecednyssum,
150 þonne hi ne mihton hi sylfe ahreddan?"
      Hwæt ða Datianus gedihte þisne cwyde
and het ðus acwellan þone Godes cempan:
"Nimað þisne scyldigan, þe mid scin-cræfte
towende ure ar-wurðan godas mid ealle to duste,
155 and dragað hine niwelne his neb to eorðan
geond ealle ðas stræt and stænene wegas
and ofsleað hine syþþan mid swurdes ecge."
Þa tugon þa hæðenan þone halgan wer
swa Datianus him gediht hæfde
160 oðþæt hi comon to ðære cwealm-stowe,
and se martyr bæd þæt he hine gebiddan moste
to ðam ælmihtigan Gode and his gast betæcan.
He þancode ða Gode eallra his godnyssa,
þæt he hine gescylde wið þone swicolan deofol
165 and him sige forgeaf þurh soðne geleafan.
He gebæd eac swylce for eall Cristen folc
and þæt God forgeafe þære eorðan renas,

your servant's prayer and utterly destroy these base images just as wax melts away in front of a hot fire, so that people may come to know you and believe in you, that you alone are God, almighty creator." After this prayer a very sudden fire burst out of the heavens and burned up that temple, and all the gods sank completely into the earth and did not appear subsequently. Likewise the priests sank along with them and some of the heathens who were there standing nearby, and George asked the impious emperor: "In what sort of gods do you urge us to believe? How can they save you from dangers, when they cannot save themselves?"

Well then, Datianus issued this decree and ordered the soldier of God to be killed thus: "Take this guilty man, who with sorcery has completely reduced our honored gods to dust, and drag him prostrate, his face on the ground, through all these streets and stony roads and kill him afterward with a sword's blade." Then the heathens dragged the holy man as Datianus had directed them until they came to the place of execution, and the martyr asked to be allowed to pray and entrust his spirit to the almighty God. Then he thanked God for all of his acts of goodness, that he had protected him against the deceitful devil and had given him victory by means of true faith. He prayed likewise for all Christian people and that God would give rains to the land,

forþan ðe se hæða þa hynde ða eorðan.

Æfter ðisum gebæde he bletsode hine sylfne

170 and bæd his slagan þæt he hine sloge.

Mid þam ðe he acweald wæs, ða comon þyder sona

his agene land-leode geleofede on God

and gelæhton his lic and læddan to þære byrig

þe he on ðrowode and hine ðær bebyrigdon

175 mid mycelre ar-wurðnysse, þam Ælmihtigan to lofe.

Þa asende Drihten sona ren-scuras

and þa eorðan gewæterode þe ær wæs forburnen,

swa swa Georius bæd ær ðan þe he abuge to slege.

Hwæt ða Datianus wearð færlice ofslagen

180 mid heofonlicum fyre and his geferan samod,

þa ða he hamwerd wæs mid his heah-þegenum,

and he becom to helle ær ðan þe to his huse.

And se halga Georius siðode to Criste,

mid ðam he a wunað on wuldre. Amen.

because the heat was then laying waste the land. After this prayer he blessed himself and asked his slayer to kill him. 170 When he was killed, immediately his own countrymen who believed in God came there and took his body and brought it to the city in which he had suffered martyrdom and buried him there with great honor, in praise of the Almighty. 175 Then the Lord sent showers of rain immediately and watered the land that had been scorched, just as George had requested before he had submitted to slaughter.

Well then, Datianus was suddenly killed by heavenly fire 180 along with his companions, when he was traveling homeward with his chief officers, and he arrived in hell rather than at his house. And the holy George journeyed to Christ, with whom he lives forever in glory. Amen.

SAINT MARK *AND* THE FOUR EVANGELISTS

14

Saint Mark *and* The Four Evangelists

VII Kalendas Maii: Passio sancti Marci
evangelistae

Marcus se god-spellere be Godes dihte gefor
to Aegipta lande and ðær lærde þæt folc
and to fulluhte gebigde fram þam fulan hæþenscype.
He ferde þa geond eall ðæt Aegiptisce land
5   sawende Godes sæd and ða seocan gehælde.
Hreoflige he geclænsode fram ðære unclænan coðe,
wode he gehælde and on gewitte gebrohte,
and adræfde þa deofla þe derodon mannum.
Þa gelyfdon ða hæðenan on ðone soðan hælend
10 and wurdon gefullode and towurpon heora deofol-gild.
    He wearð þa æt nextan geneosod þurh God
and se Halga Gast þa het hine faran
to Alexandrian byrig and bodian geleafan.
Seo burh is mærost mid Egyptiscum man-cynne.
15 Hwæt þa se god-spellere gegrette his gebroðra
and sæde þæt se hælend hine hete faran
to Alexandrian byrig and bodian geleafan.

14

Saint Mark *and* The Four Evangelists

April 25: Passion of Saint Mark
the Evangelist

Mark the Evangelist at God's direction went to Egypt and taught the people there and converted them from foul heathenism so that they accepted baptism. Then he traveled throughout all Egypt sowing God's seed, and he healed the 5 sick. He cleansed the lepers from that unclean disease, healed the insane and brought them to sanity, and drove out the devils who harmed people. Then the heathens believed in the true savior and were baptized and destroyed their 10 idols.

Then he was visited by God next, and the Holy Spirit ordered him to go to the city of Alexandria and preach the faith. That city is the most famous among the Egyptian people. Well then, the evangelist greeted his brothers and said 15 that the savior had ordered him to go to the city of Alexan-

Hi þa sona eoden to scipe mid him
and bædon God georne þæt he his weg gewissode.

20 He ferde ða on scipe oðþæt he gesundful becom
to Alexandrian byrig and bodode ðær geleafan
and fela wundra worhte and ðær wunode lange.

Sum sutere siwode þæs halgan weres sceos
and ðurhþide his hand hetelice swyþe,

25 ac se halga wer hine gehælde sona
and to fulluhte gebigde and fela oðre mid him.
Anianus wæs gehaten se ylca sutere
and he geþeah swa for Gode þæt se god-spellere hine gesette
þam folce to bisceope þære burh-scire.

30 He gehadode eac þa ðry messe-preostas
and seofon diaconas and endleofan clericas.

Þa syrwdon ða hæðenan and hine beswican woldon
forþan þe he awende heora gewunelican ðeawas
and heora goda offrunga mid ealle adwæscte.

35 Þa ferde se god-spellere fram ðære byrig
to ðam geleaffullum ðe he ær lærde
and ðær þurhwunode wel twa gear mid him
and getrymede ða gebroðra ðe he ær to Gode gebigde
and þær bisceopas gehadode and halige preostas.

40 And ferde eft ongean to Alexandrian byrig
and gemette þær fela, gemenigfealde on geleafan
and on Godes gife ðeonde, and he ðæs þancode Gode.
Hi hæfdon eac aræred on hrædincge ane cyrcan
and weox se geleafa and Godes wuldor scean.

45 Þa worhte Marcus myccle wundra.
He gehælde untrume on ðæs hælendes naman,
blinde and deafe, and bodode geleafan,
and ða hæðenan cepton hu hi hine acwealdon.

dria and preach the faith. They then immediately went to the ship with him, and they eagerly beseeched God to direct his journey. Then he traveled on the ship until he arrived 20 safely at the city of Alexandria, and he preached the faith there and performed many miracles and lived there for a long time.

A shoemaker was sewing the holy man's shoes and he pierced his hand very severely, but the holy man immedi- 25 ately healed him and converted him so that he was baptized and many others with him. That same shoemaker was called Anianus, and he achieved such favor in the eyes of God that the evangelist appointed him as bishop for the people of the city. He also ordained three priests and seven deacons and 30 eleven clerics in lower orders.

Then the heathens plotted and wished to entrap him because he had changed their customary practices and had put an end entirely to offerings to their gods. Then the evange- 35 list went from that city to the faithful whom he had previously taught and remained there with them a full two years, and he strengthened the brothers whom he had previously converted to God and consecrated bishops and holy priests there. And he went back again to the city of Alexandria and 40 found many there, multiplied in the faith and flourishing in God's grace, and he thanked God for this. They had also hurriedly built a church, and the faith grew and God's glory shone. Then Mark performed many miracles. He healed the 45 sick in the savior's name, the blind and the deaf, and preached the faith, and the heathens sought how to kill him.

Þa com seo halige Easter-tid and þa hæðenan cepton
50 hwær se god-spellere mæssode and mærsode his Drihten,
þe on ðam ylcan dæge of deaðe aras,
and urnon endemes to and hine gelæhton.
Becnytton ða his swuran sona mid rape
and tugon geond ða stræt, swa þæt þa stanas wæron
55 mid his blode begotene and mid his flæsce begleddode,
and se halga Marcus micclum þancode
þam hælende Criste þæt he for hine þrowode.
Þa siððan on æfen-timan hi setton hine on cweart-ern
oðþæt hi beðohton hu hi hine acwealdon.
60 Efne þa on middere nihte wearð mycel eorð-styrung
and Godes encgel fleah færlice to þam cweart-erne
and awræhte þone god-spellere and ðas word him sæde:
"Þu Godes þeowa, þin nama is awriten
on ðære liflican bec and ðin gemynd ne ateorað
65 and ðu eart gefera ðære upplican mihte,
þær ðu a lyfast, and þin gast bið on heofonum
and þin rest ne losað næfre on worulde."
Þa astrehte se halga his handa and cwæð:
"Ic ðancie ðe, Drihten, þæt ðu me ne forlete,
70 ac gemundest min mid þinum halgum.
Ic bidde þe nu, hælend Crist, onfoh mine sawle on sibbe
and ne geðafa þu þæt ic beo fram ðe ascired."
Mid þam ðe he þis cwæð, þa com Crist sylf him to
on þære ylcan gelicnysse þe he leofode on worulde
75 and hine mid sibbe gegrette and sæde him þas word:
Pax tibi, Marce, noster evangelista.
"Sy þe syb, Marce, ure god-spellere."

Then the holy Easter time came and the heathens observed where the evangelist was saying Mass and was glorifying his Lord, who on that same day had arisen from death, and they ran there together and seized him. They tied his neck at once with a rope and dragged him through the streets, so that the stones were drenched with his blood and stained with his flesh, and the holy Mark greatly thanked the savior Christ that he was suffering for him. Then afterward in the evening time they put him in prison until they had considered how to kill him.

Truly then in the middle of the night there was a great earthquake and God's angel flew without warning to the prison and aroused the evangelist and said these words to him: "You servant of God, your name is written in the book of life and the memory of you will not fail, and you are a companion of the celestial power, where you will live forever, and your spirit will be in heaven and your eternal rest will never fail." Then the saint stretched out his hands and said: "I thank you, Lord, that you have not abandoned me, but that you have remembered me with your saints. I beseech you now, savior Christ, receive my soul in peace and do not permit that I be separated from you." While he was saying this, Christ himself came to him in the same appearance in which he had lived in the world and greeted him by wishing him peace and said these words to him: *Peace be with you, Mark, our evangelist.* "Peace be with you, Mark, our evan-

And Marcus him cwæð to: "Min Drihten hælend,"
and se hælend siðode sona to heofonum.

80   Hwæt þa on ærne-merigen comon ða arleasan hæðenan
and becnytton his swuran eftsona mid rape
and drogon hine eft swa swa hi ær dydon,
huxlice sprecende be ðam halgan were.
And se eadige Marcus mycclum þæs ðancode

85   þam hælende Criste and cwæð þis gebæd:
In manus tuas, Domine, commendo spiritum meum.
"On þine handa, Drihten, ic betæce minne gast."
And he gewat mid þam worde of worulde to Gode,
mid ðam he a blyssað butan earfoðnyssum.

90   Þa woldon þa hæðenan his lic forbernan
and worhten mycel ad, ac hit wearð adwæsced,
swa þæt God asende swyðe mycelne ren
ofer ealne þone dæg mid egeslicum ðunore
swa þæt manega hus hetelice feollon

95   and eac manega menn mid ðam þunore swulton
and þa oðre flugon, mid fyrhte fornumene.
Comon þa syððan sona þa Cristenan,
eawfæste weras, and hi aweg feredon
þæs god-spelleres lic and ledon on anre þryh

100   and mid ar-wurðnysse bebyrigdon, mid gebedum þancigende
þæt hi swilcne halgan mid him habban moston,
him to mund-boran, to þam ælmihtigan Gode,
þam sy wuldor and lof a to worulde. Amen.

74

gelist." And Mark said to him: "My Lord savior," and the savior immediately went to heaven.

Well then, in the early morning the impious heathens 80 came, and once again they tied his neck with a rope and dragged him again as they had done previously, speaking scornfully about the holy man. And for this the blessed Mark fervently thanked the savior Christ and said this 85 prayer: *Into your hands, Lord, I commend my spirit.* "Into your hands, Lord, I commend my spirit." And with that utterance he departed from the world to God, with whom he rejoices eternally without tribulations.

Then the heathens wished to burn up his body and built a 90 large pyre, but it was extinguished, in that God sent very heavy rainfall throughout the whole day with terrifying thunder, so that many houses fell violently and many people 95 also died as a result of the thunder and the others fled, gripped by fear. Then afterward the Christians came immediately, devout men, and they took away the evangelist's body and laid it in a coffin and buried it with honor, with 100 prayers giving thanks that they had been permitted to have such a saint among them, as their protector, to the almighty God, to whom be glory and praise eternally. Amen.

Item alia

We habbaþ nu gesæd sceortlice on ðysum gewryte
105 hu se halga Marcus wæs gemartyrod.
Nu wylle we eow secgan hu se halga Hieronimus
be ðam feower god-spellerum, ðe Gode gecorene synd,
awrat on ðære fore-spræce þa ða he awende Cristes-boc
of Ebreiscum gereorde, and sume of Greciscum,
110 to Læden-spræce on þære ðe we leorniað.
He cwæð þæt Lucas sæde, swa swa hit ful soð is,
þæt manega menn ongunnon god-spel to writenne
butan þam Halgan Gaste and þæs hælendes wissunge
and be heora gewille sædon, swa swa him geþuhte,
115 and þam gelamp seo awyrigung þe se witega cwæð:
"Wa þam þe witegað be heora agenre heortan
and farað æfter heora gaste and cwæðaþ þæt hit God sæde
þæt þæt hi secgað, and God hi ne sende."
Be swilcum cwæð se hælend eac on sumere stowe:
120 "Warniað eow georne wið lease witegan,
þa ðe cumað to eow on sceape gelicnysse,
and hi synd wiþinnan reafigende wulfas."
Ac seo geleaffulle gelaðung þe is gelogod on Criste
and on him gefæstnod, swa swa on fæstum stane,
125 ne underfehð þa gesetnyssa þe swilce gedwolan
ðurh hi sylfe gesetton, buton soðfæstnysse.
  Se forma god-spellere is, þe Gode gecoren wæs,
Matheus gehaten, þone se hælend geceas
of woruldlicum tollere to gastlicum god-spellere,
130 and he wæs an ðæra twelfa Cristes ðegna.
He awrat on Ebreisc ærest þa god-spel

Another in the Same Manner [On the Four Evangelists]

We have now told briefly in this text how the holy Mark was 105
martyred. Now we intend to tell you what the holy Jerome
wrote about the four evangelists who are chosen by God, in
his preface when he was translating Christ's gospels from
the Hebrew language, and some from Greek, into the Latin 110
language in which we learn. He said that Luke said, as is entirely true, that many people had begun to write gospels
without the guidance of the Holy Spirit and the savior and
had spoken according to their own will, as things seemed to
them, and the curse that the prophet had uttered had come 115
upon them: "Woe to those who prophesy according to their
own hearts and follow their own spirits and say that God
said what they say, but God did not send them." About such
people the savior also said in one place: "Be keenly on guard 120
against false prophets, those who come to you in the likeness of a sheep, and inside they are ravenous wolves." But
the church of the true faith that is founded in Christ and
established on him, as on a firmly fixed stone, does not ac- 125
cept those compositions that such heretics composed by
themselves, without truth.

The first evangelist who was chosen by God is called
Matthew, whom the savior chose from being a secular tax
collector to be a spiritual evangelist, and he was one of the 130
twelve followers of Christ. He first wrote in Hebrew the

þe on ðæra forman bec beoð geendebyrde.

He awrat hi on Ebreisc þam Ebreiscum mannum
ðe on Iudea lande gelyfdon on Criste
135 and wolde mid ðam gewrite, þe hi wæron on afedde,
heora geleafan getrymman forðan þe he lufode hi
and he sceolde ða faran to fyrlenum lande
to hæþenum leodum, hi to lærenne.

Þa wolde he on ær his agenre leode
140 þæt god-spell awritan, ær ðam þe he gewende him fram.

Se oðer god-spellere is Marcus, se wæs mid þam apostole
Petre
getogen on lare and to geleafan gebiged.

Petrus wæs his god-fæder and hine Gode gestrynde,
and he swa lange folgode his fulluht-fædere Petre
145 oðþæt he gesette mid soðum geleafan
þa oðre Cristes-boc on Italia lande.

Ne geseah he Crist on life, ac he leornode swaðeah
of Petres bodunge hu he ða boc gesette
and Petrus hi sceawode and sealde to rædenne.

150 Se ðridda god-spellere is Lucas, se wæs læce on worulde
and wunode mid ðam apostolum and mid Paule syððan,
þeowigende þam Ælmihtigan butan ælcum leahtre
on clænum life, æfre buton wife, mid Godes gaste afylled.

And he ða god-spel awrat and wislice geendebyrde
155 and *actus apostolorum* eac he gesette.

He awrat his god-spell on Achaian lande
and gewat to Gode, mid ðam Halgan Gaste afylled,
ða þa he wæs on ylde feower and hundeahtatig geara.

Se feorða god-spellere is Iohannes, Cristes moddrian
sunu,
160 se wæs Criste swa leof þæt he hlynode uppan his breoste,

gospel passages that are recorded in the first book. He wrote them in Hebrew for those Hebrew people who believed in Christ in the land of Judea, and he intended by this writing, by which they were nourished, to strengthen their faith because he loved them, but he had to go then to distant countries to heathen peoples, in order to teach them. Then he wished to write the gospel beforehand for his own people, before he left them.

The second evangelist is Mark, who was educated in doctrine and converted to the faith by the apostle Peter. Peter was his godfather and gained him for God, and he followed his baptismal father Peter until with true faith he had written the second gospel book in Italy. He did not see Christ in life, but nevertheless he learned from Peter's preaching how he should write the book, and Peter examined it and approved it for reading.

The third evangelist is Luke, who was a doctor in secular life and lived with the apostles and afterward with Paul, serving the Almighty without any vice by means of a pure life, all the time without a wife, filled with God's spirit. And he wrote the gospel passages and set them in order wisely, and he also wrote the *Acts of the Apostles*. He wrote his gospel in the land of Achaea and departed to God, filled with the Holy Spirit, when he was eighty-four years old.

The fourth evangelist is John, the son of Christ's mother's sister, who was so dear to Christ that he leaned on his

on ðam þe wæs behyd eal se heofonlica wisdom,
swylce he of ðam drunce þa deopan lare
þe he siððan awrat on wundorlicre gesetnyssa,
swa þæt he oferstah ealle gesceafta
165 and þa word geopenade þe englas ne dorston.
He wæs ærest gecoren eallra þæra god-spellera,
ac he is forði se feorða forþan þe he sette þa feorðan boc,
æfter ðam þe ða oðre geendebyrde wæron
and wide geond þas woruld awritene wæron.
170 On Asia he wæs þa he awrat þa boc
and he leofode lange on life æfter Criste,
oðþæt þa oðre apostolas geendoden heora lif
and sigefæste ferdon to ðan soþan life.
    Ðas feower god-spelleras syndon Gode gecorene
175 and hi ealne middan-eard mid heora lare onlihton,
swa swa þa feower ean ðe yrnað of neorxne-wange
ealne þisne embhwyrft endemes wæteriað,
and ðas feower god-spelleras God geswutelode gefyrn
on ðære ealdan æ Ezechihele þam witegan.
180 He geseah on his gesihðe swylce feower nytenu:
an þæra nytena wæs gesewen swilce mannes ansyn
and þæt oðer wæs gelic anre leon hiwe
and þæt þridde stod anum styrce gelic
and þæt feorðe wæs fagum earne gelic.
185 Þes mannes gelicnyss belimpð to Mathee
forðan þe he ongan his god-spell be Cristes menniscnysse.
Seo leo belimpð, swa swa þa geleaffullan secgaþ,
to Marces gelicnysse, forðan þe he hlud-swege clypode,
swa swa leo grimmeteð gredig on westene:
190 *Vox clamantis in deserto: Parate viam Domini; rectas facite semitas eius.*

breast, in which all the heavenly wisdom was hidden, as if he might drink from there the profound doctrine that he subsequently wrote down in a wonderful work, so that he rose above all created things and disclosed the words that the angels did not dare to. He was chosen first of all of the evangelists, but he is the fourth because he composed the fourth book after the others had been written and widely copied throughout the world. He was in Asia when he wrote this book, and he lived his life for a long time after Christ, until the other apostles had ended their lives and had gone, victorious, to the true life.

These four evangelists are chosen by God and they illuminated all the world with their teaching, just as the four rivers that run from paradise together water all this orb, and God long ago revealed these four evangelists in the old law to Ezekiel the prophet. He saw in his vision something resembling four beasts: one of these beasts was seen as if with the face of a man, and the second was like the form of a lion, and the third stood like a calf, and the fourth was like a particolored eagle. The likeness of a man is assigned to Matthew because he began his gospel with Christ's humanity. The lion, as the faithful say, is assigned to the likeness of Mark, because he called out loudly, just as the greedy lion roars in the desert: *The voice of one crying in the desert: Prepare ye the way of the Lord; make his paths straight.* "A voice crying in the

"Clypiende stemn on westene: Gearciað Godes weg; doð
                                  rihte his paðas."
Þæs celfes gelicnyss belimpð to Lucan
forðan þe he ongan his god-spell, swa swa God him gedihte,
fram ðam sacerde þe Zacharias hatte,
195   forðan þe man offrode on ða ealdan wisan
cealf for ðæne sacerd and ofsloh æt ðam weofode.
Þæs earnes gelicnys belimpð to Iohanne,
forðan þe se earn flyhð ealra fugela ufemest
and mæg swyðost starian on þære sunnan leoman.
200   Swa dyde Iohannes, se driht-wurða writere:
he fleah feor upp, swylce mid earnes fyðerum,
and beheold gleawlice hu he be Gode mihte mærlicost
                                          writan.
Se fore-sæda witega sæde on his gesihðe
þæt þæra feower nytena fet wæron rihte
205   and hi eodon æfre æfter ðam gaste
and hæfdon eagan him on ælce healfe.
    Þus is on ðære ealdan æ awriten be ðam god-spellerum
and eft on ðære niwan gecyðnysse æfter Cristes
                                     menniscnysse.
Apocalypsis seo boc be ðisum ylcum segð
210   þæt Iohannes gesawe þa fore-sædan nytenu
on þam ylcan hiwe þe we ær sædon
and hi sungon þisne sang mid singalum dreame:
*Sanctus, sanctus, sanctus, Dominus Deus omnipotens, qui erat et
qui est et qui venturus est.*
"Halig, halig, halig, Drihten God ælmihtig,
215   se ðe wæs and se ðe nu is and se ðe towerd is."
Se halga sang geswutelað þa halgan Þrynnysse,

desert: Prepare the way of God; make his paths straight."
The calf's likeness is assigned to Luke because he began his
gospel, as God directed him, with the priest who was called
Zachariah, because in the old manner a calf was offered for   195
the priest and killed at the altar. The eagle's likeness is assigned to John, because the eagle flies highest of all birds
and can gaze most directly at the rays of the sun. So did   200
John, the divine writer: he flew far up, as if with the feathers
of an eagle, and considered wisely how he could write most
gloriously about God. The prophet whom we have already
mentioned said in his vision that the feet of the four beasts
were straight and they always walked in accordance with the   205
spirit and they had eyes on every side.

This is what is written in the old law about the evangelists and again in the new testament after Christ's incarnation. The book of the Apocalypse says about this same subject that John saw the beasts that we have mentioned in the   210
same form that we mentioned previously, and they sang this
song with continual joy: *Holy, holy, holy, Lord God almighty,*
who was and who is and who is to come. "Holy, holy, holy, Lord
God almighty, who was and is now and will be in the future."   215
This holy song signifies the holy Trinity, eternally living in

83

on anre godcundnysse æfre wunigende,
seo ðe æfre wæs and eac nu wunað
and æfre is towerd butan ateorunge.
220   Nu we habbað gesæd, on ðisre sceortnysse,
hu God geswutelode þa soðfæstan god-spelleras
on þære ealdan æ and eac on þære niwan.
And þas feower ana syndon to underfonne
on geleaffulre gelaðunge and forlætan þa oðre,
225   þe lease gesetnysse gesetton ðurh hi sylfe,
na þurh þone Halgan Gast, ne ðurh ðæs hælendes
                                   gecorennysse.

We geendiað þus ðas gesetnysse her.

one divine nature, which was eternally and is now also and will be eternally in the future without coming to an end.

Now we have told, in this brief account, how God re- 220
vealed the true evangelists in the old law and also in the new. And these four alone are to be accepted in the church of the true faith and the others are to be ignored, those who wrote 225
false works by themselves, not by the Holy Spirit, nor by the savior's choosing. Thus we end this composition here.

MEMORY OF SAINTS

Memory of Saints

Sermo de memoria sanctorum

Spel loca hwænne mann wille.

1

"Ego sum Alfa et Omega, initium et finis," dicit Dominus Deus, qui est et qui erat et qui venturus est, Omnipotens. Ðæt is on Englisc: "'Ic eom angin and ende,' cwæþ Drihten God, se ðe is and se ðe wæs and se ðe towerd is, ælmihtig." An ælmihtig God is on þrym hadum æfre wunigende, se þe ealle þincg gesceop. Nu habbe we anginn þurh hine, forðan þe he us gesceop þa ða we næron and us eft alysde þa þa we forwyrhte wæron. Nu sceole we hogian mid mycelre gymene þæt ure lif beo swa gelogod, þæt ure ende geendige on God, þanon þe us þæt angin com.

2. We magon niman gode bysne, ærest be ðam halgum heah-fæderum, hu hi on heora life Gode gecwemdon, and eac æt þam halgum þe þam hælende folgodon. Ærest Abel, Adames sunu, wæs Gode swa gecweme þurh unsceðþignysse and rihtwisnysse þæt Crist sylf hine het Abel *iustus,* þæt is se

15

Memory of Saints

A Sermon on the Memory of the Saints

A sermon for any occasion.

1

"*I am Alpha and Omega, the beginning and the end" saith the Lord God, who is and who was and who is to come, the Almighty.* That is in English: "'I am beginning and end,' said the Lord God, he who is and he who was and he who is to come, almighty." There is one almighty God eternally existing in three persons, who created all things. Now we have our beginning through him, because he created us when we did not exist and redeemed us afterward when we were lost. Now we must with great care take heed that our lives be so ordered that our end may end in God, from whom our beginning came.

2. We can take good example, first from the holy patriarchs, how they pleased God in their lives, and also from the holy ones who followed the savior. First Abel, Adam's son, was so pleasing to God because of his innocence and righteousness that Christ himself called him *just* Abel, that is

rihtwisa Abel. Eft Enoch, se seofoða mann fram Adame, wæs swa estful on his mode and Gode swa lic-wurðe þæt God hine genam, andsundne on sawle and on lic-haman, butan deaðe up to heofonum þa ða he on ylde wæs þreo hund geara and fif and sixtig geara and he þurhwunað swa andsund butan deaðe and butan geswince oð Antecristes tocyme. Noe eac for his rihtwisnysse ofercom þæt miccle flod þe ealne middan-eard ofereode swa þæt ðurh hine wearð eft eall man-cynn geedstaþelod.

3. Abraham, for his micclan geleafan to Gode and for his gehyrsumnysse, underfeng swilce bletsunge æt Gode þæt eall man-cynn ða þe gelyfað on God is gebletsod on his cynne, and his sunu Isaac æfter him leofode mid bletsunge and God hine lufode. Eft Iacob, Isaaces sunu, for his geswincum soðlice wearð gebletsod, ærest æt his fæder, and siððan æt Godes engle, and God him gesette þa oðerne naman, Israhel, þæt is *vir videns Deum:* se wer þe God gesihð. And mid ðam naman wæron þa getacnode, þe nu on Cristendome ðuruh geleafan God geseoð.

2

Iob se eadiga and se an-ræda Godes ðegn
wæs swa fulfremed on eallum godnyssum þæt God sylf
                                                cwæð be him
þæt his gelica nære ða on ðam life ofer eorðan.
Þa bæd se deofol æt Gode þæt he moste his fandian,
5   hwæðer he ðurhwunian wolde on his godnysse
and bile-witnysse oð his lifes ende
oððe he wolde fram Gode abugan þurh ða ormætan ehtnysse

the righteous Abel. Likewise Enoch, the seventh man from Adam, was so devout in his heart and so agreeable to God that God took him, sound in soul and body, without dying up to heaven when he was three hundred and sixty-five years of age, and he will continue as sound without dying and without hardship until Antichrist's coming. Noah also because of his righteousness overcame the great flood that covered the entire world, so that through him all humankind was restored again.

3. Abraham, because of his great faith in God and because of his obedience, received such a blessing from God that all humankind that believes in God is blessed in his line of descendants, and his son Isaac lived after him with the blessing of God and God loved him. Likewise Jacob, Isaac's son, was truly blessed on account of his labors, first by his father, and afterward by God's angel, and God then gave him a second name, Israel, that is *the man seeing God:* the man who sees God. And those who in the Christian era now see God through faith were signified by that name.

2

Job the blessed and the steadfast servant of God was so perfect in all virtues that God himself said concerning him that there was not his like then living upon the earth. Then the devil asked of God that he might be allowed to test him, to 5 find out whether he would be willing to persevere in his goodness and innocence until his life's end, or whether he would be willing to turn away from God by reason of the

þe se niðfulla deofol him on asende.

Hwæt ða se deofol anes deges ealle his æhta acwealde,

10 and his seofon suna and ðreo dohtra, and hine sylfne eac
        siððan
mid egeslicre untrumnysse geswencte.

Ac se an-ræde Iob nolde næfre abugan fram Godes lufe,
ne for ehtnysse ne for untrumnysse ne for his bærna lyre,
ne nan dyslic word ongean God ne cwæð,

15 ac mid micclum geþylde he ðancode æfre Gode
and mid innewerdre heortan his Drihten æfre herode.

God hine ða gehælde fram ðam egeslican broce
and his æhta him forgeald ealle be twifealdum
and he leofode ða gesælig forðan þe he oferswiðde þone
        deofol.

20 Dauid for his man-þwyrnysse and mild-heortnysse
wearð Gode gecweme and to cynincge gecoren,
swa þæt God sylf cwæð þus be him:
"Ic afunde me Dauid, Iessan sunu, æfter minre heortan,
se ðe minne willan mid weorcum gefremð."

25 Eft Helias se æðela witega, forðan þe he wan wið
        unrihtwisnysse,
wearð on heofenlicum cræte to heofonum ahafen
and ðær, swa swa Enoch, on orsorhnysse wunað.

Forðan þe nan gastlic lac nis Gode swa gecweme
swa him bið þæt man winne wið unrihtwisnysse symle

30 for manna rihtinge (mid man-þwærnysse swaðeah,
and mid gemetfæstnysse and mild-heortnysse)
þæt man unriht alecge and Godes riht arære,
swa swa Helias se witega wan wið unrihtwisnysse
oðþæt God hine ferode on fyrenum cræte to heofonum

35 fram eallum ehtnyssum þyssere yðegan worulde.

exceptionally great tribulation that the malicious devil would inflict on him. Well then, the devil one day killed all that he possessed, together with his seven sons and three daughters, and afterward also afflicted him with a horrible illness. But the steadfast Job refused to turn away from love of God, neither on account of tribulation nor illness nor the loss of his children, nor did he speak one foolish word against God, but with great patience he always thanked God and in his innermost heart always praised his Lord. Then God healed him from that horrible disease and restored all his possessions to him twofold, and then he lived blessed because he had defeated the devil.

David, because of his meekness and mercifulness, was pleasing to God and was chosen as king, so that God himself spoke thus about him: "I have found David, the son of Jesse, who will do my will in his deeds, to be after my own heart."

Likewise Elijah the noble prophet, because he fought against unrighteousness, was raised up to heaven in a heavenly chariot and there, like Enoch, he lives free from care. Because no spiritual offering is as pleasing to God as is that one should always fight against unrighteousness in order to correct people (yet with gentleness and with restraint and mercifulness) so that wrong may be put down and God's truth may be advanced, just as Elijah the prophet fought against unrighteousness until God conveyed him to heaven in a fiery chariot, away from all the tribulations of this stormy world.

Eac swilce þa ðry cnihtas on Chaldea lande,
Sidraac, Misaac, and Abdenago, þe for ðan soðan geleafan
on þam byrnendan ofne gebundene wurdon
to cwale aworpene, ac him sona cydde God
40 hwylcne geleafan hi hæfdon, þa ða se lig ne moste
furðon heora fex forswælan on þam ade,
ac hi ealle ut eodon ansunde to ðam cynincge.

Ealswa eft Danihel, se deor-wurða witega,
for his anfealdnysse and an-rædum geleafan,
45 wearð tua aworpen þurh ða wodan Chaldeiscan
into leona seaðum, ac hi leofodon be hungre
seofon niht metelease and ne mihton him derian.

Manega oðre heah-fæderas and halige witegan
wæron wuldorfulle weras and wundra gefremedon
50 on þære ealdan æ and hi ealle cyddon
mid wordum oððe mid weorcum þæt se wuldorfulla hælend
wolde us alysan fram helle-wite ðurh hine sylfne.
Eft us secgað bec hu ða synfullan forferdon
and ða arleasan æfre for heora yfelnysse losodon,
55 forðan þe God is swa rihtwis þæt þa rihtwisan men
ne beoð bereafode heora rihtwisnysse mede.
Ne eft ða arleasan, þe hine mid yfelnysse gremiað,
ne magon næfre ætwindan ðam ecum witum ahwar.

Eft on þæs hælendes tocyme wearð se halga Iohannes
60 ætforan him asend swa swa heofonlic bydel,
þæt he Cristes wegas gerihtlæhte mid wordum
and to rihtum weorcum gewende þa leode.
Witegung and seo ealde æ wunodon oð þæt
and Iohannes astealde þa stiðan drohtnunge
65 on þære niwan gecyðnysse, swa swa Crist him gewissode.
And he wæs ægðer ge ælic ge god-spellic,

Likewise with the three young men in the country of the Chaldeans, Sidrach, Misach, and Abdenago, who for the true faith were bound and cast to death in the burning fur- nace, but immediately God revealed in them what faith they 40 had, when the flame was not permitted even to singe their hair in that pyre, but they all came out to the king, un- harmed.

Again Daniel too, the esteemed prophet, because of the simplicity of his nature and his steadfast faith, was twice 45 thrown by the furious Chaldeans into lions' pits, but they lived in hunger for seven days without food and could not harm him.

Many other patriarchs and holy prophets were glorious men and performed miracles in the time of the old law, and 50 they all showed by their words or by deeds that the glorious savior was willing to save us from hell torment by means of himself. Likewise books tell us how the sinful perished and the impious were always lost on account of their evil, be- 55 cause God is so righteous that the righteous people will not be deprived of the reward of their righteousness. On the other hand the impious, who provoke him to anger by evil, can never escape eternal punishments anywhere.

Later at the savior's coming, the holy John was sent be- 60 fore him as a heavenly herald, so that with his words he might make Christ's paths straight and convert the people to righteous deeds. Prophecy and the old law lasted until then, and John established the austere way of life in the new 65 testament, as Christ had directed him. And he belonged to both the law and to the gospel, like a boundary between

swa swa gemæru betwux Moysen and us,
swa an-ræde Godes man þæt God sylf cwæð be him
þæt nan mærra man næs on middan-earde
70 acenned of were and of wife—þus hine wurðode God.

Hwæt ða ure hælend, þæs heofonlican Godes Sunu,
cydde his mycclan lufe þe he to us mannum hæfde
swa þæt he wearð acenned of anum clænan mædene
butan weres gemanan and man wearð gesewen
75 on sawle and on lic-haman, soð God and soð man,
to ðy þæt he us alysde, þa ðe gelyfað on hine,
fram ðam ecan deaðe mid his unscyldigan deaðe.
Be þam we magon tocnawan Cristes ead-modnysse,
þæt se healica God hine sylfne swa geeadmette
80 þæt he ðam deaðe underhnah and þone deofol oferswyðde
mid þære menniscnysse and man-cynn swa alysde.
He is ofer ealle þincg, ælmihtig scyppend,
and he wolde swaðeah wite ðrowian for us.

Nu is his ead-modnys us unwiðmetenlic,
85 forðan þe we synd synfulle and sceolan beon ead-mode,
wille we, nelle we, and he wolde sylf-willes
us syllan ða bysne, swa swa he sylf cwæð:
Discite a me, quia mitis sum et humilis corde, et invenietis requiem
animabus vestris.
"Leorniað æt me þæt ic man-þwære eom
90 and ead-mod on heortan and ge gemetað reste
eowrum sawlum." Þis sæde Drihten.
Ne het he us na leornian heofonas to wyrcenne,
ac het us beon ead-mode þæt we to heofonum becomon,
forðan þe þa modigan ne magon to heofonum.
95 Crist clypode on his bodunge and cwæð to eallum mannum:

Moses and us, so steadfast a man of God that God himself said concerning him that there was no greater person on earth born of man and woman—thus God honored him. 70

Well then, our savior, Son of the heavenly God, showed his great love that he had for us human beings in such a way that he was born of a pure virgin without intercourse with a man and was seen as a human being in soul and in body, true 75 God and true man, in order that he might redeem us, those who believe in him, from eternal death with his guiltless death. By this we can discern Christ's humility, in that the heavenly God so humbled himself that he submitted to that 80 death and overcame the devil by that incarnation and so redeemed humankind. He is above all things, the almighty creator, and nevertheless he was willing to suffer punishment for our sake.

Now his humility is not comparable with ours, because 85 we are sinful and ought to be humble, whether we wish to or do not wish to, and he was willing voluntarily to give us this example, as he himself said: *Learn of me, because I am meek and humble of heart, and you shall find rest for your souls.* "Learn from me because I am meek and humble of heart, and you will 90 find rest for your souls." The Lord said this. He did not command us to learn how to make the heavens, but he commanded us to be humble so that we might go to heaven, because the proud cannot go to heaven. In his preaching 95 Christ proclaimed and said to all people: *Do penance, for the*

Penitentiam agite, adpropinquabit enim regnum caelorum.
"Wyrcað dæd-bote eowra misdæda,
forðan þe heofonan rice efne genealæchð."
    Crist ferde ða abutan geond þa Iudeiscan byrig
100 bodigende god-spel and ða blindan onlihte
and ealle untrumnysse and adla gehælde.
His hlisa asprang þa to Syrian lande
and man ferode untrume feorran and nean,
myslice geuntrumode, and monað-seoce and wode,
105 and eac swilce bedd-rydan, and brohton to ðam hælende,
and he hi ealle gehælde forðan þe he hælend is.
Þas ylcan mihte he forgeaf his mæran apostolum,
þæt hi mihton gehælan, on ðæs hælendes naman,
ealle untrumnyssa, and eac ða deadan aræran
110 and aclænsian ða hreoflian, swa swa Crist sylf dyde.
Twelf apostolas wæron þe wunedon mid him
and twa and hundseofontig he geceas him to bydelum,
þa ferdon twam and twam ætforan him gehwyder.
Þas feower and hundeahtatig þe folgodon ðam hælende
115 synd ða grund-weallas on Godes gelaðunge
and þa fyrmestan bydelas and hi ure bec setton
swa swa hi geleornodon æt heora lareowe Criste,
and heora lar becom to ðam ytemestum landum.
    Hit gelamp þa sume dæg, ða ða se hælend siðode,
120 þæt sum man him cwæð to: "Ic wille siþian mid ðe
and ðe folgian swa hwider swa ðu færst."
Ða cwæð se hælend him to: "Foxas habbað holu
and fugelas habbað nest and ic næbbe wununge
hwider ic min heafod ahyldan mæge."
125 Crist sceawode his heortan and geseah his prættas,
forðan þe he mid soðfæstnysse ne sohte þone hælend,

kingdom of heaven is at hand. "Do penance for your evil deeds, because the kingdom of heaven draws near right now."

Christ then went about throughout the Jewish cities preaching the gospel, and he gave sight to the blind and 100 healed all sicknesses and diseases. Then his fame spread abroad to Syria, and sick people were carried from far and near, variously afflicted by sicknesses, and lunatics and the insane, and likewise the bedridden, and they brought them 105 to the savior, and he healed them all because he is the savior. He gave that same power to his great apostles, so that they could heal, in the savior's name, all sicknesses, and also raise up the dead and cleanse the lepers, as Christ himself did. 110 There were twelve apostles who were with him, and he chose seventy-two as his disciples, who went two by two ahead of him everywhere. These eighty-four who followed the savior are the foundations in God's church and the first 115 preachers, and they composed our books as they had learned from their teacher Christ, and their teaching reached the most remote lands.

One day it happened, when the savior was on a journey, that a man said to him: "I wish to go with you and follow you 120 wherever you go." Then the savior said to him: "Foxes have holes and birds have nests, and I have no dwelling in which I can lay down my head." Christ looked into his heart and saw 125 his tricks, because he was not seeking the savior with truth,

ac foxunga wæron wunigende on him
and up-ahefednys, swilce healice fugelas;
ða ne mihte swilc mann siðian mid Criste.
130   Crist eft þa siððan cwæð to sumum oðrum:
"Fylig me on minre fare," and he afyrht andwyrde:
"Læt me ærest, Drihten, ardlice faran
and minne fæder bebyrigan." Þa cwæð Crist to þam menn
                                                        eft:
"Geþafa þæt þa deadan heora deadan bebyrion.
135   Gang ðu sylf soðlice and Godes rice boda."
Þa synd soðlice deade þe heora scyppende ne ðeowiað
and ða þe Godes beboda mid biggengum ne healdað.
Þas magon bebyrigan þyllice oðre
and mid lyffetungum to leahtrum gehnexian.
140   Þa cwæð sum þridda man to Criste eft ðus:
"Ic wylle fylian þe, leof, ac læt me ærest faran
and cyðan minum hiwum hu ic hæbbe gemynt."
Him andwyrde þus se hælend: "Gif se yrðlincg behylt
underbæc gelome, ne bið he gelimplic tilia."
145   Þæt is on ðisum andgite: swa swa se yrðlincg amyrð
his furuh gif he locað to lange underbæc,
swa eac se ðe wile gewendan to Gode,
and bihð eft to woruld-þingum, ne bið he Gode andfencge.
    Mænigfealde wæron þæs hælendes wundra
150   and his halige lar, swa we leorniað on bocum,
and ealle his folgeras forleton ealle þincg,
ægðer ge wif ge æhta, and wunodon on clænnysse
for his fægeran behate and for heofonan rice.
Eft æfter his æriste and up-stige to heofonum,
155   þa þa se geleafa aras and man alede deofol-gyld,
þa wurdon ða halgan martiras swa micclum onbryrde

but there were foxlike wiles in him and arrogance, like haughty birds; then such a man could not go with Christ.

Afterward Christ then said to another man: "Follow me on my journey," and, frightened, he answered: "Let me first, Lord, go quickly and bury my father." Then Christ in reply said to the man: "Let the dead bury their dead. Truly, as for you, you go and proclaim God's kingdom." Those people are truly dead who do not serve their creator and who do not practice God's commandments. Those people can bury others of their kind and with their flatteries make them yield easily to vices.

Then a third man in turn spoke to Christ thus: "I wish to follow you, sir, but let me first go and tell my household what I have determined." The savior answered him thus: "If the plowman looks back frequently, he is not a competent tiller." The meaning of that is: just as the plowman mars his furrow if he looks behind him for too long, so also he who wishes to turn to God but turns back to worldly things will not be acceptable to God.

The savior's miracles and his holy teaching were numerous and varied, as we learn in books, and all of his followers renounced everything, both wives and possessions, and lived in chastity for the sake of his delightful promise and for the kingdom of heaven. Moreover after his resurrection and ascension to heaven, when the faith was springing up and idolatry was being put down, then the holy martyrs

þæt hi sweltan woldon ær ðan þe hi wiðsocon Gode
and heora lif aleton ær ðan þe heora geleafan
and wurdon ofslagene for ðam soðan geleafan,
160 fela þusenda martira on myslicum witum,
and hi habbað þa ecan myrhðe for heora martyrdome.
　Se arleasa deofol, þe is æfre embe yfel,
astyrode þa ehtnysse ðurh arlease cwelleras
and wolde mid slege oferswiðan þa Cristenan
165 and Godes geleafan alecgan gif he mihte,
ac swa man ma ofsloh, swa þær ma gelyfdon
ðurh þa micclan wundra þe ða martyras gefremedon.
　Eft ða ða God sealde sibbe his gelaðunge,
þa wolde se deofol mid gedwylde amyrran þone soðan
　　　　　　　　　　　　　　　　　　　　geleafan
170 and seow ða gedwyld on dyrstigum mannum.
An ðæra wæs Arrius, þe þæt yfel ongann,
ac him eode se innoð ut æt his forð-gange.
Manega wæron eac þe myslice dwelodon,
oðþæt þa halgan fæderas heora yfel adwæscton
175 and þone soþan geleafan gesetton ðurh God,
swa swa se hælend hine tæhte his halgum apostolum.
Þa wæron halige bisceopas, gehealtsume on þeawum,
and wise mæsse-preostas þe wunodon on clænnysse
and manega munecas on mycelre drohtnunge
180 and clæne mædenu þe Criste þeowodon
on gastlicre drohtnunge for heora Drihtnes lufan.
And ða synd nu ealle on þam ecan wuldre
for heora clænnysse, mid Criste wunigende.
　Nu on urum dagum, on ende þyssere worulde,
185 swicað se deofol digollice embe us,
hu he þurh leahtras forlære ða Cristenan

were so greatly inspired that they were willing to die rather than deny Christ, and they gave up their lives rather than their faith, and they were killed for the true faith, many 160 thousands of martyrs by various tortures, and they have eternal happiness as a reward for their martyrdom. The wicked devil, who is always occupied with evil, stirred up those persecutions by wicked murderers, and he wished to defeat the Christians by killing them and put an end to faith 165 in God if he could, but the more that were killed, the more believed there because of the great miracles that the martyrs performed.

Afterward when God gave peace to his church, then the devil wished to corrupt the true faith with heresy and he 170 sowed heresy among presumptuous people. One of them was Arius, who began that evil, but his intestines came out through his anus. There were also many who erred in various ways, until the holy fathers put an end to their evil and they 175 wrote down the true faith with the aid of God, as the savior had taught it to his holy apostles. Then there were holy bishops, continent in their habits, and wise priests who lived in purity and many monks living an excellent life and 180 pure virgins who served Christ in a spiritual way of life for love of their Lord. And now they are all in eternal glory because of their purity, dwelling with Christ.

Now in our days, at the end of this world, the devil 185 practices deceit with respect to us, as to how he may lead Christians astray by means of vices and may direct their

and to mislicum synnum heora mod awende,
ac ða beoð gesælige þe his swicdomas tocnawað
and his lot-wrencas mid geleafan oferswyðað.

190 He wet nu swiðe and wynð on ða Cristenan,
forðan þe he wat geare þæt þysre worulde geendung
is swyðe gehende and he onet forði.

We sceolan eac onettan and urum sawlum gehelpan
þurh gode biggengas, Gode to gecwemednysse,

195 forðan þe we ne motan lange on ðysum life beon,
and þæt is Godes mild-heortnyss, þeah ðe hit digle sy.

On anginne ðissere worulde, þa þa heo wynsum wæs
and menn moston lybban be heora lustum ða,
þa wæs langsum lif, swa þæt hi leofodon

200 sume nigon hund geara on ðæra heah-fædera timan,
sume eahta hund geara, and sume eac leng.

Nu is ure lif ungelic heora,
forðan þe we ne moton lybban be urum lustum nu,
ac we sceolan gehyrsumian ures hælendes bebodum

205 and mid earfoðnyssum þæt ece lif geearnian.

And seo earfoðnys ongan on ðære god-spell-bodunge.

Nu hæfð God eac gescyrt swyþe ure dagas,
swylce he swa cwæde: "Ne sceole ge swincan to lange,
ac beoð eow an-ræde to þam ecan life,

210 þær ðær ge butan geswince gesælige lybbað."

Nu synd ðreo heah-mægnu ðe menn sceolan habban,
fides, spes, caritas, þæt is geleafa and hiht and seo soðe lufu.

Þæt is se geleafa, þæt he gelyfe mid mode
on ða halgan Ðrynnysse and soðe annysse.

215 And þæt is se hiht, þæt he hopige to Gode,
ægðer ge on gelimpe ge on ungelimpe,
and næfre ne ortruwige be Godes arfæstnysse.

hearts to various sins, but those who discern his deceits and
who overcome his cunning tricks with faith will be blessed.
He is in a great rage now and is attacking Christians, be- 190
cause he knows clearly that the end of this world is very near
at hand and for this reason he is hurrying. We must also
hurry and help our souls by good habits, to please God, be- 195
cause we are not permitted to live long in this life, and that
is the mercy of God, though it be difficult to understand.

In the beginning of the world, when it was delightful and
people were allowed to live according to their desires, then
life was long lasting, so that some people lived for nine hun- 200
dred years in the time of the patriarchs, some for eight hundred years, and some even longer. Now our life is not like
theirs, because we are not now permitted to live according
to our desires, but we must be obedient to our savior's commandments and earn the eternal life by toil. And this toil be- 205
gan in the preaching of the gospel. Now God has also short-
ened our days greatly, as if he were to say: "You must not
labor too long, but be steadfast with regard to the eternal
life, where you will live blessed without hardship." 210

Now there are three chief virtues that people must have,
faith, hope, love, that is faith and hope and true love. This is
faith, that he believe with his mind in the holy Trinity and
true unity. And this is hope, that he hope in God, both in 215
good fortune and in bad fortune, and never despair of God's

Þæt is seo soðe lufu, þæt man his scyppend lufige
mid unametenre lufe, and ða menn þe wel willað,
220 swa swa hine sylfne, on soðfæstnysse æfre.
For Godes lufon we sceolon eac lufian ure fynd,
swa þæt we ðone man lufian and his misdæda onscunian.
Us is to understandenne ðas ende-byrdnysse:
Crist cwæð on his god-spelle þæt we God lufian sceolan
225 mid ealre ure heortan ofer ealle ðincg
and siððan ure nextan swa swa us sylfe.
And eac ure fynd he het us lufian,
ac he ne ihte ðær-to mid ealre heortan,
ne swa swa us sylfe, forðan þe him soðlice genihtsumað
230 þæt we hi lufian and læððe to nabban,
þeah ðe we mid ealre heortan ne swa swa us sylfe hi lufian.
        Nu syndon eahta heafod-leahtras þe us onwinnað swiðe.
An is gecwæden *gula,* þæt is gyfernyss on Englisc:
seo deð þæt man yt ær timan and drincð,
235 oððe he eft to micel nimð on æte oððe on wæte.
Seo fordeð ægðer ge sawle ge lic-haman,
forðan þe heo macað þam menn mycele untrumnysse
and to deaðe gebrincgð mid ormætum dræncum.
Heo fordeð eac ða sawle, forðan ðe he sceall syngian oft
240 ðone he sylf nat hu he færð for his feondlicum drencum.
        Se oðer leahtor is forligr and ungemetegod galnyss.
Se is gehaten *fornicatio* and he befylð þone mannan
and macað of Cristes limum myltestrena lima
and of Godes temple gramena wununge.
245   Se þridda is *avaritia,* þæt is seo yfele gitsung,
and seo is wyrtruma ælcere wohnysse.
Heo macað reaflac and unrihte domas,

mercy. This is true love, that one should love one's creator and those people who are of good will, with unlimited love, as oneself, always in truth. For the love of God we must also 220 love our enemies, in such a way that we love the person and abhor his evil deeds. We must understand these precepts: Christ said in his gospel that we must love God with all our 225 hearts above all things and then our neighbor as ourselves. And he also commanded us to love our enemies, but he did not add with all our hearts, nor as ourselves, because truly it is sufficient for him that we love them and do not have 230 hatred toward them, though we may not love them with all our hearts nor as ourselves.

Now there are eight capital sins that attack us fiercely. The first is called *gluttony*, that is greed in English: it makes one eat and drink before the proper time or on the other 235 hand to take too much in food and drink. It destroys both soul and body, because it causes a person much illness and leads him to death with excessive drinking. It also destroys the soul, because he will often sin when he himself does not 240 know how he is behaving because of his diabolical drinking.

The second vice is fornication and intemperate lust. It is named *fornication* and it defiles a person and makes prostitutes' limbs out of Christ's limbs and a dwelling of fiends out of God's temple.

The third is *avarice,* that is evil avarice, and it is the root 245 of all wrong. It causes robbery and unjust judgments, theft

stala and leasunga and forsworennysse.
Heo is helle gelic forðan þe hi habbað butu
250 unafylledlice grædignysse, þæt hi fulle ne beoð næfre.
   Se feorða leahtor is *ira,* þæt is on Englisc wea-modnyss.
Seo deð þæt se man nah his modes geweald
and macað man-slihtas and mycele yfelu.
   Se fifta is *tristitia,* þæt is ðissere worulde unrotnyss,
255 þone se man geunrotsoð ealles to swyðe
for his æhta lyre, þe he lufode to swyðe,
and cid þonne wið God and his synna geeacnað.
Twa unrotnyssa synd: an is þeos yfele
and oðer is halwende, þæt man for his synnum geunrotsige.
260 Se sixta leahter is *accidia* gehaten,
þæt is asolcennyss oþþe slæwð on Englisc,
ðonne ðam menn ne lyst on his life nan god don
and bið him ðonne mycel yfel þæt he ne mæge nan god don
and bið æfre ungearu to ælcere duguðe.
265 Se seofoða leahter is *iactantia* gecweden,
þæt is ydel gylp on Ængliscre spræce,
ðonne se man bið lof-georn and mid licetunge færð
and deð for gylpe, gif he hwæt dælan wile.
And bið þonne se hlisa his edlean ðære dæde
270 and his wite andbidað on ðære toweardan worulde.
   Se eahteoðe leahter is *superbia* gehaten,
þæt is on Ænglisc modignyss gecweden.
Seo is ord and ende ælcere synne.
Seo geworhte englas to atelicum deoflum
275 and ðone man macað eac, gif he modigað to swyðe,
þæs deofles geferan, ðe feol ær ðurh hi.
   Nu syndon eahta heafod-mægnu ðe magan oferswiðan
þas fore-sædan deoflu þurh Drihtnes fultum.

and lies and perjury. It is like hell because they both have insatiable greed, so that they will never be full. 250

The fourth vice is *anger,* that is anger in English. It causes a person to have no control over his mind and results in manslaughters and many evils.

The fifth is *sadness,* that is sadness of this world, when 255 a person is all too sad on account of the loss of his possessions, which he loved too much, and then complains against God and adds to his sins. There are two sadnesses: one is this evil one and the second is salutary, in that one is sad on account of one's sins.

The sixth vice is named *sloth,* that is indolence or sloth in 260 English, when a person does not desire to do any good in his life, and then it will be a great evil for him that he cannot do any good, and he will always be unprepared for any virtuous action.

The seventh vice is called *vainglory,* that is vainglory in 265 the English language, when a person is eager for praise and behaves with hypocrisy and, if he is willing to give something in alms, does it for vainglorious display. And then the good reputation will be his reward for the deed and his pun 270 ishment will await him in the next world.

The eighth vice is named *pride,* which is called pride in English. It is the beginning and end of every sin. It changed angels into horrible devils and will also make man, if he is 275 too proud, into the companion of the devil, who formerly fell because of it.

Now there are eight capital virtues that can overcome the aforementioned devils with the help of the Lord. One is

An is *temperantia,* þæt is gemetegung on Englisc,
280 þæt man beo gemetegod and to mycel ne ðicge
on æte and on wæte ne ær timan ne gereordige.
Nytenu ætað swa ær swa hi hit habbað,
ac se gesceadwise man sceal cepan his mæles
and ðonne mid gesceade his gesetnysse healdan.
285 Þonne mæg he oferswiðan swa ða gyfernysse.

Seo oðer miht is *castitas,* þæt is clænnyss on Ænglisc,
þæt se læweda hine healde butan forligre
on rihtum synscipe, mid gesceadwisnysse,
and se gehadode Godes ðeowa healde his clænnysse.
290 Þonne bið oferswyðed swa eac seo galnyss.

Seo ðrydde miht is *largitas,* þæt is cystignyss on Englisc,
þæt man wislice aspende (na for woruld-gylpe)
þa ðincg þe him God lænde on ðysum life to brucenne.
God nele þæt we beon grædige gytseras,
295 ne eac for woruld-gylpe forwurpan ure æhta,
ac dælan hi mid gesceade, swa swa hit Drihtne licie,
and gif we ælmyssan doð, don hi butan gylpe.
Þonne mage we fordon swa ða deofollican gitsunge.

Seo feorðe miht is *patientia,* þæt is geðyld gecwæden,
300 þæt se mann beo geðyldig and ðol-mod for Gode
and læte æfre his gewitt gewyldre þonne his yrre,
forðan þe se hælend cwæð þus on his god-spelle:
In patientia vestra possidebitis animas vestras.
Þæt is on Engliscre spræce: "On eowrum geðylde
305 ge habbað eowre sawla soðlice gehealdene."
Se heofonlica wisdom cwæð þæt þæt yrre hæfð wununge
on ðæs dysegan bosme, ðonne he bið to hræd-mod,
and se eal-wealdenda dema demð æfre mid smyltnysse,
and we sceolan mid geðylde oferswyðan þæt yrre.

temperance, that is temperance in English, that a person be 280
temperate and not consume too much in food and in drink,
nor eat before the proper time. Beasts eat as soon as they
have it, but the rational person must keep to the proper
times for meals and then observe his established practice
with reason. Then he will be able to overcome gluttony in 285
this way.

The second virtue is *chastity,* that is chastity in English,
that the lay person should keep himself free from adultery
in lawful marriage, with rationality, and the consecrated servant of God should preserve his chastity. Then lust will like- 290
wise be overcome.

The third virtue is *generosity,* that is generosity in English,
that one should spend wisely (not for worldly ostentation)
the things that God has lent one to enjoy in this life. God
does not wish that we should be greedy misers, nor throw 295
away our possessions for the sake of worldly ostentation,
but that we should give them charitably with discrimina-
tion, as it may please the Lord, and if we give alms, give them
without ostentation. Then we can destroy diabolical avarice
in this way.

The fourth virtue is *patience,* that is called patience, that a 300
person should be patient and forbearing for God and always
let his understanding be more powerful than his anger, because the savior spoke thus in his gospel: *In patience you shall
possess your souls.* That is in the English language: "By your patience you shall truly possess your souls." The heavenly wis- 305
dom said that anger has its dwelling in the bosom of the fool
when he is too hasty, but the all-ruling judge always judges
with calm, and we must overcome anger with patience.

310   Seo fifte miht is *spiritalis laetitia,*
     þæt is seo gastlice blys, þæt man on God blyssige
     betwux unrotnyssum þysre reðan worulde,
     swa þæt we on ungelimpum ormode ne beon
     ne eft on gesælðum to swyðe ne blyssian.
315   And gif we forleosað þas lænan woruld-ðingc,
     þonne sceole we witan þæt ure wunung nis na her
     ac is on heofonum, gif we hopiað to Gode.
     Þyder we sceolan efstan of ðyssere earfoðnysse
     mid gastlicre blisse; þonne bið seo unrotnyss
320   mid ealle oferswyðed mid urum geðylde.
      Seo syxte miht is *instantia boni operis,*
     þæt is an-rædnyss godes weorces.
     Gif we beoð an-ræde on urum godum weorcum,
     ðonne mage we oferswyðan þa asolcennysse swa,
325   forðan þe hit bið langsum bysmor gif ure lif bið unnyt her.
      Seo seofoðe miht is seo soðe lufu to Gode,
     þæt we on godum weorcum Godes lufe cepon,
     na ideles gylpes, þe him is andsæte.
     Ac uton don ælmyssan swa swa he us tæhte,
330   Gode to lofe, na us to hlisan,
     þæt God sy geherod on urum godum weorcum
     and se idela gylp us beo æfre unwurð.
      Seo eahteoðe miht is seo soðe ead-modnyss,
     ge to Gode ge to mannum, mid modes hluttornysse,
335   forðan se ðe wis byð, ne wurð he næfre modig.
     On hwan mæg se mann modigan þeah he wille?
     Ne mæg he on geðincðum, forðan þe fela synd geþungenran;
     ne mæg he on his æhtum, forðan þe he his ende-dæg nat,
     ne on nanum þingum he ne mæg modigan, gif he wis bið.

The fifth virtue is *spiritual happiness,* that is spiritual hap- 310
piness, that one should rejoice in God amid the sadnesses of
this cruel world, so that we be not too despairing in misfortunes nor on the other hand that we not rejoice too much in
good fortunes. And if we lose these transitory worldly pos- 315
sessions, then we must know that our dwelling is not here
but is in heaven, if we hope in God. We must hasten there
with spiritual happiness, away from this hardship; then this
sadness will be entirely overcome by our patience. 320

The sixth virtue is *perseverance in good work,* that is perseverance in good work. If we are steadfast in our good works,
then we can overcome sloth in this way, because it will be a 325
long-lasting disgrace if our life here is useless.

The seventh virtue is true love for God, that through
good deeds we seek to have God's love, not vainglory, which
is repugnant to him. But let us give alms as he taught us, for 330
the glory of God, not for the sake of our own reputations, so
that God may be praised in our good deeds, and let vainglory always be worthless in our eyes.

The eighth virtue is true humility, both toward God and
toward people, with purity of mind, because he who is wise 335
will never become proud. Even if a person may wish it, of
what can he be proud? He cannot be proud of his rank, because many are more distinguished; he cannot be proud of
his possessions, because he does not know his final day; nor
can he be proud of anything, if he is wise.

340   Nu ge habbað gehyred hu þas halgan mægnu
oferswyðaþ ða leahtras þe deofol besæwð on us,
and gif we nellað hi oferswiðan, hi besencað us on helle.
We magon þurh Godes fylst ða feondlican leahtras
mid gecampe oferwinnan, gif we cenlice feohtað,
345   and habban us on ende þone ecan wurð-mynt
a mid Gode sylfum, gif we swincað nu her.

Now you have heard how these holy virtues overcome   340
the vices that the devil sows among us, and if we are not willing to overcome them, they will plunge us into hell. Through
God's help we can defeat the diabolical vices by combat, if
we fight boldly, and can in the end have eternal honor for   345
ourselves forever with God himself, if we toil here now.

ON OMENS

16

On Omens

De Auguriis: Sermo in Laetania maiore

1

Se apostol Paulus, ealra ðeoda lareow, manode ða Cristenan þe he sylf ær to geleafan gebigde on anum pistole, þæt is ærend-gewrit, ðus cwæðende: *Fratres, spiritu ambulate, et desideria carnis non perficietis, et cetera.* "Mine gebroðra, farað on gaste, þæt is on gastlicre drohtnunga, and ne gefremme ge eowres flæsces lustas." Þæt flæsc soðlice gewilnað ongean ðone gast and se gast ongean þæt flæsc. Þas ðincg soðlice, ðæt is se lic-hama and seo sawl, winnað him betweonan. Ac seo sawl is ðæs flæsces hlæfdige and hire gedafnað þæt heo simle gewylde ða wylne, þæt is þæt flæsc, to hyre hæsum. Þwyrlice færð æt ðam huse þær seo wyln bið þære hlæfdian wissigend and seo hlæfdige bið þære wylne underðeodd. Swa bið eac þæs mannes lif onhinder gefadod, gif þæt flæsc þe is brosnigendlic and deadlic sceal gewyldan þone gast, ðe is ece and unateorigendlic, to his fracodum lustum ðe hi buta fordoð and to ecum tintregum gebringað.

16

On Omens

On Omens: A Sermon for Rogationtide

I

The apostle Paul, the teacher of all peoples, exhorted the Christians whom he himself had converted to the faith in an epistle, that is a letter, saying thus: *Brethren, walk in the spirit, and you shall not fulfill the lusts of the flesh, et cetera.* "My brothers, walk in the spirit, that is in a spiritual manner of living, and do not let yourselves carry out the desires of your flesh." Truly the flesh desires what is contrary to the spirit and the spirit what is contrary to the flesh. Truly these things, that is the body and the soul, oppose one another. But the soul is the flesh's mistress, and it is fitting for it always to make the maidservant, that is the flesh, subject to its commands. Things go awry in the house where the maidservant directs the mistress of the house and where the mistress of the house is subject to the maidservant. So also a person's life will be upside down, if the flesh, which is decaying and mortal, should make the spirit, which is eternal and unfading, subject to its wicked desires that will destroy them both and bring them to eternal torments.

2. Se apostol cwæð: "Gif ge beoð þurh ðone gast gelædde, ðonne ne synd ge na under æ." He cwæð on oðre stowe: "Nis nan æ rihtwisum menn gesett, ac unrihtwisum and na underþeoddum, arleasum and forscyldegodum"; forðan þe seo æ, þæt is seo rihtwise steor, ne gegret þone rihtwisan mid nanum yfele, ac heo gewitnað þa unrihtwisan be heora gewyrhtum. Se rihtwisa soðlice ne þearf him ondrædan þa stiðan steora þe Godes æ tæcð, gif he him sylfum styrð fram eallum stuntnyssum.

3. Paulus cwæð: "Swutele synd þæs flæsces weorc, þæt is forligr and unclænnyss, estfulnyss oððe galnyss, hæðen-gild and unlybban, feond-ræden and geflit, anda and yrre, sacu and twi-rædnyss, dwollic lar and nið, man-sliht and druncennyss, ofer-fyll and oðre ðyllice, þe ic eow foresecge swa swa ic foresæde; forðan þa ðe ðyllice weorc wyrcað, ne begitað hi Godes rice." Gehwa mot yfeles geswican and gebetan, ac gif he ðurhwunað on yfelnysse and forsihð his scyppendes beboda and deofla gecwemð, þonne sceal he unðances on ecnysse ðrowian, on ðam unadwæscendlicum fyre betwux ðam wyrrestan wurm-cynne, þe næfre ne bið adyd, ac ceowað symle þæra arleasra lic-hama on ðam hellican lige.

4. Eft cwæð se apostol on oðrum pistole: *Fratres, nolite errare: neque fornicarii neque idolis servientes neque adulteri neque molles neque fures neque avari neque ebriosi neque maledici neque rapaces regnum Dei non possidebunt.* "Mine gebroðra, nelle ge dwelian: naðor ne unriht-hæmeras, ne ða ðe hæðen-gildum þeowiað, ne ða þe oðre manna wif habbað, ne ða hnescan, þæt synd þa ðe nane stiðnysse nabbað ongean leahtras, ne

2. The apostle said: "If you are led by the spirit, then you are not under the law." He said in another place: "The law is not decreed for righteous people, but for the unrighteous and those who are not obedient, the impious and the guilty"; because the law, that is just rule, does not assail the righteous person with any evil, but it punishes the unrighteous according to their deserts. Truly the righteous person need not fear the strict rule that God's law teaches, if he restrains from all foolishness.

3. Paul said: "The works of the flesh are manifest, that is fornication and impurity, licentiousness or lust, idolatry and witchcraft, enmity and dissension, envy and anger, strife and discord, heretical teaching and envy, murder and drunkenness, excessive eating and other such things, of which I foretell you as I have foretold you before; because those who do such deeds will not obtain God's kingdom." Everyone must cease from evil and atone, but if he perseveres in evil and holds his creator's commands in contempt and pleases the devil, then he will have to suffer against his will for eternity, in the inextinguishable fire among the worst kind of serpent, which will never be put to death, but will continually chew the bodies of the impious in the fire of hell.

4. Likewise the apostle said in another epistle: *Brethren, be not deceived: neither fornicators nor idolaters nor adulterers nor the effeminate nor thieves nor covetous nor drunkards nor railers nor extortioners shall possess the kingdom of God.* "My brothers, do not be mistaken: neither fornicators, nor those who serve idols, nor those who have intercourse with other men's wives, nor those who are morally soft, that is those who have no firmness in resisting vices, nor thieves, nor covetous

ðeofas, ne gytseras, ne drinceras, þæt synd þa ðe druncennysse lufiað, ne wyrgendras, þæra muð bið symle mid geæt-
trode wyrigunge afylled, ne reaferas, nabbað hi næfre Godes
rice." He cwæð þa git eft forð to þam folce ðus: "Þis ge
wæron. Ac ge synd nu afeormode; ac ge synd gehalgode; ac
ge synd gerihtwisode on Drihtnes naman ures hælendes
Cristes, and on Gaste ures Godes."

2

Deofol-gild bið þæt man his Drihten forlæte and his
                                                    Cristendom
and to deofollicum hæðenscype gebuge, bysmrigende his
                                                    scyppend.
Oðer deofol-gild is, derigendlic þære sawle,
ðonne se man forsihð his scyppendes beboda
5   and þa sceandlican leahtras begæð þe se sceocca hine lærð.
Þæs Gastes wæstmas synd þa godan ðeawas:
þæt se man lufige þone lifigendan God
and hæbbe ða soðan lufe symle on his mode
and ða gastlican blysse and beo gesibsum,
10 geðyldig and ðol-mod, and on ðeawum hæbbe
godnysse and glæd mod and man-ðwærnysse,
geleafan and gemetfæstnysse and modes clænnysse
and forhæfednysse butan higeleaste.
Nis nan æ wiðerræde þus geworhtum mannum,
15 ac ða þe Cristes synd cwylmiað heora flæsc
swa þæt hi nellað onbugan ðam bysmorfullum leahtrum
ne ðam yfelum gewilnungum, ac winnað him togeanes
oðþæt hi sigefæste siðiað to Criste
and to ðam ecan wuldre for ðam sceortan gewinne
20 and hi blyssiað on ecnysse, bliðe mid Criste.

people, nor drinkers, that is those who love drunkenness, nor those who curse, whose mouths are always filled with poisonous cursing, nor robbers, will ever possess the kingdom of God." He spoke moreover still further to the people thus: "This is what you were. But now you are cleansed; but you are sanctified; but you are justified in the name of the Lord our savior Christ, and in the Spirit of our God."

2

It is idolatry to abandon one's Lord and one's Christian faith and submit to diabolical heathenism, insulting one's creator. It is a different idolatry, harmful to the soul, when a person holds his creator's commands in contempt and engages in 5 the shameful vices that the devil teaches him. The fruits of the Spirit are these good practices: that a person should love the living God; and always have true love in his heart and spiritual joy; and be peaceful, patient, and forbearing; and 10 habitually have goodness and a joyous heart and gentleness, faith, and moderation and purity of heart and abstinence without recklessness. There is no law against people of such dispositions, but those who are Christ's mortify their flesh 15 so that they refuse to yield to shameful vices or to evil desires, but they fight against them until they go victoriously to Christ and to the eternal glory as a reward for that short conflict, and they will rejoice in eternity, joyous with Christ. 20

Agustinus se snotera bisceop sæde eac on sumere bec:
"Mine gebroðra þa leofestan, gelome ic eow warnode
and mid fæderlicre carfulnysse ic eow cuðlice manode
þæt ge þa andsætan wiglunge þe unwise men healdað
25 mid ealle forlætan, swa swa geleaffulle men,
forðan butan ic eow warnige and þone wol eow forbeode,
ic sceal agyldan gescead þam soðfæstan deman
minre gymeleaste and mid eow beon fordemed."
Nu alyse ic me sylfne wið God and mid lufe eow forbeode
30 þæt eower nan ne axie þurh ænigne wicce-cræft
be ænigum ðinge oððe be ænigre untrumnysse
ne galdras ne sece to gremigenne his scyppend
forðan se ðe þys deð, se forlysð his Cristendom,
and bið þam hæðenum gelic þe hleotað be him sylfum
35 mid ðæs deofles cræfte, þe hi fordeð on ecnysse.
And butan he manega ælmyssan and mycele dæd-bote
his scyppende geoffrige, æfre he bið forloren.
    Hleotan man mot mid geleafan swaþeah
on woruld-ðingum, butan wicce-cræfte,
40 þæt him deme seo ta, gif hi hwæt dælan willað;
þis nis nan wiglung, ac bið wissung foroft.
Eallswa gelice se ðe gelyfð wiglungum,
oððe be fugelum oððe be fnorum
oððe be horsum oððe be hundum,
45 ne bið he na Cristen, ac bið forcuð wiðersaca.
    Ne sceal nan Cristen man cepan be dagum,
on hwilcum dæge he fare oððe on hwylcum he gecyrre,
forðan þe God gesceop ealle ða seofan dagas,
þe yrnað on þære wucan oð þysre worulde geendunge.
50 Ac se ðe hwider faran wille, singe his *Pater noster*

Augustine the wise bishop also said in a book: "My most beloved brothers, I have frequently warned you and I have clearly exhorted you with fatherly solicitude that you abandon entirely, like people of the true faith, the repugnant omens that foolish people engage in, because unless I warn you and forbid this plague, I will have to render an account to the true judge for my negligence and be condemned with you." Now I will acquit myself before God, and with love I will forbid that any one of you should by means of any witchcraft ask about any thing or about any sickness or seek out sorcerers to anger his creator, because he who does this renounces his Christian faith, and will be like those heathens who cast lots concerning themselves by the devil's evil power, that will damn them for eternity. And unless he offer many alms and much penance to his creator, he will be lost forever.

One may, however, cast lots in secular matters with faith, without witchcraft, so that, if people wish to divide something into parts, the lot will decide for them; this is no omen, but is very often a direction. In like manner also he who believes omens, either from birds or from sneezes or from horses or from dogs, is not a Christian, but is a despicable apostate.

No Christian person ought to pay attention to the days, on which day he may travel or on which he may return, because God created all seven days that will go by in the week until the end of this world. But he who may wish to go somewhere, let him sing his *Our Father* and creed, if he knows

and credan, gif he cunne, and clypige to his Dryhtne
and bletsige hine sylfne and siðige orsorh
þurh Godes gescyldnysse, butan ðæra sceoccena wiglunga.
   Us sceamað to secgenne ealle ða sceandlican wiglunga
55 þe gedwæs-menn drifað ðurh deofles lare,
oððe on wifunge oððe on wadunge
oððe on bryw-lace oððe gif hi man hwæs bitt
þonne hi hwæt onginnað, oþþe him hwæt bið acenned.
Ac wite ge to soðan þæt se sceocca eow lærð
60 þyllice scin-cræftas þæt he eowre sawla hæbbe
ðonne ge gelyfað his leas-brædnysse.
   Nu cwyð sum wiglere þæt wiccan oft secgað
swa swa hit agæð mid soðum ðincge.
Nu secge we to soðan þæt se ungesewenlica deofol
65 þe flyhð geond þas woruld, and fela ðincg gesihð,
geswutelað þæra wiccan hwæt heo secge mannum,
þæt þa beon fordone þe ðæne dry-cræft secað.
Fela sædon þa dry-men þurh deofles cræft,
Iamnes and Mambres, swa swa Moyses awrat,
70 and hi Pharao forlærdon mid heora lot-wrencum,
oððæt he adranc on ðære deopan sæ.
Eallswa eac Symon, se swicola dry,
swa lange he wan wið Petre oðþæt he wearð afylled,
ða þa he wolde fleon to heofonum, þæt he on feower tobærst
75 and swa ferde wæl-hreow mid wite to helle.
Fela oðre forferdon þe folgodon dry-cræfte,
swa swa we on bocum rædað, ac heora racu is langsum.
Ne sceal se Cristena befrinan þa fulan wiccan
be his gesundfulnysse, þeah ðe heo secgan cunne
80 sum ðincg þurh deofol, forðan þe hit bið derigendlic

how, and call to his Lord and bless himself and travel free from care with God's protection, without the demons' omens.

We are ashamed to relate all the shameful omens that foolish people engage in at the devil's instigation, either in marrying, or in traveling, or in brewing, or if someone asks them for something when they are beginning something, or when a child is born to them. But know in truth that the devil teaches you such magic arts so that he may possess your soul when you believe his deception.

Now one sorcerer says that witches often tell something as it will truly come to pass. Now we say in truth that the invisible devil who flies throughout the world and sees many things reveals to the witch what she should say to people, so that those who resort to magic may be ruined. The sorcerers Jamnes and Mambres said many things through the devil's cunning, as Moses wrote, and they led Pharaoh astray with their deceitful tricks, until he drowned in the deep sea. Simon also, the deceitful sorcerer, fought against Peter for a long time, until he was cast down when he wished to fly to heaven, so that he burst into four parts and in this way the savage man went to hell in torment. Many others who practiced sorcery perished, as we read in books, but their stories are lengthy. The Christian must not ask the foul witch about his health, although she may be able to say something through the devil, because it will be harmful and everything

and eall hit við ættrig þæt him of cymð
and ealle his folgeras forfarað on ende.

Sume men synd swa ablende þæt hi bringað heora lac
to eorðfæstum stanum and eac to treowum
85 and to wyl-springum, swa swa wiccan tæcað,
and nellað understandan hu stuntlice hi doð
oððe hu se deada stan oððe þæt dumbe treow
him mæge gehelpan oððe hæle forgifan,
þone hi sylfe ne astyriað of ðære stowe næfre.

90 Se Cristene man sceall clypian to his Drihtne
mid mode and mid muðe and his munda abiddan,
þæt he hine gescylde wið deofles syrwunga,
and besettan his hiht on ðone soðan God,
se ðe ana gewylt ealra gesceafta,
95 þæt he foresceawige be his gesundfulnysse,
loca hu he wille, swa swa eal-wealdend God.

We sceolan on ælcne timan and on ælcere styrunge
bletsian us sylfe mid soðum geleafan
and mid rode-tacne þa reðan aflian,
100 forðan þe se reða deofol wearð þurh ða rode oferswiðed,
and heo is ure sige-beacn ongean þone sceoccan a.

Eac sume gewitlease wif farað to wega gelætum
and teoð heora cild þurh ða eorðan
and swa deofle betæcað hi sylfe and heora bearn.

105 Sume hi acwellað heora cild ær ðam þe hi acennede beon,
oððe æfter acennednysse, þæt hi cuðe ne beon
ne heora manfulla forligr ameldod ne wurðe,
ac heora yfel is egeslic and endeleaslic morð.

Þær losað þæt cild, laðlice hæðen,
110 and seo arleasa modor, butan heo hit æfre gebete.

that comes from him is poisonous and all his followers will perish in the end.

Some people are so blinded that they bring their offerings to stones fixed in the earth and also to trees and to springs, as witches direct, and refuse to understand how foolishly they are acting or how the dead stone or the dumb tree would be able to help them or give them health, when they themselves never stir from that place. The Christian person must call to his Lord with his heart and with his mouth and pray for his protection, that he may defend him from the devil's plotting, and must place his hope in the true God, he who alone rules all creatures, so that he may provide for his health, however he may wish, as the omnipotent God. At every time and in every trouble we must bless ourselves with true faith and put the cruel ones to flight with the sign of the cross, because the cruel devil was defeated by means of the cross, and it is always our sign of victory against the devil.

Likewise some stupid women go to crossroads and drag their children through the earth and in this way commit themselves and their children to the devil. Some of them kill their children before they are born, or after birth, so that they may not be known nor their wicked fornication exposed, but their evil is terrible and their perdition everlasting. The child perishes there, a loathsome heathen, and the impious mother too, unless she atones for it always. Some of

Sume hi wyrcað heora wogerum drencas,
oððe sumne wawan, þæt hi hi to wife habbon.
Ac þyllice sceandas sceolan siðian to helle,
þær hi æfre cwylmiað on þam cwealm-bærum fyre
115 and on egeslicum witum for heora gewitleaste.

Ac Cristene men sceolan campian wið deofla
mid strangum geleafan, swa swa gelærede cempan,
and forhogian þa hætsan and ðyllice hæðen-gyld
and þæs deofles dydrunga, and heora Drihten arwurðian.
120 Þonne gesihþ se deofol þæt ge hine forseoð
and him bið þonne wa on his awyrigedum mode,
þæt ge swa an-ræde beoð, and nimð andan to eow
and wile eow geswencan mid sumere untrumnysse
oððe sum eowre orf ardlice acwellan,
125 forðan þe he mot ælces mannes afandian
on manega wisan, hwæðer his mod wille
abugan þurh ða ehtnysse fram ðam ælmihtigan Gode.
Ac wite ge to gewissan þæt se wæl-hreowa deofol
ne mæg mannum derian mid nanre untrumnysse
130 ne heora orf adydan butan Drihtnes geþafunge.

God is eall godnyss and he æfre wel wile,
ac manna yfelnysse mot beon gestyrod;
þonne geðafað God þam sceoccan foroft,
þæt he men geswence for heora misdædum.
135 Us is to secenne, gif we geswencte beoð,
þa bote æt Gode, na æt ðam gramlican wiccum,
and mid ealra heortan urne hælend gladian,
forðan þe his mihte ne mæg nan ðincg wiðstandan.
He cwæð on his god-spelle þæt buton Godes dihte
140 furðon an fugel ne befylð on deaðe.
Wen is þæt he wille bewitan a his menn,

them make drinks for their wooers, or some kind of trouble, so that they may take them as their wives. But such shameful women will have to go to hell, where they will forever suffer in the deadly fire and in terrible torments for their stupidity. 115

But Christian people must fight against devils with a strong faith, like trained warriors, and scorn those sorceresses and such idolatry and the devil's delusions, and worship their Lord. Then the devil will see that you scorn him, 120 and he will be grieved in his accursed mind because you are so resolute, and he will conceive malice toward you and will wish to afflict you with some illness or quickly kill one of your cattle, because he is allowed to test every person in 125 many ways, to see whether his mind may be willing to turn from the almighty God because of that tribulation. But know for certain that the cruel devil cannot harm people with any illness or kill their cattle without the Lord's per- 130 mission.

God is all goodness and he is always benevolent, but people's evil may be aroused; then God very often permits the devil to afflict people because of their evil deeds. If we are 135 afflicted, we must seek the remedy from God, not from the cruel witches, and appease our savior with all our hearts, because nothing can withstand his power. He said in his gospel that without God's direction not even one bird falls to its 140 death. It is to be expected that he should wish to watch over

ge on life, ge on deaðe, þonne se lytla fugel
ne befylþ on grin butan Godes willan.
Ure Drihten adræfde deoflu mid his hæse of anum wodum
menn;

145 þa wæs ðær gehende an heord swina
and hi sona bædon þæt hi moston faran into ðam swynum
and Drihten geðafode þa ðam deoflum þæt.
Hi ða into þam swynum and hi ealle aweddan
and urnon to ðære sæ and sona adruncon.

150 Ne mæg se deofol mannum derian butan Godes geðafunge,
ne heora ðincg amyrran, þonne he ne moste faran
furðon on þa swin, butan him geðafode þæs se hælend.
Gif us deofol drecð oþþe ure þincg adyd,
þæt getimað þonne swa for twam intingum:

155 oþþe God swa þreað ure ðwyrlican dæda
oððe he ure afandað on ðære frecednysse.
And se sceocca sceall aswæman æt us
gif we an-ræde beoð on urum geleafan
and Crist hine adræfð þæt he us derian ne mæg,

160 gif we ða ehtnysse ead-modlice forberað
and butan ceorunge symle Gode þanciað.
Us becymð swaþeah eall þæt to gode
gif we beoð geðyldige and þanciað urum Drihtne
and on ðære fandunge his fultumes biddað

165 se þe eaðelice mæg us æfre ahreddan
fram eallum fræcednyssum feondlicra costnunga.
      Læcedom is alyfed for lic-hamena tyddernysse
and halige gebedu, mid Godes bletsunge,
and ealla oðre tilunga syndon andsæte Gode,

170 swa swa Paulus awrat, þysum wordum cweðende:
"Ne mage ge samod drincan ures Drihtnes calic

his people always, both in life and in death, when the little
bird does not fall into a trap without God's will. Our Lord
drove devils out of an insane person with his command;
then nearby there was a herd of pigs, and they immediately   145
entreated to be allowed to go into the pigs, and then the
Lord permitted this to the devils. Then they went into the
pigs, and they all became insane and ran to the sea and
drowned at once. The devil cannot harm people without   150
God's permission, nor destroy their possessions, when he
was not allowed to go even into the pigs, unless the savior
permitted him this. If the devil afflicts us or destroys our
possessions, then that happens for two reasons: either God   155
is punishing our perverse deeds like this, or he is testing us
in that danger. And the devil will be obliged to be ashamed
before us if we are resolute in our faith, and Christ will drive
him away so that he will not be able to harm us, if we humbly   160
endure the tribulation and always thank God without com-
plaint. All that will, however, turn out well for us if we are
patient and thank our Lord and during the testing pray for
help from him who can easily save us always from all the   165
dangers of diabolical temptations.

Medicine and holy prayers are permitted for physical in-
firmity with God's blessing, and all other treatments are repugnant to God, as Paul wrote, speaking in these words: 170
"You cannot drink both the chalice of our Lord and the cup

and ðæs deofles cuppan, to deaðe eowre sawle."
And ure Drihten cwæð þæt man gecwæman ne mæg
twam hlafordum ætsomne, þæt he ne forseo þone oðerne,
175 ne we ne magon gecwæman Criste and deofle.

Nu secgað sume menn þæt him sceole gelimpan
swa swa him gesceapan wæs and geset æt fruman
and ne magon forbugan þæt hi misfaran ne sceolan.
Nu secge we to soðan, gif hit swa beon sceall,
180 þæt hit is unnyt bebod ðe God bebead þurh Dauid:
Declina a malo, et fac bonum.
"Buh fram yfle, and do god." And eft se apostol cwæð:
"Swa man swyðor swincð for Gode, swa he selran mede
hæfð."

Gif ælces mannes lif æfre sceola swa gan
185 þæt he ne mæge forbugan bysmorlice dæda,
þonne bið unrihtlic þæt ða unrihtwisan onfon
ænige witnunge for heora wohnysse.
Eac ða arfæstan beoð wolice gearwurðode,
gif þæt soð beon mæg þæt him swa gesceapen wæs.
190 And on unnyt we swincað on urum þeowdome,
oððe on ælmyssum oþþe on oðrum dædum,
gif we his na maran edlean æt urum Drihtne nabbað
þonne ða receleasan menn, þe butan gerade lybbað
and on eallum þingum wadað on heora agenum willan
195 and on heora lustum heora lif aspendað.

God ælmihtig gesceop manega gesceafta
and heora nanum ne forgeaf agenne freodom
oþþe gesceadwisnysse, butan ðam scinendum englum
and menniscum gesceafta, þe he mid his handum gesceop.
200 Þas twa gesceafta habbað gesceadwisnysse
and ælc man hæfð agenne freodom,

of the devil, to the death of your souls." And our Lord said that one cannot please two masters at once, lest he hold the second in contempt, nor can we please Christ and the devil. 175

Now some people say that it must turn out for them as it was ordained for them and appointed in the beginning, and that they cannot avoid going wrong. Now we say truly, if this must be the case, that what God commanded though David 180 is a useless command: *Decline from evil, and do good.* "Turn from evil, and do good." And again the apostle said: "The more one labors for God, the greater reward he will have." If each person's life must always proceed in such a way that he 185 cannot abstain from shameful deeds, then it is unjust that the unrighteous should receive any punishment for their wickedness. Also the virtuous are wrongly honored, if it can be true that it was so ordained for them. And we labor in 190 vain in our service, or in alms or in other deeds, if we have no greater reward from our Lord than negligent people, who live without reason and proceed according to their own wills in all things and squander their lives in their pleasures. 195

God almighty created all creatures and did not give any of them their own freedom or rationality, except for the shining angels and human creatures, whom he created with his own hands. These two creatures have rationality and 200 each person has his own freedom, so that he knows what he

þæt he wat hwæt he wile and wat hwæt he nele,
ac God us ne nyt swaþeah þæt we god don sceolon
ne eac us ne forwyrnð yfel to wyrcenne,
205 forðan þe he us forgeaf agenne cyre.
He sealde swiðe fæste gife and swyþe fæste æ
mid þære gife ælcum menn oð his ende, earmum and
           eadigum.
Þæt is seo gifu þæt se man mot don þæt he wile
and þæt is seo æ þæt God forgylt ælcum menn be his
          gewyrhtum,
210 ægðer ge on þysre worulde ge on þære toweardan,
swa god swa yfel, swa hwæðer swa he begæð.
 Gif hwa nu wundrige hwi God wolde
forgifan þam yfelum mannum agenne freodom,
þone he wat on ær þæt hi yfel don willað,
215 nu cweðe we þæt hit ne gerist nanum ricum cynincge
þæt ealle beon þeowe menn ðe him þenian sceolon,
and on his anwealde ne beo furðon an frig man.
Swa eac ne gedafnode þam ælmihtigan Drihtne
þæt on eallum his rice nære ænig gesceaft
220 þe nære on þeowte þearle genyrwed.
Nu behofað ure freodom æfre Godes fultumes
forþan ðe we ne doð nan god butan Godes gife.
Se us gewissige a on ðysre worulde
and to þam ecan life gelæde þurh hine sylfne,
225 swa swa he þam eallum behet þe hine lufiað.
Sy him wuldor and lof a to worulde. Amen.

desires and knows what he does not desire, but nevertheless God does not compel us to do good nor does he prevent us from doing evil, because he gave us our own free choice. He gave a very enduring gift and a very enduring law with that gift to each person until his death, to poor and rich. The gift is that a person may do what he wishes and the law is that God will requite each person according to his actions, both in this world and in the future one, whether good or evil, whichever he does. 205 210

If anyone should wonder now why God would be willing to give evil people their own freedom, when he knows in advance that they intend to do evil, we say now that it is not fitting for any powerful king that they who must serve him should all be slaves, and that there should not be even one free person in his realm. So also it would not be fitting for the almighty Lord that in all his kingdom there would not be any creature who was not strictly confined in servitude. Now our freedom always needs God's help because we do no good without God's grace. May he always guide us in this world and lead us in person to the eternal life, as he promised to all those who love him. Glory and praise be to him forever and ever. Amen. 215 220 225

KINGS

17

Kings

Sermo excerptus de Libro regum

Saul hatte se forma cyning þe ofer Godes folc rixode.
Se wæs to cynincge ahafen swyðor for folces gecorennysse
þonne ðurh Godes ræd. Fela oðre cynincgas rixodon ær
geond ealne middan-eard ofer hæðenum leodum,

5 ac ofer Israhela folc þe on God belyfde
næs nan eorðlic cynincg ær ðan þe Saul,
swa swa hi sylfe gecuron, ofer hi cyne-rice underfencg.
Se beah hrædlice fram þæs ælmihtigan Godes willan
and nolde be his wissunge and be his witegan lare faran

10 and se yfela gast hine drehte mid deofollicum sticelsum
and on ungewitte his mod awende.
    Þa forseah se ælmihtiga God þone Saul æt nextan
and hine of his rice awearp be his agenum gewyrhtum
and ceas to cynincge þone cenan Dauid,

15 se ðe butan wæpnum gewylde ða leon
and þæs beran ceaflas tobræc mid his handum
and ahredde þæt gelæhte scep of his scearpum toðum.
He ofwearp eac syððan þone swyþlican ent,
Goliam ðone gramlican, þe Godes naman hyrwde,

17

Kings

A Sermon Excerpted from the Book of Kings

The first king who reigned over God's people was called
Saul. He was raised up as king by the choice of the people
rather than through the counsel of God. Many other kings
had reigned over heathen peoples throughout the world,
but over the people of the Israelites who believed in God 5
there was no earthly king until Saul, as they themselves had
chosen, assumed royal authority over them. He soon turned
away from the will of the almighty God and refused to act
according to his direction and his prophet's teaching, and 10
the evil spirit disturbed him with diabolical goading and altered his mind to insanity.

Then finally the almighty God rejected Saul and deserv-
edly cast him out of his kingdom and chose the brave David
as king, he who had overpowered the lion without weapons 15
and had shattered the jaws of the bear with his hands and
had rescued the captured sheep from his sharp teeth. Moreover he had then killed with a stone the powerful giant,
Goliath the fierce, who had slandered the name of God,

20 and mid gebeote clypode bysmor Godes folce,
gearu to an-wige mid ormettre wæpnunge.

Hwæt þa Dauid eode togeanes þam ente
and ofwearp mid his liþeran þone geleafleasan ent
bufon ðam eagan, þæt he beah to eorðan.

25 Gelæhte þa of ðam ente his agen swurd
and his ormæte heafod mid þam of asloh
and hæfde ða gewunnen sige his leode.

Be þysum Dauide cwæð se ælmihtiga wealdend
þæt he hine gecure, þus cweðende:

30 "Ic afunde me Dauid æfter minre heortan,
þæt he ealne minne willan mid weorcum gefremme."

Þes Dauid wæs witega and wuldorful cyningc
and Gode gelicode oð his lifes ende
and mid ealre heortan him gehyrsumode a.

35 He wæs forði mære on micclum geðincþum,
forðan þe he cepte symle hu he gecwemde Gode.

Æfter him rixodon on Israhela rice
manega cyningas, mislice geworhte.

Sume hi gelyfdon on þone lyfigendan God,
40 sume on hæðen-gild, him sylfum to forwyrde,
and þa ðe God wurðodon wurdon gemærsode
and sigefæste wæron symle on gefeohte.

Þa ðe fram Gode bugon to bysmorfullum hæðenscype,
þa wurdon gescynde and a unsigefæste.

45 An þæra wæs Achab, se arleasa cyning
þe forseah his scyppend and geceas him Baal,
þæra hæðenra god, þe næfde nane godcundnysse,
ac wæs gramlic deofol, mid gedwylde afunden.

Þyses cyninges cwen wæs forcuþost wifa,
50 Gezabel gehaten, hetelice gemodod.

and with a vow to do harm had called down insult upon 20
God's people, ready for single combat with his enormous ar-
mor.

Well then, David went against the giant and struck the
unbelieving giant above the eyes with a stone from his sling,
so that he sank to the ground. Then he seized the giant's 25
own sword from him and with it struck off his enormous
head and won the victory for his people. The almighty ruler
said concerning this David that he had chosen him, saying
thus: "I have found David to be after my own heart, in that 30
he will do all my will in his deeds." This David was a prophet
and a glorious king and pleased God until the end of his life
and always obeyed him with all his heart. For this reason he 35
was distinguished with great honors, because he always
heeded how he might please God.

After him many kings reigned in the kingdom of Israel, of
various dispositions. Some of them believed in the living
God, some in idolatry, resulting in their own damnation, 40
and those who honored God were glorified and were always
victorious in battle. Those who turned away from God to
shameful heathenism were put to shame and always defeated.

One of them was Ahab, the impious king who scorned his 45
creator and chose Baal, the god of the heathens, who had no
divinity, but was a fierce devil, to be found by means of heresy. This king's queen, called Jezebel, was the most depraved 50
of women, of a violent disposition. She incited her husband

Seo tihte hyre wer to ælcere wæl-hreownysse
and hi tyrgdon God mid gramlicum weorcum.
On ðam dagum wæs Helias, halig Godes witega,
se abæd æt Gode þæt he ðam yfelan cynincge
55 ren-scuras oftuge for his reðnysse.
Eode þa forð feorðe healf gear
butan ren-scurum and reocendum deawe
and se witega Helias gewende of ðam lande
and God hine afedde þurh fugela ðenunga,
60 oðþæt he hine asende to sumere wydewan
on Sidoniscum earde, and hire sæde se witega:
"Ðus cwæð Israhela God, þæt ðe ele ne ateorað,
ne melu on þinum mittan, oðþæt mannum becymð
ren ofer eorðan, eow to wæstme."
65 Þa afedde seo wudewe þone Godes witegan
mid ðam lytlan melewe and þam gehwædan ele
and funde ða fatu æfre fulle eft,
oðþæt God eft forgeaf eorðlice wæstmas.
Betwux ðysum gelamp þæt of life gewat
70 þære wudewan sunu and se witega hine arærde
eft of deaðe þurh his Drihtnes mihte.
    Eft ða se Ælmihtiga het þone witegan
faran to his earde and to ðam arleasan cynincge:
cwæð þæt he wolde sendan syððan ren-scuras.
75 Helias ða ferde and efne hine gemette
Abdias se æðela and se ar-wurðfulla Godes ðegn
se fægnode his tocymes and cwæð him þus to:
"Swyðe we axodon embe ðe gehwær
and se cyning sende swyðe fela ærend-racan
80 to gehwylcum eardum embe þe axiende.
Næs ðe, leof, gecyd þæt ic cuce behydde

to every cruelty, and they provoked God with terrible deeds. In those days lived Elijah, God's holy prophet, who requested of God that he would take rain showers away from 55 that evil king on account of his ferocity. Three and a half years went by without rain showers and rising dew, and the prophet Elijah left that land, and God fed him by the ministrations of birds, until he sent him to a widow in the region 60 of Sidon, and the prophet said to her: "Thus said the God of the Israelites, that oil will not run out for you, nor the flour in your jar, until rain comes upon the earth for people so that it will produce a crop for you." Then the widow fed the 65 prophet of God with the little flour and the small amount of oil and found the containers always full afterward, until God gave the fruits of the earth again. Meanwhile it happened that the widow's son died and the prophet raised him up 70 again from death through the power of his Lord.

After that the Almighty commanded the prophet to go to his own country and to the impious king: he said that he was willing to send rain showers. Elijah then went and truly the 75 noble Obadiah met him, and the honored servant of God rejoiced at his coming and spoke to him thus: "We asked assiduously about you everywhere, and the king sent very many messengers to every country, asking about you. Is it 80 not known to you, my lord, that I hid a hundred living

hundteontig witegan and hi mid wistum afedde
ða ða Gezabel acwealde ealle Godes witegan
þe heo ofaxian mihte on ealre ðysre leode?"

85 Helias ða becom to ðam cyninge Achab
and he befran sona þone soðfæstan witegan:
"Eart ðu la Helias, ðe Israhel gedrefst?"
Þa andwyrde se witega þam wæl-hreowan and cwæð:
"Ne gedræfde ic Israhel, ac gedrefdest ðu sylf

90 and þines fæder hiw-ræden, ge þe forleten God
and fyligdon Baal mid fulum biggencgum.
Hat nu gelangian to me ealle þa leasan witegan
ðe þeowiað Baal and etað mid Gezabel."

Þa sende se cyning and cydde his leode þæt

95 and het Israhela folc and ða facenfullan witegan
ealle endemes cuman to Helian spræce.
Þa cwæð Helias to eallre þære meniu:
"Hu lange wille ge healtian on twa healfe ðus?
Gif ure Drihten is God, fyliað þonne him;

100 gif Baal is god, fyliað his biggengum."
Þa suwode þæt folc and Helias feng eft on:
"Ic belaf ana ealra Godes witegena
and Baal hæfð feower hund and fiftig witegan.
Nimon hi anne oxan and geoffrian heora gode

105 and ic oðerne oxan geoffrige minum Gode
and beon hi begen beworpene mid wuda wiðneoðan.
Uton biddan syððan onsundron æt Gode,
ic æt minum Gode þæt he mine lac forbærne
mid upplicum fyre, and ge eac swa don:

110 beo þonne se soð god þe asent þæt fyr ufan."
Þa cwæð eall þæt folc þæt he ænlice spræce.
Ða namon þa deofol-gildan þone dumban oxan:

prophets and fed them with provisions when Jezebel killed all the prophets of God among all this people that she could find out about?" Then Elijah came to Ahab the king and at once he asked the true prophet: "Oh are you Elijah, who is disturbing Israel?" Then the prophet answered the cruel man and said: "I have not disturbed Israel, but you yourself and your father's household have disturbed it, you who have abandoned God and have followed Baal with foul rites. Order now all the false prophets who serve Baal and eat with Jezebel to be summoned to me."

Then the king sent a message and told his people this, and he ordered the people of the Israelites and the fraudulent prophets to come all together to speak with Elijah. Then Elijah said to all the multitude: "How long do you intend to sit on the fence like this? If God is our Lord, then follow him; if Baal is a god, follow his rites." Then that people was silent and Elijah took up the subject again: "I alone am left of all God's prophets, and Baal has four hundred and fifty prophets. Let them take one ox and offer it to their god, and I will offer a second ox to my God, and let them both be surrounded by wood placed beneath them. Let us then separately make requests of God, I of my God that he burn up my offering with heavenly fire from above, and you do likewise: then let him be the true God who sends fire from above." Then all the people said that he had spoken excellently. Then the idol worshippers took the dumb ox:

beworhton mid wudu on heora wisan to offrunga
and clypodon to Baal þæt he heora bene gehyrde.

115 Stodon ða fram ærne-mergen earmlice hrymende
oð ofer midne deg, gedrehte forðearle;
ne him answaru ne com ne seo offrung næs forbærned.
Þa cwæð Helias to ðam leasum witegum:
"Clypiað git hluddor—uncuð þeah þe he slæpe—
120 þæt he huru awacnige and eow wið spræce."
Hi clypodon þa swyðor and hi sylfe gewundodon,
ac se leasa Baal ne mihte hi geblyssian.

Þa genam Helias þone oþerne oxan:
beworhte mid wuda on ða ealdan wisan.
125 Het ða gewæterian ealne þone wudu
and clypode an-modlice to þam ælmihtigan Gode:
"Þu ælmihtiga God, þe Abraham on belyfde
and his sunu Isaac and eac swilce Iacob,
geswutela on þysum dæge þæt ðu eart soð God
130 and þis folc oncnawe cuðlice mid geleafan
þæt þu eart Drihten God þe heora heortan gebigst."
Æfter ðisre clypunge com fyr of heofonum
and forbærnde þone oxan and ealne ðone wudu
and ða twelf stanas ðe stodon under ðam oxan.

135 Þa feol eall þæt folc forht on gebedum
and clypode mid geleafan to ðam lyfigendan Gode:
"Drihten sylf is God, Drihten sylf is God."
Him cwæð þa to Helias: "Gelæccað þa witegan
þe Baale ðeowdon þæt heora nan ne ætberste."
140 Hi wurdon ða gelæhte and gelædde to Helian
and he hi acwealde þæt þær nan ne belaf cucu.

He astah ða ardlice up to anre dune
and gebigedum cneowum bæd ðone ælmihtigan God

they surrounded it with wood as an offering in their manner, and they called to Baal to hear their prayer. Then they stood calling miserably from early morning until after midday, greatly troubled; no answer came to them nor was the offering burned up. Then Elijah said to the false prophets: "Cry out still louder—it is not known if he is asleep—so that he may at least wake up and speak with you." Then they cried out more loudly and wounded themselves, but the false Baal could not comfort them.

Elijah then took the second ox: he surrounded it with wood in the old manner. Then he ordered that water be poured on all the wood and cried out boldly to the almighty God: "Almighty God, in whom Abraham believed and his son Isaac and likewise Jacob, reveal on this day that you are the true God and may this people recognize clearly with faith that you are the Lord God who converts their hearts." After this cry came fire from heaven and burned up the ox and all the wood and the twelve stones that were under the ox. Then all that people, frightened, knelt in prayers and cried out with faith to the living God: "The Lord himself is God, the Lord himself is God." Then Elijah said to them: "Seize the prophets who served Baal so that none of them may escape." Then they were seized and brought to Elijah, and he killed them so that not one remained alive there.

Then he went quickly up a mountain and on bended knees entreated the almighty God to give rains to the inhab-

þæt he renas forgeafe eorð-bugiendum
145 and het his cnapan ða hwile hawian to ðære sæ,
gif ænig mist arise of ðam mycclum brymme.
Þa gecyrde se cnapa seofon siðum him to
and on ðam seofoðan cyrre sæde ðam witegan
þæt an gehwæde wolcn of ðære wid-gillan sæ
150 efne þa upp astige mid þære unscæðþigan lyfte.
Efne ða aras se wind and ða wolcnu sweartodon
and com ormæte scur of ðære lyfte.

  Þa gewende se cyning aweg mid þam rene
and cydde his wife ðæs witegan dæda
155 and hu he ofsloh ða hæðen-gildan.
Þa asende Gezabel ongean to Helian
and swor þurh hire godas, mid syrwigendum mode,
þæt Helias sceolde ðæs on mergen sweltan
and beon anum gelic hire leasra witegena.
160 Þa forfleah Helias þæt fracode wif,
ut to anum westene and wearð ðær on slæpe.
Ac hine awrehte sona an scinende Godes engel:
het hine arisan and hine gereordian.
He geseah þær licgan ænne snaw-hwitne focan
165 and fæt ful wæteres þa þa he awacnode.
He æt ða and dranc and eft wearð on slæpe,
ac se encgel hine awrehte oþre siðe and cwæð:
"Aris hraðe and et; þu hæfst swyþe langne weg."
He æt eft and dranc and eode be ðam mete
170 feowertig daga on an butan ælcum gereorde.

  Sum þegen hatte Naboð; se hæfde ænne win-eard
wið ðæs cynincges botl. Þa cwæð se cynincg him to:
"Syle me ðinne win-eard me to wyr-tune
and ic þe oðerne finde on fyrlene forhwega

itants of earth, and he ordered his servant meanwhile to 145
look at the sea, to see if any mist were rising up from that
great ocean. Then the servant returned seven times to him,
and the seventh time he said to the prophet that one little
cloud was indeed rising up from that broad sea in the middle 150
of the unthreatening sky. Indeed then the wind rose and the
clouds grew dark and a very heavy fall of rain came from the
sky.

Then the king went away at the same time as the rain and
told his wife the prophet's deeds and how he had killed the 155
idolaters. Then Jezebel sent a message back to Elijah and,
with a scheming mind, swore by her gods that Elijah would
have to die the next morning and be like one of her false
prophets. Then Elijah fled from that wicked woman out to a 160
wilderness, and he fell asleep there. But immediately a shining angel of God woke him: he commanded him to rise and
to eat. He saw lying there when he awoke a snow-white cake 165
and a vessel full of water. Then he ate and drank and fell
asleep again, but the angel woke him a second time and said:
"Arise quickly and eat; you have a very long journey." He ate
once more and drank and, sustained by that food, walked for 170
forty days continuously without any meal.

A certain nobleman was called Naboth; he had a vineyard
next to the king's palace. Then the king said to him: "Give
me your vineyard as a garden, and I will find you another one

175 oððe mid feo ofgange, forðan þe he is me gehende."
Þa cwæð Naboð him to þæt he ne mihte alætan
his yldrena yrf-weardnysse swa eaðelice him to handa.
Þa gebealh hine se cynincg and to his bedde eode:
wende hine to wage, wodlice gebolgen.

180 Him eode þa to Gezabel and cwæð:
"Hwi eart ðu geunrotsod and þe gereordian nelt?"
Þa sæde se arleasa his yfelan wife
hu he þæs win-eardes gyrnde and him forwyrnde Naboð.
Þa olæhte Gezabel þam unrihtwisan and cwæð:

185 "Aris and gereorda ðe mid rædfæstum mode;
ic ðe forgife þone win-eard þe ðu gewilnodest."
Þa sende Gezabel sona anne pistol
to Naboðes neh-geburum mid þisum gebanne:
"Habbað eow gemot and tomiddes settað Naboð,

190 eowerne neh-gebur. Biddað lease gewitan
þæt hi hine forsecgan on eowere gesamnunge ðus:
'Naboð wyrigde on ure gewitnysse God
and his cyne-hlaford.' Acwellað hine siððan."
Þa dydon þa heafod-menn swa swa þæt hetelice wif

195 him on gewrite bebead and budon to gemote.
Fundon ða lease gewitan þe forlugon Naboð,
þæt he sceolde wyrigan wæl-hreowlice God
and his cyne-hlaford, and acwealdan hine mid stanum.
Cyddon ða Gezabele þæt Naboð cucu næs.

200   Hwæt ða Gezabel eode mid blysse
to þam unrihtwisan and cwæð him ðus to:
"Aris nu and hafa ðe Naboðes win-eard,
þeah ðe he þe ðæs ne uðe — he is nu unlifes."
Þa aras se arleasa ardlice and ferde

205 to Naboðes win-earde: wolde hine habban.

somewhere at a distance or I will acquire it with money, be- 175
cause it is near me." Then Naboth said to him that he could
not let the inheritance of his ancestors go so lightly into his
hands. Then the king became enraged and went to his bed:
he turned himself to the wall, insanely enraged. Then Jeze- 180
bel went to him and said: "Why are you sorrowful and do
not wish to eat?" Then the impious man told his evil wife
how he had desired the vineyard and Naboth had refused
him. Then Jezebel soothed the unrighteous man and said:
"Arise and eat with a resolute mind; I will give you the vine- 185
yard that you desired." Then Jezebel immediately sent a letter to Naboth's neighbors with this command: "Have a
meeting and put Naboth, your neighbor, in the middle. Di- 190
rect false witnesses to accuse him thus in your assembly: 'In
our presence, Naboth has cursed God and his royal lord.'
Kill him then." Then the elders did as that malevolent
woman had commanded them in the letter and summoned 195
him to an assembly. Then they found false witnesses who
told lies about Naboth, alleging that he had cursed God and
his royal lord savagely, and they killed him with stones. Then
they told Jezebel that Naboth was not alive.

Well then, Jezebel went joyfully to the unrighteous man 200
and spoke to him thus: "Arise now and have Naboth's vineyard for yourself, even though he did not grant it to you—he
is now dead." Then the impious man arose quickly and went
to Naboth's vineyard: he intended to possess it. Then God's 205

Þa com him gangende to se Godes witega Helias,
asend fram Gode, and sæde him ðas word:
"Ðus cwæð se ælmihtiga God: 'Þu ofsloge and geagnodest:
swa swa hundas lapodon Naboðes blod,

210 swa hi sceolon lapian and liccian þin blod.
Ic adilegie þinne hired and fordo þinne ofspring,
forðan þe ðu me getyrgdest and min folc mistihtest,
and Gezabel sceolon etan æl-grædige hundas.'"
    Hwæt ða æfter fyrste ferde Achab se cyning

215 togeanes Syrian cynincge mid swyðlicre fyrdinge:
wolde mid gewinne wanian his rice.
Þa het Syrian cyning sona his cepan
þæt he ana feolle of eallum his folce.
Þa gebende an scytta sona his bogan

220 and ascet ana flan, swylce on ungewis,
and atæsde ðone cyning betwux þære lungene,
þæt he feallende sweolt on ðam gefeohte ærest.
Þa gewende his here aweg swyðe hraðe
and leddon ðone cyning on his cræte swa deadne

225 and his blod ða fleow binnon ðam cræte,
þæt liccodon hundas ða ða hi ham comon.
    Ða feng his sunu sona to his rice,
Oozias gehaten, swyðe yfel-dæda.
He ferde swa swa his fæder and swa swa his fracode modor

230 him yfele gebysnodon and binnon twam gearum
his lifes ðolode and his lænan rices.
He feoll of anre stægere and forðy gelæg.
Sende ða to hæðen-gilde: het axian be him.
And Helias gemette þa menn ðe he asende.

235 Cwæð him sona to, swa swa him sæde Godes engel:
"Hwæt la, nis se ælmihtiga God on Israhela ðeode,

prophet Elijah came to meet him, sent from God, and said these words to him: "Thus said the almighty God: 'You have killed and taken possession: just as dogs have lapped Naboth's blood, so they shall lap and lick your blood. I will cut off your house and put your offspring to death, because you have provoked me and led my people astray, and voracious dogs shall eat Jezebel.'"

Well then, after a time Ahab the king advanced against the Syrian king with a great army: he wished to reduce his kingdom by battle. Then the Syrian king immediately ordered his men to take heed that he alone should fall out of all his people. Then an archer straightaway bent his bow and shot an arrow, at random as it were, and struck the king between the lungs, so that, falling, he died first in that battle. Then his army turned away very quickly, and they brought the king in his chariot, dead like this, and then his blood flowed into the chariot, so that dogs licked it when they came home.

Then his son, called Ahaziah, immediately succeeded to power, a great evildoer. He behaved according to the evil example his father and his wicked mother had set him and within two years had lost his life and his transitory kingdom. He fell from a staircase and lay sick because of that. Then he sent messengers to a heathen god: he ordered them to ask about him. And Elijah met the men whom he had sent. He immediately said to them, as God's angel had said to him: "What then, is not the almighty God among the people of

210

215

220

225

230

235

and ge farað to hæðen-gilde eowre hæle to axienne?
Nu cwæð se Ælmihtiga forði þæt se cynincg ne sceall arisan
of ðam bedde þe he on lið, ac sceall beon dead."
240 Þa gewendon ða ærend-racan eft to ðam cynincge
and cyddon hwæt se witega him be wege sæde.
  Þa sende se cyning sona fiftig manna
to ðam Godes witegan: wolde hine gelangian.
  Ða cwæð se yldosta to ðam ar-wurðan witegan:
245 "Gang nu, Godes man, of þære grædan dune:
se cynincg gewilnað þæt þu cume him to."
  Þa andwyrde Helias an-rædlice and cwæð:
"Gif ic Godes man eom, forbærne eow Godes fyr."
Hwæt þa mid ðam worde wand fyr of heofonum
250 and forbærnde þa fiftig manna mid ealre heora fare.
  Þa asende se cynincg eft oðre fiftig
up to ðære dune þær Helias sæt
and him eallswa getimode swa swa ðam oðrum flocce,
þæt hi wurdon forbærnde mid brastligendum lige
255 heofonlices fyres færlice ealle.
  Þa asende se cynincg gyt ðriddan siðe him to
fiftig his ðegna; ða feollan ealle on cneowum,
biddende þone witegan mid bifigendre heortan
þæt he hi ne forbærnde ðeah ðe hi heora ærende abudon,
260 swa swa ða oþre ðe him ær to comon.
  Ða het Godes engel þæt he gan sceolde
forð mid ðam mannum, unforht to ðam cynincge.
  Elias ða eode to þam adlian cyninge
and him sylfum sæde þæt he sweltan sceolde,
265 forðan þe he asende to þam sceandlican hæðen-gilde
to befrinenne his hæle swylce God nære on Israhel.
  Ða gewat se cyning, swa swa se witega cwæð,

156

the Israelites, and you are going to a heathen god to ask for healing? Now therefore the Almighty has said that the king shall not arise from the bed on which he lies, but he shall be dead." Then the messengers returned to the king and re- 240 ported what the prophet had said to them along the way.

Then the king at once sent fifty men to the prophet of God: he wished to summon him. Then the chief one said to the honored prophet: "Come down now, man of God, from 245 the grassy hill: the king desires that you come to him." Then Elijah answered resolutely and said: "If I am a man of God, let God's fire burn you up." Well then, with that utterance fire flew from the heavens and burned up the fifty men with 250 all their equipment. Then the king again sent a second fifty up to the hill where Elijah was sitting, and it happened to them just as to the other troop, that they were all suddenly burned up by a roaring flame of heavenly fire. Yet a third 255 time then the king sent fifty of his officers to him; then they all fell on their knees, beseeching the prophet with trembling hearts that he would not burn them up even though they were announcing their message, like the others who 260 had come to him previously. Then God's angel commanded that he must go away with those men to the king, without fear.

Elijah then went to the sick king and told him that he was destined to die, because he had sent a messenger to the vile 265 heathen god to ask about his healing as if there were no God in Israel. Then the king died, as the prophet had said, and

and his broðor Ioram feng to his rice
and hit endlyfan gear yfele geheold,
270 and his modor Gezabel manfullice leofode
on fulum forligere and on ælcere fracodnysse,
oþþæt Godes wracu hire wæl-hreownysse geendode.

Betwux ðysum wearð se witega Helias
up to heofonum ahafen hal, butan deaðe,
275 and lyfað git on lic-haman mid langsumre strangunge.
Heliseus his gingra eode mid him on ær.
Ða cwæð se lareow Helias to his leorning-cnihte:
"Bide me loca hwæs þu wille ær ðan þe ic beo genumen
of ðinre gesihðe and of ðysum geswince."
280 Ða cwæð Eliseus to ðam ar-wurðan witegan:
"Ic bidde þe, min fæder, þæt ic beo afylled
mid þam witegendlicum gaste þe on ðe nu wunað."
Ða cwæð Helias to his leorning-cnihte:
"Myceles þu bæde, ac ðu bist swaþeah tiða
285 gif ðu most geseon hu ic siþige heonon:
gif ðu hit ne gesihst, soðlice hit ne bið."
Betwux heora spræce com an heofonlic cræt,
swylce eall fyren, mid fleogendum horsum,
and Helias ferde on ðam fægeran cræte
290 upp geond ða lyft and let afeallan his basincg.
Ða geseah Heliseus hu he siðode up
and clypode hlude æfter his lareowe þus:
Pater mi, pater mi! Currus Israhel et auriga eius!
"Fæder min, fæder min! Israheles cræt
295 and his wissigend!" (þæt is cræt-wisa).
He ne geseah hine siððan ac genam sona his basincg,
ðe of þam cræte ætfeoll, and ferde ongean
and wæs Godes witega, swa wis swa se oðer,

his brother Jehoram succeeded to his kingdom and held it evilly for eleven years, and his mother Jezebel lived wickedly in foul fornication and in every abomination, until God's vengeance ended her ferocity.

In the meantime the prophet Elijah was taken up to heaven in good health, without dying, and he lives still in the body with lasting vigor. Elisha his disciple accompanied him beforehand. Then the master Elijah said to his disciple: "Ask me for whatever you wish before I am taken from your sight and from this toil." Then Elisha said to the honored prophet: "I beseech you, my father, that I may be filled with the prophetic spirit that dwells now in you." Then Elijah said to his disciple: "You have asked for much, but nevertheless you will receive it if you are able to see how I go from here: if you do not see it, truly it will not come to pass." During their conversation a heavenly chariot came, as if all of fire, with flying horses, and Elijah went in that beautiful chariot up through the air and let fall his cloak. Then Elisha saw how he was going up and called out loudly after his teacher thus: *My father, my father! The chariot of Israel and the driver thereof!* "My father, my father! Israel's chariot and its driver!" (that is, charioteer). He did not see him subsequently but straightaway took his cloak, which had fallen from the chariot, and went back and was God's prophet, as wise as the other man,

270

275

280

285

290

295

and fela wundra worhte and witegode fela ðincg.

300 He arærde ænne deadne þurh Drihtnes mihte,
ænne on his life and oðerne æfter forð-siðe.

Æfter þæs witegan forð-siþe wearð
an lic gebroht to ðæs halgan byrgene
and sceaðan þa afligdon færlice ða lic-menn,

305 þæt hi forleton þone deadan uppan his byrgene
and urnon aweg swa hraðe swa hi besawon on ðone reþan
floc.

Þa aras se deada mid ðam þe he hrepode þa byrgene
and eode ham gesund for Heliseus geearnungum.

Heliseus gehælde eac ænne ealdor-man

310 fram atelicum hreoflan (se hatte Naaman,
of Syrian lande) and he gelyfde on God
þurh þæt mycele wundor ðe God on him geworhte.

Fela oðre tacna gefremede God þurh hine
on Israhela ðeode, on þam yfelan timan.

315 Heliseus ða asende sumne oðerne witegan
mid Godes ærende to anum ealdor-menn,
Hieu gehaten: het hine halgian to cynincge.

Ða ferde se geonga witega to þam fore-sædan ealdor-menn,
begeat his heafod mid ele, swa swa se Ælmihtiga het,

320 and abead him Godes ærende an-rædlice and cwæð:
"God ælmihtig cwæð be þe: 'Ic ðe to cynincge gesmyrode
ofer Israhela folc, þæt þu eall adilegie
Achabes ofsprincg, ðæs arleasan cynincges,
þæt ic beo gewrecen on þære awyrigendan Gezabel.

325 Heo bið hundum to mete, na bebyrged on eorðan.'"

Hwæt ða Hieu, se ni-gehalgode cynincg,
ferde mid fultume to gefremmenne þa þincg
ðe him God bebead, betwux his gebroðrum.

and performed many miracles and prophesied many things. He raised up a dead man by the Lord's power, one during his 300 life and a second after his death.

After the prophet's death a body was brought to the holy man's grave, and then robbers suddenly put the pallbearers to flight, so that they left the dead man on top of his grave 305 and ran away as soon as they saw the fierce gang. Then the dead man got up when he touched the grave and went home healthy on account of Elisha's merits. Elisha also healed a commander from hideous leprosy (he was called Naaman, 310 from Syria), and he believed in God because of the great miracle that God had performed on him. God performed many other miracles through him among the people of the Israelites, in that evil time.

Elisha then sent another prophet with God's message to 315 a commander called Jehu: he ordered that he be consecrated as king. Then the young prophet went to the commander whom we have already mentioned, sprinkled his head with oil, as the Almighty had commanded, and without hesita- 320 tion announced God's message to him and said: "God almighty said concerning you: 'I have anointed you as king over the people of the Israelites, so that you may destroy all the offspring of Ahab, the impious king, that I may be avenged on the accursed Jezebel. She will be food for dogs, 325 not buried in the earth.'"

Well then, Jehu, the newly consecrated king, went with support to do the things that God had commanded him to

Þa com him togeanes Ioram se cyning:

330 axode hwæðer he come mid sibbe swa caflice.

Ða andwyrde Hieu and cwæð unforht him to:

"Git ðinre modor manfullan forligr

and fela unlybban syndon forðgenge."

Þa gewende Ioram awæg sona and cwæð:

335 "Ðis synd syrwunga." And Hieu him scet to

bæftan his bæce, þæt him tobærst seo heorte.

Het hine ða wurpan of þam wege swa deadne.

Þa fleah Iudea cyning þe com mid ðam oþrum,

ac Hieu hine offerde and him his feorh benam.

340 Wende þa to Gezabel þe wæs on þære byrig

and stod uppon anre up-flora, ænlice geglencged,

and gehiwode hire eagan and hire neb mid rude

togeanes Hieu and beheold his tocyme.

Þa beseah Hieu to þære sceande up

345 and het hi asceofon sona underbæc.

Heo wearð ða afylled ætforan ðam horsum

and þa hors hi oftrædan huxlice under fotum.

   Hieu þa eode to his gereorde sittan

and æfter his ðenunge cwæð to his þegnum:

350 "Gað to þære hætse þe ic het niþer asceofan

and bebyriað hire lic for hire gebyrdum."

Hi eoden ardlice to ac heo wæs eall freten,

butan þam handum anum and þam hæfde ufweardum,

and þam fot-wylmum, þurh fule hundas.

355 Þa cyddon ða cnihtas þam cynincge þæt

and he cwæð to andsware þæt hit wæs ær swa gewitegod.

   Þa wæran on Samarian hundseofontig aðelinga,

Achabes suna, þæs ealdan cynincges,

Iorames gebroðra. Þa het se bealda Hieu

do, among his brothers. Then Jehoram the king came to meet him: he asked whether he was coming so boldly in peace. Then Jehu answered and without fear said to him: "Your mother's wicked fornications and many magical practices are still going on continuously." Then Jehoram turned away immediately and said: "These are treacherous plots." And Jehu shot at him behind his back, so that his heart burst asunder. He ordered him to be thrown out of the way then, dead like this. Then the king of Judea, who had come with the others, fled but Jehu overtook him and deprived him of his life. He went then to Jezebel, who was in the city and was standing upon an upper floor, splendidly adorned, and she had colored her eyes and her face with red to meet Jehu, and she was watching his arrival. Then Jehu looked up at the shameful woman and ordered that she be cast down immediately. She was then thrown down in front of the horses, and the horses trampled her ignominiously under their feet.

Jehu then went to sit at his meal and after his meal said to his followers: "Go to that witch whom I ordered to be cast down and bury her body on account of her birth." They went quickly to her, but she had been all devoured, except for the hands only and the top of the head, and the soles of her feet, by foul dogs. Then the servants told the king this, and he said in answer that it had been so prophesied beforehand.

Then there were seventy princes in Samaria, sons of Ahab, the old king, Jehoram's brothers. Then the bold Jehu

360 ða ceaster-gewaran þæt hi of ðam hundseofontigum
ænne æðeling gecuron him to cynincge
and fuhton him togeanes for heora hlafordum.
Þa sende seo burh-waru to ðam breman Hieu:
budon him man-rædene to eallum his bebodum.
365 Þa het Hieu him to gebringan
þæra æðelinga heafdu ealle þæs on mergen
and he acwealde siððan ælc þincg ðæs cynnes.
    Gewende ða to Samarian, þære fore-sædan byrig,
and het him to gelangian þa leasan deofol-gildan
370 þe Baal wurðodon: wolde hi gespræcan.
Het ða gedreohlæcan þæs deofles templ:
sæde þæt he wolde hine wurðian for God
swa swa Achab dyde and eac git swyðor.
Þa comon þa sacerdas to þam cynincge ealle
375 and he het hi ingan to ðam gode Baal
and him geoffrian þa estfullan onsægednysse.
Hwæt ða Hieu het hi ealle ofslean
and forbærnan þone Baal and tobræcan his templ.
Worhton þa gang-tun þær ðær se god Baal
380 ær wæs gewurðod wolice oð þæt.
Þa com Godes word to ðam cynincge þus:
"Forðan þe þu geworhtest minne willan geornlice
on Achabes ofsprincge and hi ealle adilogodest,
þine suna gesittað þæt cyne-setl on Israhel
385 oð ða feorþan mægðe, mid fæderlicre æfter-gengnysse."
    Manega cynegas wæron, myslice geworhte,
æfter þysum rixiende on Israhela rice,
and eac on Iudea lande, oðþæt se geleaffulla cynincg,
Ezechias gehaten, mid ealre heortan gebeah
390 to ðam ælmihtigan Gode and his biggengas arærde

ordered the inhabitants of the city that, of the seventy, they 360
choose one prince as their king and that they fight against
him in support of their lords. Then the citizenry sent to the
renowned Jehu: they offered to be subject to all his commands. Then Jehu ordered them to bring him all the princes' 365
heads the next morning, and he subsequently killed every
one of that kindred.

Then he went to Samaria, the city that we have already
mentioned, and commanded the false idol worshippers who
honored Baal to be summoned to him: he wished to speak to 370
them. He commanded that the devil's temple be put in order: he said that he wished to honor him as God as Ahab had
done, and even more too. Then all the priests came to the
king and he commanded them to go in to the god Baal and 375
to offer him their devout sacrifices. Well then, Jehu commanded them all to be killed and Baal to be burned up and
his temple destroyed. Then they made a lavatory where the
god Baal had been wrongly honored until then. Then God's 380
word came to the king thus: "Because you have diligently
carried out my will with respect to Ahab's offspring and have
destroyed them all, your sons will sit on the throne in Israel
until the fourth generation, in lineal succession." 385

There were many kings, of various dispositions, reigning
after this in the kingdom of the Israelites, and also in the
land of the Jewish people, until the devout king, called Hezekiah, with all his heart submitted himself to the almighty 390

and towearp þa deofol-gild þe dwollice oþþæt
wæron gewurðode mid wolicum biggencgum.
He rixode on Iudea lande an leas ðryttig geara
and wislice leofode forðan þe he lufode God.

395 And God hine gescylde wið Syrian cyning,
Sennacherib gehaten, þe mid hole him on wan
and mid ormætre fyrdincge hine afyllan wolde
and asende his here-togan to, ðe huxlice spræc be Gode
and be Ezechian mid mycclum gebeote.

400 Hwæt ða Ezechias an-modlice clypode
to ðam ælmihtigan Gode þæt he hine ahredde.
Ða asende God his engel to þam Syriscan here
and ofsloh on anre nihte an hund þusend manna
and hundeahtatig ðusend and sumne eacan ðær-to.

405 Þa geseah Sennacherib sona ðæs on mergen
þæt his here wæs ofslagen mid heofonlicum swurde.
Wende þa sona ham and his twægen suna
hine ofslogon mid swurdes ecge.
Swa ahredde se Ælmihtiga þone æþelan cynincg

410 and eac his leode, for his geleafan.
Æfter ðysum wearð geuntrumod Ezechias oð deað,
and him com gangende to Godes witega Isaias.
Abead him Godes ærende þus bealdlice and cwæð:
"God cwæð be ðe, cynincg, þæt þu becweðe þine ðincg,

415 forðan þe ðu sweltan scealt and þu soðlice ne leofast."
Þa awende Ezechias to wage his ansyne
and clypode to Gode, þus cweðende mid wope:
"Ic bidde þe, min Drihten, þæt þu beo gemyndig
hu ic ætforan ðe ferde on fulfremedre heortan

420 and on soðfæstnysse þe symle gecwemde."
Isaias se witega wæs awæg farande,

God and fostered his rites and destroyed the idols that until then were heretically honored with evil rites. He reigned in the land of the Jewish people for thirty years less one and lived wisely because he loved God. And God protected him 395 against the king of Syria, called Sennacherib, who fought against him with false speech and wished to kill him with a huge army, and who had sent the leader of his army to him, who spoke contemptuously about God and about Hezekiah with a great threat.

Well then, Hezekiah called steadfastly to the almighty 400 God to save him. Then God sent his angel to the Syrian army and in one night he killed a hundred and eighty thousand people and some more besides. Then Sennacherib saw 405 at once the following morning that his army had been killed by a heavenly sword. He went home immediately and his two sons killed him with the sword's edge. In this way the Almighty saved the noble king and also his people, on ac- 410 count of his faith.

After this Hezekiah became sick to the point of death, and God's prophet Isaiah came to him. He announced God's message to him thus boldly and said: "God said concerning you, king, that you should bequeath your property, because 415 you must die and truly you will not live." Then Hezekiah turned his face to the wall and called to God, speaking thus with weeping: "I beseech you, my Lord, to be mindful how I have walked before you with a perfect heart and in my truth 420 have always pleased you." Isaiah the prophet was going away,

ac God hine gecyrde, þus him eft secgende:
"Gecyr to Ezechian and sege him ðas word:
'Drihten God gecwæð, þe Dauid on gelyfde:
425 ic gehyrde þin gebed and ic beheold þinne wop
and efne ic ðe gehælde þæt þu hal gæst
nu embe þry dagas to þines Drihtnes temple.
And ic fiftyne gear þe to fyrste læte
ðinum dagum toeacan and ic eac þas burh gescylde.'"
430 Þa het se witega Isaias wyrcan ænne clyþan
to þæs cynincges dolge and him com ða hælu.
He leofode þa siððan oðþæt sixteoðe gear
and mid ealre godnysse Gode gecwemde.
    Mannases wæs gecyged Ezechias sunu
435 and se feng to rice æfter his fæder geendunge
and mid manegum yfelum dædum þone Ælmihtigan
                                           gremode.

Þa asende him God to swyðlice steore,
swa þæt him comon to ða Chaldeiscan leoda
and hine gebundenne geleddon to Babiloniscre byrig
440 and on cweart-erne bescufon, to sceame his kynescipe.
Þa behreowsode Mannases mycclum his synna
and mid eallre heortan to þam Ælmihtigan clypode,
biddende miltsunge ealra his man-dæda,
and behet geswicennysse and hit eac swa gelæste.
445 Hwæt ða se ælmihtiga God þas earman cynincges
bene gehyrde and gebrohte hine
eft to his cyne-rice of ðam reðan cweart-erne
and he gebette syððan þæt ðæt he ær tobræc.
He oncneow þa Godes mihte and his mild-heortnysse on
                                           him
450 and awende his dæda to his Drihtnes willan
and wel geendode, þeah ðe he yfele ongunne.

but God caused him to turn back, speaking again to him thus: "Return to Hezekiah and say these words to him: 'The Lord God, in whom David believed, has said: I have heard 425 your prayer and I have seen your weeping, and truly I have healed you so that in good health you will go now after three days to your Lord's temple. And I will allow you fifteen years as a respite added to your days, and I will also protect this city.'" Then the prophet Isaiah ordered a poultice to be 430 made for the king's sore, and then he was healed. He lived afterward until the sixteenth year and pleased God with every virtue.

Hezekiah's son was named Manasseh, and he succeeded 435 to power after his father's death and he angered the Almighty with many evil deeds. Then God sent him a severe punishment, so that the Chaldean people came to him and brought him bound to the city of Babylon and shoved him 440 into prison, as a disgrace to his kingship. Then Manasseh repented greatly of his sins and with all his heart called to the Almighty, praying for mercy for all his evil deeds, and he made a promise to stop and moreover he carried it out. Well 445 then, the almighty God heard the prayer of the miserable king and brought him back to his kingdom from the cruel prison, and he afterward restored what he had previously destroyed. Then he perceived God's power and his mercifulness to him, and he directed his deeds to his Lord's will and 450 ended well, although he had begun badly.

His sunu Amon, swyðe ungesælig,
feng to his rice and hit unrihtlice heold,
swa þæt he forlet þone lyfigendan God
455 and deofol-gild beeode and dæd-bote ne geworhte.
Twa gear he rixode unrædfæstlice.
Ða gewearð his þegnum þæt hi hine acwealdon
and Iosias his sunu sona feng to rice
on iunglicre ylde and geefenlæhte Dauide
460 on ealre godnysse and Godes wyllan gefremode.
He awearp yfelnysse and ða unrihtan biggengas
ðæra leasra goda þe his fæder on gelyfde
and geedniwode Godes æ, mid eallum biggencgum,
and wiccan fordyde and wigleras afligde
465 and dry-cræft towearp, his Drihtne to gecwemednysse.
Næs soðlice nan cynincg þe gecyrde swa geornlice
mid ealre heortan to ðam ælmihtigan Gode
beforan Iosian, ne eac siððan ne com
nan his gelica ðe swa gelyfde on God.
470 An and þryttig geara he rixode þrymlice on Hierusalem
and myld-heortnysse weorc be Moyses æ
symle beeode, swa swa us secgað gewrytu.
    Ne mage we awritan ða mænigfealdan gerecednyssa
ealra Iudeiscra cyninga on ðisum lytlan cwyde,
475 oððe Israhela ðeode hu hi ealle leofodon,
ac we cweðað to soðum: se þe synnum gehyrsumað
and Godes beboda forsyhð, nu on þæs god-spelles timan,
þæt he bið þam cynincgum gelic ðe gecuron deofol-gild
and heora scyppend forsawon, se ðe soþlice is
480 ana God ælmihtig, æfre rixigende.
Þam sy a wuldor on ealra worulda woruld. Amen.

His son Amon, very evil, succeeded to his power and held
it unrighteously, in that he deserted the living God and wor- 455
shiped idols and did not do penance. He reigned for two
years imprudently. Then his servants conspired to kill him,
and Josiah his son immediately succeeded to power at a
young age, and he imitated David with every virtue and did 460
God's will. He cast off evil and the evil rites of the false gods
in whom his father had believed and restored God's law,
with all its rites, and put wizards to death and expelled sorcerers and put an end to magic, to please his Lord. Truly 465
there was never a king who turned so eagerly with all his
heart to the almighty God before Josiah, nor did his equal
come afterward who believed in God in this way. He reigned 470
gloriously for thirty-one years in Jerusalem, and in accordance with the law of Moses he always performed works of
mercy, as books tell us.

We cannot set down in writing the numerous histories of
all the Jewish kings in this little sermon, or of the people of 475
the Israelites, how they all lived, but we say in truth: he who
is obedient to sins and holds God's commandments in contempt, now in the time of the gospel, he will be like those
kings who chose idolatry and held their creator in contempt, he who truly is the one God almighty, ruling everlast- 480
ingly. To him be glory eternally, world without end. Amen.

SAINT ALBAN *AND*
ON THE UNJUST

18

Saint Alban *and* On the Unjust

Passio sancti Albani martyris

Sum hæðen casere wæs gehaten Dioclitianus.
Se wæs to casere gecoren, þeah ðe he cwealm-bære wære,
æfter Cristes acennednysse twam hund gearum
and syx and hundeahtatigum ofer ealne middan-eard
5 and he rixode twentig geara, reðe cwellere,
swa þæt he acwealde and acwellan het
ealle ða Cristenan þe he ofaxian mihte
and forbærnde cyrcan and berypte ða unscæððigan.
And þeos arleasa ehtnyss unablinnendlice eode
10 ofer ealne middan-eard ealles tyn gear,
oðþæt heo to Englalande eac swylce becom
and þær fela acwealde ða þe on Criste gelyfdon.
An ðæra wæs Albanus, se æþela martyr,
se ðe on þære ehtnysse eac wearð acweald
15 for Cristes geleafan, swa swa we cyðaþ her.
    On þam dagum becom seo cwealm-bære ehtnyss
to Englalande fram ðam arleasan casere
and þa cwelleras cepton ðæra Cristenra gehwær
mid ormetre wodnysse. Þa ætwand him an preost.

18

Saint Alban *and* On the Unjust

The Passion of Saint Alban the Martyr

A certain heathen emperor was called Diocletian. He was chosen as emperor over the entire world, murderous though he was, two hundred and eighty-six years after Christ's incarnation, and he reigned for twenty years, a fierce killer, in such a way that he killed and ordered the killing of all the Christians whom he could discover and burned down churches and robbed the innocent. And this impious persecution spread ceaselessly over the entire world for ten years in all, until it came also to England and killed many there who believed in Christ. One of these was Alban, the noble martyr, who was also killed in that persecution for the sake of his faith in Christ, as we will tell here.

In those days the murderous persecution by the impious emperor came to England, and the killers seized the Christians everywhere with enormous fury. Then a priest escaped

20   Se arn digollice to Albanes huse
     and ðær ætlutode his laðum ehterum,
     and Albanus hine underfeng, þeah ðe he gefullod nære.
     Þa began se preost, swa swa he God lufode,
     his gebedu singan and swyðe fæstan
25   and dæges and nihtes his Drihten herian
     and betwux ðam secgan ðone soðan geleafan
     þam ar-wurþan Albane, oþþæt he gelyfde
     on ðone soðan God and wiðsoc þam hæðenscype
     and wearð soþlice Cristen and swyðe geleaffull.
30   Þa wunode se preost mid ðam ar-wurðan were
     oðþæt se ealdor-mann ðe ehte ða Cristenan
     hine ðær geaxode and hine ardlice het
     to him gefeccan mid fullum graman.
     Þa comon ða ærend-racan to Albanes huse,
35   ac Albanus eode ut to þam ehterum
     mid ðæs preostes hakelan, swylce he hit wære,
     and hine nolde ameldian ðam manfullum ehterum.
     He wearð þa gebunden and gebroht sona
     to ðam arleasan deman, þær he ða defollican lac
40   his godum offrode mid his gegadum eallum.
     Þa wearð se dema deofollice gram
     sona swa he beseah on þone soðfæstan martyr,
     forðan þe he underfeng þone fleondan preost
     and hine sylfne sealde to slege for hine.
45   Het hine þa lædan to ðam hæðen-gilde and cwæþ
     þæt he sylf sceolde ða swaran wita onfon
     þe he þam preoste gemynte, gif he mihte hine gefon,
     butan he hraðe gebuge to his bysmorfullum godum.
     Ac Albanus næs afyrht for his feondlicum þeow-racan
50   forðan þe he wæs ymbgyrd mid Godes wæpnum

from them. He ran secretly to Alban's house and hid there   20
from his hateful persecutors, and Alban took him in, although he was not baptized. Then the priest, since he loved
God, began to chant his prayers and to fast strictly and to   25
praise his Lord day and night and meanwhile to explain the
true faith to the honorable Alban, until he believed in the
true God and renounced heathenism and truly became a
Christian and very devout.

Then the priest stayed with the honorable man until the   30
ruler who was persecuting the Christians learned that he
was there and, filled with anger, commanded that he be
fetched urgently to him. Then the messengers came to Alban's house, but Alban went out to the persecutors wearing   35
the priest's cloak, as if it were he, and refused to inform
against him to the evil persecutors. Then he was bound and
immediately brought to the impious judge, where he was offering diabolical sacrifices to his gods with all his compan-   40
ions. Then the judge became diabolically angry as soon as he
looked at the faithful martyr, because he had taken in the
fleeing priest and had given himself to be killed in his place.
He commanded that he be led to the heathen idol and said   45
that he himself would have to undergo the severe tortures
that he had intended for the priest, had he been able to
catch him, unless he immediately submitted to his shameful
gods. But Alban was not afraid of his hostile threats because   50
he was equipped with God's weapons for the spiritual bat-

to þam gastlicum gecampe and cwæð þæt he nolde
his hæsum gehyrsumian ne to his hæðen-gilde bugan.
   Þa axode se dema ardlice and cwæð:
"Hwylcere mægþe eart þu oððe hwylcere manna?"
55 Ða andwyrde Albanus þam arleasan þus:
"Hwæt belympð to þe hwylcere mægðe ic sy?
Ac gif ðu soð wylt gehyran, ic þe secge hraðe
þæt ic Cristen eom and Crist æfre wurðige."
Se dema him cwæð to: "Cyð me þinne naman
60 butan ælcere yldinge, nu ic axie ðus."
Se Godes cempa cwæð to þam cwellere þus:
"Ic hatte Albanus and ic on þone hælend gelyfe,
se ðe is soð God and ealle gesceafta geworhte;
to him ic me gebidde and hine æfre wurðige."
65 Se cwellere andwyrde þam arfæstan were:
"Gif ðu þæs ecan lifes gesælþe habban wylt,
þonne ne scealt ðu elcian þæt ðu offrige
þam mærum godum mid mycelre underðeodnysse."
Albanus him andwyrde: "Eowre offrunga ne magon,
70 þe ge deoflum offriað, eower gehelpan
ne eowerne willan gefremman, ac ge underfoð to medes
ða ecan wita on ðære wid-gillan helle."
   Hwæt ða se dema deofollice yrsode
and het beswingan þone halgan martyr:
75 wende þæt he mihte his modes an-rædnysse
mid þam swingelum gebigan to his biggengum.
Ac se eadiga wer wearð þurh God gestrangod
and ða swingle forbær swyðe geþyldiglice
and mid glædum mode Gode ðæs þancode.
80 Ða geseah se dema þæt he oferswyðan ne mihte
þone halgan wer mid þam hetelicum witum

tle, and he said that he was not willing to obey his commands nor to submit to his idolatry.

Then the judge urgently questioned him and said: "What family are you from or from what people?" Alban then answered the impious man thus: "What concern is it of yours what family I am from? But if you wish to hear the truth, I will tell you immediately that I am a Christian and I always honor Christ." The judge said to him: "Tell me your name without any delay, now that I am asking like this." The soldier of God said to the killer thus: "I am called Alban and I believe in the savior, he who is the true God and who created all created things; to him I pray and I honor him always." The killer answered the pious man: "If you wish to have the happiness of eternal life, then you must not delay in offering to the glorious gods in full submission." Alban answered him: "Your offerings, that you are offering to devils, cannot help you nor accomplish your desire, but you will receive as your reward eternal torments in the vast hell."

Well then, the judge became diabolically angry and commanded that the holy martyr be flogged: he thought that he could convert the constancy of his mind to his own rituals by means of the lashes. But the blessed man was strengthened by God and very patiently endured the lashes and with a glad heart thanked God for this. Then the judge saw that he could not defeat the holy man with those savage tortures

ne fram Criste gebigan and het hine acwellan
mid beheafdunge, for ðæs hælendes naman.

    Þa dydon þa hæðenan swa swa hi het se dema
85 and leddon ðone halgan to beheafdigenne,
ac hi wurdon gelette lange æt anre brycge
and stodon oð æfnunge for ðam ormætan folce
wæra and wifa þe wurdon onbryrde
and comon to ðam martyre and him mid eoden.

90 Hit gelamp ða swa þæt se geleafleasa dema
ungereordod sæt on ðære ceastra oð æfen,
butan ælcere ðenunge, unþances fæstende.

    Hwæt ða Albanus efstan wolde to slege
and eode to þære ea, þa ða he ofer þa brycge ne mihte,
95 and beseah to heofonum, þone hælend biddende,
and seo ea þær-rihte adruwode him ætforan
and him weg rymde, swa swa he gewilnode æt Gode.
Þa wearð se cwellere þe hine acwellan sceolde
þurh þæt wundor abryrd and awearp his swurd.

100 Arn ða ardlice þa ða hi ofer ða ea comon
and feoll to his fotum mid fullum geleafan:
wolde mid him sweltan ær ðan þe he hine sloge.
He wearð þa geanlæht, mid an-rædum geleafan,
to ðam halgan were þe he beheafdian sceolde
105 and þæt swurd læg þær scynende him ætforan
and heora nan nolde naht eaðe hine slean.

    Ða wæs ðær gehende þam halgan wære
an myrige dun mid wyrtum amet,
mid eallre fægernysse, and eac ful smeðe.
110 Þa eode Albanus ardlice ðyder
and bæd sona æt Gode þæt he him sealde wæter
uppan ðære dune and he dyde swa.

nor turn him from Christ, and commanded that he be killed
by beheading, for the sake of the savior's name.

Then the heathens did as the judge had commanded and 85
took the saint in order to behead him, but they were delayed
for a long time at a bridge and were standing until the evening because of the huge crowd of men and women who
were inspired and came to the martyr and accompanied
him. Then it happened that the faithless judge sat unfed in 90
the town until evening, unattended, fasting unwillingly.

Well then, Alban wished to hasten to his death and, when
he could not get over the bridge, went to the river and 95
looked to the heavens, praying to the savior, and straightaway the river dried up in front of him and cleared a way for
him, as he had desired of God. Then the executioner who
was supposed to kill him was spurred on by that miracle and
threw down his sword. When they had come over the river, 100
he then ran quickly and fell at his feet with complete faith:
he wished to die with him rather than to kill him. He was
then united, with resolute faith, to the holy man whom he
was supposed to behead, and the sword lay there shining in 105
front of them, and none of them wished to kill him willingly.

Then near to the holy man there was a pleasant hill
adorned with plants, with every beauty, and very smooth
also. Then Alban went there quickly and immediately asked 110
God to give him water at the top of the hill, and he did so.

Þær arn þa wyl-spryncg æt Albanes fotum
þæt men mihton tocnawan his mihte wið God,
115 þa ða se stream arn of ðære sticolan dune.
He wearð þa beheafdod for ðæs hælendes naman
uppan ðære dune and to his Drihtne ferde
mid sigefæstum martyrdome and soðum geleafan.
Ac his slaga ne moste gesundful lybban
120 forðam þe him burston ut butu his eagan
and to eorðan feollon mid Albanes heafde,
þæt he mihte oncnawan hwæne he acwealde.
Hi beheafdodon syððan þone soðfæstan cempan
þe nolde beheafdian ðone halgan wer
125 and he læg mid Albane, gelyfed on God,
mid his blode gefullod, and ferde to heofonum.
    Eft ða ða cwelleras comon to heora hlaforde
and hi sædon þa syllican tacna ðe Albanus worhte
and hu se wearð ablend þe hine beheafdode,
130 ða het he geswican þære ehtnysse and ar-wurðlice spræc
be ðam halgum martyrum þe he ne mihte gebigan
fram Godes geleafan þurh ða gramlican witu.
    On ðære ylcan ehtnysse wurdon ofslagene
Aaron and Iulius and oðre manega,
135 wera and wifa, wide geond Englaland,
for Cristes geleafan gecwylmede on witum,
and hi ferdon sigefæste to þam soðan life.
Seo ehtnys geswac ða and eoden þa Cristenan
of wudum and of wæstenum þær hi wæron behydde
140 and comon to mannum and Cristendom geedniwodon
and gebetton cyrcan þe tobrocene wæron.
Wunodon ða on sybbe mid soðum geleafan.

Then a spring ran there at Alban's feet, so that people could know what power he had in the eyes of God when the stream ran out from the high hill. Then he was beheaded for the sake of the savior's name on the top of that hill, and he went to his Lord with victorious martyrdom and true faith. But his killer was not permitted to live happily because his two eyes burst right out of him and fell to the earth at the same time as Alban's head, so that he could realize whom it was that he had killed. Afterward they beheaded the faithful soldier who had refused to behead the holy man, and he lay together with Alban, believing in God, baptized by his blood, and went to heaven.

Afterward when the killers came to their lord and they spoke of the wonderful miracles that Alban had worked and how the man who had beheaded him had been blinded, then he commanded that the persecution cease and spoke reverently about the holy martyrs whom he could not turn from belief in God by his terrible tortures.

In that same persecution Aaron and Julius were killed and many others, men and women, far and wide throughout England, killed by tortures on account of their faith in Christ, and they went victoriously to the true life. The persecution ceased then, and the Christians came out from the woods and the wildernesses where they were hidden, and came among people and restored Christianity and repaired the churches that had been destroyed. Then they lived in peace with true faith.

Hi worhton eac þa wurðlice cyrcan
þam halgan Albane, ðær he bebyrged wæs,
145 and þær wurdon gelome wundra gefremode,
þam hælende to lofe ðe leofað a on ecnysse.
Þis wæs geworden ær ðæt gewinn come
ðurh Hengest and Horsan, þe hyndon ða Bryttas,
and se Cristendom wearð geunwurðod syððan
150 oðþæt Agustinus hine eft astealde
be Gregories lare, þæs geleaffullan papan.
Sy wuldor and lof þam wel-willendan scyppende
se ðe ure fæderas feondum ætbræd
and to fulluhte gebigde þurh his bydelas. Amen.

Item alia

155 Is nu eac to witenne þæt man witnað foroft
ða arleasan sceaðan and þa swicolan ðeofas
ac hi nabbað nan edlean æt þam ælmihtigan Gode,
ac swyðor þa ecan witu for heora wæl-hreownysse,
forðan þe hi leofodon be reaflace swa swa reðe wulfas
160 and þam rihtwisum ætbrudon heora bigleofan foroft.
Wolde huru se earming hine sylfne beþencan
and his synna geandettan mid soðre behreowsunge,
huru ðonne he on bendum bið and gebroht to cwale,
swa swa se sceaða dyde, þe forscylgod hangode
165 mid þam hælende Criste and cwæð him to mid geleafan:
"Drihten leof, gemiltsa me þonne ðu becymst to ðinum
rice."
Se hælend him andwyrde: "Soð ic þe secge,
nu todæg þu bist mid me on neorxna-wange."

Then they also built a fitting church for the holy Alban, where he was buried, and frequent miracles were performed 145 there, in praise of the savior who lives always into eternity. This occurred before that conflict took place because of Hengest and Horsa, who conquered the Britons, and subsequently Christianity was dishonored until Augustine estab- 150 lished it again at the instigation of Gregory, the devout pope.

Glory and praise be to the benevolent creator who rescued our fathers from their enemies and converted and baptized them through his preachers. Amen.

Another in the Same Manner [On the Unjust]

Let it also be known now that very often impious robbers 155 and treacherous thieves are punished, but they will not have any reward from almighty God, but rather eternal torments on account of their cruelty, because they lived by robbery like fierce wolves and very often stole their means of liveli- 160 hood from the just. Would that the wretch were even willing to reflect and confess his sins with true repentance, even when he is in bonds and being led to death, like the robber did who hung condemned with the savior Christ and said to 165 him with faith: "Dear Lord, have mercy on me when you come into your kingdom." The savior answered him: "Truly I say to you, now you will be with me in paradise today."

Þus geearnode se arleasa sceaða
170 on his deaðes þrowunge þæt ece lif mid Criste,
forðan ðe he gelyfde on hine and his miltsunga bæd.
Yfele deð him sylfum þe mid swicdome his tilað
and he bið sceaðena gefera þe man sceandlice witnað.
Se swicola bedyddrað his dæda wið menn
175 ac hi beoð geopenode, oft unþances,
huru on domes-dæg, þær nan ðincg digle ne bið,
and he hæfð þonne ece wite forðan þe his wærscype ne
dohte.
Se sceaða bið nu ofslagen and to sceame getucod
and his earme sawl syððan syðað to helle,
180 to ðam ecum suslum on sweartum racen-teagum.
    We wenað swaðeah þæt se wealdenda hælend
wille gemiltsian þam manfullan sceaðan,
gif he mid eallre heortan and incundre geomerunge
clypað to ðam Ælmihtigan and his arfæstnysse bit
185 ær ðan þe þæt scearpe swurd swege to his hneccan
and gif he bemænð his synne swyðor þonne his lif
and mid wope gewilnað þæs wealdendes miltsunge.
Ac se swicola deofol þe beswac ðone þeof
and æfre forlærde oð his lifes ende
190 nele naht eaðe on his ende geðafian
þæt he þonne gecyrre mid soðre behreowsunge
and mid incundum wope to þam wel-willendan hælende,
ac cunnað mid eallum cræfte hu he hine Criste ætbrede.
Eac swylce hlaford-swican losiað on ende,
195 swa swa us bec secgað soðlice gehwær.
    Sum woruld-wita wæs swyðe wis on ræde
mid Dauide þam cynincge, þe Gode wæs gecweme,
on ðam timan þe Absalon, his agen sunu,

Thus the impious robber in his death throes merited that   170
eternal life with Christ, because he believed in him and
asked for his mercy. He who provides for himself by deceit
acts in an evil manner toward himself, and he will be a companion of robbers who will be shamefully punished. The deceitful person conceals his actions from people, but they   175
will be revealed, often against his will, at least on judgment
day, where nothing will be hidden, and he will have eternal
punishment then because his cunning was no use. The robber will be put to death now and ignominiously punished
and afterward his wretched soul will go to hell, to eternal   180
torments in dark chains.

Nevertheless we think that the ruling savior may be willing to have mercy on the wicked robber, if with all his heart
and profound lamentation he cries out to the Almighty and
begs for his mercy before the sharp sword descends with a   185
crash on his neck, and if he laments over his sins more than
over his life and with weeping desires the ruler's mercy. But
the deceitful devil who deceived the thief and always led
him astray until the end of his life will not lightly be willing   190
to permit him at his end to turn then with true repentance
and with heartfelt weeping to the benevolent savior, but he
will try with all his ability to lure him from Christ. Likewise
traitors to their lords will perish in the end, as books truly   195
tell us in many places.

A certain counselor, a layman, was very wise in advising
David the king, who was pleasing to God, at the time when
Absalom, his own son, began to fight against his father and

ongan winnan wið þone fæder and wolde hine adræfan
200 of his cynedome and acwellan gif he mihte.
Þa wæs se Acitofel mid Absalone on ræde
and rædde him sona hu he beswican mihte
his agenne fæder ðær he on fleame wæs.
Ac sum oðer þægn wiðcwæð his geðeahte wislice
205 and tæhte Absalone oðerne ræd,
wyrsan to his willan, forðan þe hit God wolde swa
þæt Dauid wurde fram heora wodnysse ahræd.
Þa gebealh hine Acitofel and mid bealwe wearð afylled
forðan þe his ræd ne moste þam reðan gelician,
210 for ðæs oðres ræde, and rad him ham sona,
becwæð þa his ðincg and acwealde hine sylfne
on healicum grine, þæt he hangigende sweolt.
Swa geendode se wita his wæl-hreowe geþeaht,
se ðe wolde berædan his rihtwisan hlaford.
215 Absalon ða ferde forð mid his unræde
and wolde his agenum fæder feores benæmen
and habban his anweald, ac hit nolde God.
He rad ða on his mule mid mycelre fyrde
þurh ænne heahne holt mid hetelicum geþance;
220 þa gefeng hine an treow be ðam fexe sona,
forðan þe he wæs sid-fæxede, and he swa hangode.
And se mul arn forð fram þam arleasan hlaforde
and Dauides þegnas hine þurhðydon.
Swa geendode se fæder-swica mid his feore his ræd.
225 Eallswa eac Iudas, ðe wæl-hreowlice belæwde
urne hælend Crist, acwealde hine sylfne
hangiende on grine, Godes wiðersaca,
ecelice fordemed swa swa Drihtnes belæwa.
Ælc man bið eac fordemed þe hine sylfne adyt

wished to drive him away from his kingdom and kill him if   200
he could. Then this Achitophel was advising Absalom and
immediately advised him how he could entrap his own father in the place where he was in his flight. But some other
attendant wisely opposed his plan and gave Absalom other   205
advice, worse for his purpose, because God wished that David would be saved from their insanity. Then Achitophel became angry and was filled with malice because his advice
could not please that fierce man on account of that other   210
man's advice, and he immediately rode home, then be-
queathed his property and killed himself in a high noose, so
that he died hanging. Thus the counselor, who wished to betray his righteous lord, brought his cruel plan to an end.

Absalom then proceeded with his ill-advised plan and   215
wished to deprive his own father of his life and have his
power, but God did not wish it. He was riding then on his
mule with a great army through a tall wood with malevolent
intent; then at once a tree caught him by the hair, because   220
he was long haired, and he was hanging like this. And the
mule ran away from the impious lord, and David's servants
pierced him through. This is how the traitor to his father
ended his plan along with his life.

Likewise Judas, who cruelly betrayed our savior Christ,   225
killed himself hanging in a noose, an apostate from God,
eternally damned as the Lord's betrayer. Every person who
kills himself will also be damned, and every suicide will   230

230 and ælc agen-slaga a on ecnysse ðrowað
and hlaford-swican losiað on ende
mid þam getreowleasan deofle þe hi tihte to ðam swicdome.
  Eallswa þa unrihtwisan deman þe heora domas awendað,
æfre be þam sceattum, na be soðfæstnysse,
235 and habbað æfre to cepe heora soðfæstnysse
and swa hi sylfe syllað wið sceattum:
þonne habbað hi on ende, for heora unrihtwisnysse,
mid þam swicolan deofle þa ecan susle.
  Se rihtwisa dema sceall deman æfre riht
240 and fyrðrian þa rihtwisnysse for Godes lufon symle,
forðan þe ða sceattas ablendað, swa swa us bec secgað,
þæra manna mod þe hi manfullice nimað
and ða domas awendað to wohnysse swa.
  Ne sceall nan Godes þegn for sceattum riht deman
245 ac healdan þone dom, gif he Drihtnes man sy,
buton lyðrum sceattum, symle to rihte,
þæt he on þam ecan life his edlean underfo.
  Sume menn syllað eac cyrcan to hyre,
swa swa waclice mylna, þæt mære Godes hus
250 þe wæs Gode betæht to his biggencgum,
to ðam Cristendome þe Crist sylf astealde.
Ac hit ne gedafnað þæt man do Godes hus
anre mylne gelic for lyðrum tolle
and se ðe hit deð he singað swyðe deope.
255 Gescylde us se scyppend þe gesceop us to mannum
wið þæs deofles swicdom, þe syrwð embe us,
and us mild-heortlice gelæde to ðam ecan life,
on ðam is ece wuldor on eallra worulda woruld. Amen.

always suffer in eternity, and traitors to their lord will perish in the end with the false devil who incited them to the treachery.

Likewise unjust judges who change their judgments, always according to the bribes, not according to truth, and always have their truth for sale and sell themselves in this way for bribes: in the end they will then have, because of their injustice, eternal torments with the deceitful devil. The just judge must always judge according to justice and always promote justice for the love of God, because, as books tell us, bribes blind the minds of those people who wickedly accept them and thus pervert their judgments into crookedness. A follower of God must not decide justice for bribes, but he must preserve just judgment, if he be the Lord's man, without vile bribes, always according to what is right, so that he may receive his reward in the eternal life.

Some people also rent out a church for payment, just like common watermills, that glorious house of God that was dedicated to God for his rituals, for that Christianity that Christ himself established. But it is not fitting that God's house be made like a mill for a vile rent, and he who does this sins very deeply.

May the creator who created us as human beings protect us against the deceit of the devil, who plots against us, and lead us mercifully to the eternal life, in which there is eternal glory for ever and ever. Amen.

SAINT ÆTHELTHRYTH

Saint Æthelthryth

IX Kalendas Iulii: Natale sanctae
Æðeldryðae virginis

We wyllað nu awritan, þeah ðe hit wundorlic sy,
be ðære halgan Æðeldryðe, þam Engliscan mædene,
þe wæs mid twam werum and swaðeah wunode mæden,
swa swa þa wundra swuteliað þe heo wyrcð gelome.
5　Anna hatte hyre fæder, East Engla cynincg,
swyðe Cristen man, swa swa he cydde mid weorcum,
and eall his team wearð gewurðod þurh God.
Æðeldryð wearð þa forgifen anum ealdor-menn to wife,
ac hit nolde se Ælmihtiga þæt hire mægðhad wurde
10　mid hæmede adylegod, ac heold hi on clænnysse,
forðan þe he is ælmihtig God and mæg eall þæt he wile
and on manegum wisum his mihte geswutelað.
　　Se ealdor-man gewat þa ða hit wolde God
and heo wearð forgifen Ecfride cynincge
15　and twelf gear wunode ungewemmed mæden
on þæs cynincges synscype, swa swutele wundra
hyre mærða cyðaþ and mægðhad gelome.
Heo lufode þone hælend þe hi heold unwemme

19

Saint Æthelthryth

June 23: Feast of Saint Æthelthryth the Virgin

We wish to write now, astonishing as it may be, about the holy Æthelthryth, the English virgin, who had two husbands and nevertheless remained a virgin, as the miracles that she frequently performs demonstrate. Her father was called Anna, king of the East Angles, a very Christian man, as he showed in his actions, and all his family was honored by God. Then Æthelthryth was given in marriage to a ruler, but the Almighty did not want her virginity to be destroyed by sexual intercourse, but he kept her pure because he is almighty God and can do all that he wishes, and he reveals his power in many ways.

The prince died when God wished, and she was given to king Ecgfrith and for twelve years remained an unblemished virgin married to the king, so that manifest miracles frequently make known her glorious acts and her virginity. She loved the savior who kept her unblemished, and she honored God's servants. One of them was Bishop Wilfrid, whom she loved most of all, and he told Bede that Ecgfrith

and Godes ðeowas wurðode. An þære wæs Wilfrid bisceop,
20 þe heo swyðost lufode, and he sæde Bedan
þæt se cyning Ecfrid him oft behete mycel
on lande and on feo, gif he læran mihte
Æðeldryðe his gebeddan þæt heo bruce his synscipes.
Nu cwæð se halga Beda þe þas boc gesette
25 þæt se ælmihtiga God mihte eaðe gedon,
nu on urum dagum, þæt Æðeldryð þurhwunode
ungewemmed mæden, þeah ðe heo wer hæfde,
swa swa on ealdum dagum hwilon ær getimode
þurh þone ylcan God þe æfre þurhwunað
30 mid his gecorenum halgum, swa swa he sylf behet.
    Æðeldryð wolde ða ealle woruld-þincg forlætan
and bæd georne þone cynincg þæt heo Criste moste
                                    þeowian
on mynsterlicre drohtnunge, swa hire mod hire tospeon.
Þa lyfde hire se cynincg, þeah þe hit embe lang wære
35 þæs þe heo gewilnode, and Wilfrid bisceop þa
hi gehadode to mynecene and heo on mynstre wunode
sume twelf monað swa and heo syððan wearð gehadod
eft to abudissan on Elig mynstre
ofer manega mynecyna and heo hi modorlice heold,
40 mid godum gebysnungum to þam gastlican life.
Be hire is awrytan þæt heo wel drohtnode,
to anum mæle fæstende butan hit freols-dæg wære,
and heo syndrige gebedu swyðe lufode
and wyllen weorode and wolde seld-hwænne
45 hire lic baðian butan to heah-tidum
and ðonne heo wolde ærest ealle ða baðian
þe on ðam mynstre wæron and wolde him ðenian
mid hire þinenum and þonne hi sylfe baðian.

the king had often promised him much land and money, if he could persuade Æthelthryth his wife to have sexual relations with him. Now the holy Bede who wrote this book said that the almighty God could easily bring it about, now 25 in our own days, that Æthelthryth should remain an unblemished virgin, even though she had a husband, as in days of old had sometimes happened through that same God who remains eternally with his chosen saints, as he himself 30 promised.

Æthelthryth then wished to relinquish all worldly things and eagerly entreated the king that she might be permitted to serve Christ in a monastic way of life, as her spirit urged her. Then the king gave her leave, though it was long after she had desired this, and bishop Wilfrid then consecrated 35 her as a nun and she lived in a monastery in this way for some twelve months, and then she was consecrated afterward as abbess over many nuns in the monastery of Ely, and she governed them like a mother, with good examples of the 40 spiritual life. It is written about her that she conducted her life virtuously, fasting (apart from a single meal) unless it was a feast day, and she very much loved private prayers and wore woolen clothes and would seldom bathe her body ex- 45 cept at major holy days, and then she would first bathe all those who were in the monastery and would attend to them with her maidservants and then bathe herself.

Þa on þam eahteoðan geare siððan heo abbudisse wæs,

50 heo wearð geuntrumod, swa swa heo ær witegode,

swa þæt an geswel weox on hire swuran

mycel under þam cynn-bane and heo swiðe þancode

þæt heo on þam swuran sum geswinc þolode.

Heo cwæð: "Ic wat geare þæt ic wel wyrðe eom

55 þæt min swura beo geswenct mid swylcere untrumnysse,

forðan þe ic on iugoðe frætwode minne swuran

mid mænigfealdum swur-beagum. And me is nu geþuht

þæt Godes arfæstnyss þone gylt aclænsige,

þonne me nu þis geswel scynð for golde

60 and þæs hata bryne for healicum gym-stanum."

Þa wæs þær sum læce on ðam geleaffullum heape,

Cynefryð gehaten, and hi cwædon þa sume

þæt se læce sceolde asceotan þæt geswell.

Þa dyde he sona swa and þær sah ut wyrms.

65 Wearð him þa geðuht swilce heo gewurpan mihte,

ac heo gewat of worulde mid wuldre to Gode

on þam ðriddan dæge syððan se dolh wæs geopenod

and wearð bebyrged, swa swa heo bæd sylf and het,

betwux hire geswustrum on treowenre cyste.

70   Þa wearð hire swustor Sexburh gehadod

to abbudissan æfter hire geendunge,

seo ðe ær wæs cwen on Cantwarebyrig.

Þa wolde seo Sexburh æfter syxtyne gearum

don hire swustor ban of ðære byrgene up

75 and beran into þære cyrcan and sende þa gebroðra

to secenne sumne stan to swilcere neode,

forðan þe on þam fen-lande synd feawe weorc-stana.

Hi hreowan þa to Grantanceastre and God hi sona

gehradode,

Then on the eighth year after she had become abbess she 50
became ill, as she had previously prophesied, so that a large
tumor grew on her neck under the jawbone and she fervently gave thanks that she was suffering an affliction in her
neck. She said: "I know for certain that I well deserve that 55
my neck should be afflicted with such sickness, because in
youth I adorned my neck with many necklaces. And it seems
to me now that God's mercy may cleanse that guilt, when
this tumor now shines in place of gold for me and this hot 60
burning in place of precious gemstones." Then there was a
doctor in that devout company called Cynefrith, and then
some of them said that the doctor ought to lance that tumor. Then he immediately did so, and the pus oozed out.
Then it seemed to them as if she could recover, but she de- 65
parted from the world with glory to God on the third day
after the sore was opened, and she was buried, as she herself
had requested and ordered, among her sisters in a wooden
coffin.

Then her sister Seaxburg was consecrated as abbess after 70
her death, she who had been queen in Canterbury. Then this
Seaxburg after sixteen years wished to take her sister's bones
up out of the grave and bring them into the church, and she 75
sent the brothers to search for a stone for such a purpose,
because in the fenlands there are few large stones. Then
they rowed to Grantchester, and God straightaway made it

swa þæt hi þær gemetton ane mære þruh
80 wið þone weall standende, geworht of marm-stane,
eall hwites bleos, bufan þære eorðan,
and þæt hlyd ðær-to, gelimplice gefeged,
eac of hwitum marm-stane, swa swa hit macode God.
Þa naman ða gebroðra blyðelice þa ðruh
85 and gebrohton to mynstre, mycclum ðancigende Gode,
and Sexburh seo abbudisse het slean an geteld
bufan ða byrgene: wolde þa ban gaderian.
Hi sungon ða ealle sealmas and lic-sang
þa hwile þe man ða byrgene bufan geopenode.
90 Þa læg heo on ðære cyste, swilce heo læge on slæpe,
hal eallum limum and se læce wæs ðær
ðe þæt geswell geopenode and hi sceawode georne.
Þa wæs seo wund gehæled, þe se læce worhte ær.
Eac swilce þa gewæda þe heo bewunden wæs mid
95 wæron swa ansunde swylce hi eall niwe wæron.
Sexburh þa hyre swuster swiðe þæs fægnode
and hi þwogon ða syððan þone sawlleasan lic-haman
and mid niwum gewædum bewundon ar-wurðlice
and bæron into ðære cyrcan, blyssigende mid sangum,
100 and ledon hi on ðære þryh, þær ðær heo lið oð þis
on mycelre ar-wurðnysse, mannum to wundrunge.
Wæs eac wundorlic þæt seo ðruh wæs geworht,
þurh Godes fore-sceawunge, hire swa gemæte,
swylce heo hyre sylfre swa gesceapen wære,
105 and æt hire hæfde wæs aheawen se stan,
gemæte þam heafde þæs halgan mædenes.
Hit is swutol þæt heo wæs ungewemmed mæden
þonne hire lic-hama ne mihte formolsnian on eorðan,
and Godes miht is geswutelod soðlice þurh hi,

happen, so that they found there a splendid sarcophagus standing by the wall, made of marble, all white in color, 80 above the ground, and the lid for it, suitably fitted, also of white marble, just as God had made it.

Then the brothers joyfully took the sarcophagus and 85 brought it to the monastery, greatly thanking God, and Seaxburg the abbess ordered a tent to be pitched above the grave: she wished to collect the bones. Then they all sang psalms and a lament while the grave was being opened at the top. There she lay in the coffin as if she were lying asleep, 90 sound in all her limbs, and the doctor was there who had lanced the tumor, and he examined her intently. The wound had been healed then, which the doctor had made previously. Likewise the garments in which she had been wrapped were as flawless as if they were all new. Then her sister Seax- 95 burg rejoiced very much at this, and then afterward they washed the soulless body and wrapped it reverently in new clothes and carried it into the church, rejoicing with songs, and they laid her in the sarcophagus, where she lies until 100 now in great honor, to the astonishment of people. It was also astonishing that the sarcophagus was made to fit her so exactly, by God's providence, as if it had been made like this for her, and at her head the stone had been shaped by cut- 105 ting, made to fit the head of the holy virgin. It is clear that she was an unblemished virgin when her body could not decay in the ground, and God's power is truly revealed through

110 þæt he mæg aræran ða formolsnodon lic-haman,
se ðe hire lic heold hal on ðære byrgene
git oð þisne dæg. Sy him ðæs a wuldor!
    Þær wæron gehælede þurh ða halgan femnan
fela adlige menn, swa swa we gefyrn gehyrdon,
115 and eac ða þe hrepodon þæs reafes ænigne dæl
þe heo mid bewunden wæs wurdon sona hale.
And manegum eac fremode seo cyst micclum
þe heo ærest on læg, swa swa se lareow Beda
on ðære bec sæde, þe he gesette be ðysum.
120   Oft woruld-menn eac heoldon, swa swa us bec secgað,
heora clænnysse on synscipe for Cristes lufe,
swa swa we mihton reccan gif ge rohton hit to gehyrenne.
We secgað swaðeah be sumum ðegne,
se wæs þryttig geara mid his wife on clænnysse.
125 Þry suna he gestrynde and hi siððan buta
ðrittig geara wæron wunigende butan hæmede
and fela ælmyssan worhton, oðþæt se wer ferde
to munuclicere drohtnunge, and Drihtnes englas
comon eft on his forð-siðe and feredon his sawle
130 mid sange to heofonum, swa swa us secgað bec.
    Manega bysna synd on bocum be swylcum,
hu oft weras and wif wundorlice drohtnodon
and on clænnysse wunodon, to wuldre þam hælende
þe þa clænnysse astealde, Crist ure hælend,
135 þam is a wurð-mynt and wuldor on ecnysse. Amen.

her, that he can raise up decayed bodies, he who preserved 110
her body uncorrupt in the grave even to this day. Glory be to
him eternally for that!

There, through that holy virgin, many sick people were
healed, as we have heard already, and also those who touched 115
any part of the garment with which she was wrapped were
immediately healed. And the coffin in which she had first
lain also greatly helped many people, as the scholar Bede
said in the book that he wrote about this.

Often laypeople too, as books tell us, have preserved 120
their chastity in marriage for love of Christ, as we could relate if you cared to hear it. We will tell nevertheless about
one nobleman who spent thirty years in chastity with his
wife. He fathered three sons, and subsequently they both 125
lived without sexual intercourse for thirty years and gave
many alms, until the man entered a monastic way of life, and
the Lord's angels afterward came at his death and carried his
soul with song to heaven, as books tell us. 130

There are many examples of such things in books, how
men and women often conducted their lives wonderfully
and lived in chastity, to the glory of the savior who founded
that chastity, Christ our savior, to whom is honor and glory 135
in eternity. Amen.

SAINT SWITHUN *AND*
SAINT MACARIUS
AND THE SORCERERS

Saint Swithun *and* Saint Macarius and the Sorcerers

VI Nonas Iulii: Natale sancti Swyðuni episcopi

On Eadgares dagum ðæs æðelan cynincges,
þa ða se Cristendom wæs wel ðeonde þurh God
on Angelcynne under ðam ylcan cynincge,
þa geswutelode God þone sanct Swyðun
5   mid manegum wundrum þæt he mære is.
His dæda næron cuðe ær ðan þe hi God sylf cydde
ne we ne fundon on bocum hu se bisceop leofode
on þysre worulde, ær ðan þe he gewende to Criste.
Þæt wæs þære gymeleast þe on life hine cuþon
10 þæt hi noldon awritan his weorc and drohtnunge
þam towerdum mannum ðe his mihte ne cuðon,
ac God hæfð swaþeah his lif geswutelod
mid swutelum wundrum and syllicum tacnum.
Ðes Swyðun wæs bisceop on Winceastre
15 (swaþeah ofer Hamtunscire), gesælig Godes þeowa,
and eahte bisceopas wæron betwux him and Aðelwolde.
Nu næs us his lif cuð, swa swa we ær cwædon,
butan þæt he wæs bebyrged æt his bisceop-stole

20

Saint Swithun *and* Saint Macarius and the Sorcerers

July 2: Feast of Saint Swithun the Bishop

In the days of Edgar the noble king, when with the aid of God Christianity was successfully flourishing among the English people under this very king, then God made known that Swithun the saint is glorious, by many miracles. His deeds were not known before God himself made them known, nor have we found in books how the bishop lived in this world before he departed to Christ. It was negligence on the part of those who knew him in life that they were not willing to write down his deeds and his way of life for future people who did not know his power, but God has nevertheless made his life known by visible miracles and wonderful signs. This Swithun was bishop in Winchester (but over Hampshire), a blessed servant of God, and there were eight bishops between him and Æthelwold. His life is not now known to us, as we said earlier, except that he was buried at his episcopal seat to the west of the church and afterward a

be westan þære cyrcan and oferworht syððan,

20 oþþæt his wundra geswutelodon his gesælða mid Gode.

Þrym gearum ær ðan þe se sanct into cyrcan wære
gebroht

of ðære stænenan þryh þe stent nu wiðinnan

þam niwan geweorce, com se ar-wurða Swyðun

to sumum gelyfedan smyðe, on swefne æteowiende

25 wurðlice geglencged, and ðas word him cwæð to:

"Canst þu ðone preost þe is gehaten Eadzige,

þe wæs of Ealdan Mynstre mid ðam oðrum preostum
adræfed

for heora unþeawum þurh Aðelwold bisceop?"

Se smið þa andwyrde þam ar-wurðan Swyðune þus:

30 "Gefyrn ic hine cuðe, leof, ac he ferde heonon

and ic nat to gewissan hwær he wunað nu."

Þa cwæð eft se halga wer to ðam ealdan smyðe:

"Witodlice he wunað nu on Wincelcumbe hamfæst

and ic ðe nu halsige on þæs hælendes naman

35 þæt ðu him min ærende ardlice abeode

and sege him to soþan þæt Swiðun se bisceop

het þæt he fare to Aþelwolde bisceope

and secge þæt he geopenige him sylf mine byrgene

and mine ban gebringe binnan ðære cyrcan,

40 forðan þe him is getiþod þæt ic on his timan

beo mannum geswutelod." And se smið him cwæð to:

"La leof, Eadzige nele gelyfan minum wordum."

Ða cwæð se bisceop eft: "Gange him to minre byrgene

and ateo ane hringan up of ðære þryh

45 and gif seo hringe him folgað æt þam forman tige,

þonne wat he to soðan þæt ic þe sende to him.

Gif seo hringe nele up þurh his anes tige,

structure was built on top, until his miracles made known   20
his blessed state with God.

Three years before the saint was brought into the church
from the stone coffin that now stands inside the new building, the honorable Swithun came to a devout smith, appearing in a dream splendidly adorned, and spoke these words to   25
him: "Do you know the priest who is called Eadsige, who
was expelled from the Old Minster with the other priests by
Bishop Æthelwold because of their vices?" Then the smith
answered the honorable Swithun thus: "I knew him once,   30
sir, but he went away from here and I do not know for certain where he lives now." Then the holy man spoke again to
the old smith: "For certain he is settled in Winchcombe
now, and I call upon you now in the name of the savior to   35
deliver my message quickly to him and say to him truly that
Swithun the bishop has commanded him to go to Bishop
Æthelwold and say that he himself should open my grave
and bring my bones inside the church, because it is granted   40
to him that in his time I should be made known to people."
And the smith said to him: "Ah sir, Eadsige will not be willing to believe my words." Then the bishop spoke once more:
"Let him go to my grave and pull one ring up out of the coffin, and if the ring yields to him at the first pull, then he will   45
know for certain that I have sent you to him. If the ring will
not come out with his unaided pull, then he ought not to

þonne ne sceall he nates-hwon þinre sage gelyfan.
Sege him eac siððan þæt he sylf gerihtlæce
50 his dæda and þeawas to his Drihtnes willan
and efste an-modlice to þam ecan life.
Sege eac eallum mannum þæt sona swa hi
geopeniað mine byrgene, þæt hi magon ðær findan
swa deor-wurðne hord þæt heora dyre gold
55 ne bið nahte wurð wið þa fore-sædan maðmas."
    Se halga Swyðun þa ferde fram þam smiðe up
and se smið ne dorste secgan þas gesihðe ænigum menn:
nolde beon gesewen unsoð-sagul boda.
Hwæt ða se halga wer hine eft gespræc
60 and git þryddan siðe and swyðe hine þreade,
hwi he nolde gehyrsumian his hæsum mid weorce.
Se smið þa æt nextan eode to his byrgene
and genam ane hringan, earhlice swaðeah,
and clypode to Gode, þus cwæðende mid wordum:
65 "Eala ðu Drihten God, ealra gesceafta scyppend,
getiða me synfullum þæt ic ateo þas hringan
up of ðysum hlyde, gif se lið her on innan
se ðe me spræc to on swæfne þriwa."
He teah ða þæt isen up swa eaðelice of ðam stane
70 swilce hit on sande stode and he swyðe þæs wundrode.
He ða hit eft sette on þæt ylce þyrl
and þyde mid his fet and hit swa fæste eft stod
þæt nan man ne mihte hit þanon ateon.
    Þa eode se smið geegsod þanon
75 and gemette on cypincge þæs Eadzies mann
and sæde him gewislice hwæt Swyðun him bebead
and bæd hine georne þæt he hit abude him.
He cwæð þæt he wolde hit cyðan his hlaforde

believe what you say at all. Afterward say to him too that he himself should reform his deeds and behavior in accordance with his Lord's will and should hasten resolutely to the eternal life. Say also to all people that, as soon as they open my grave, they will be able to find there a treasure of such precious worth that their precious gold will be worth nothing compared to the treasures I have just mentioned."

The holy Swithun then departed upward from the smith, and the smith did not dare to tell this vision to anyone: he did not want to be seen as a lying messenger. Well then, the holy man spoke to him again and yet a third time and rebuked him strongly as to why he was not willing to obey his commands with action. Then at last the smith went to his grave and took hold, though fearfully, of a ring, and called to God, speaking thus with these words: "You Lord God, creator of all creatures, grant to me, a sinful man, that I may pull this ring up out of this lid, if he who has spoken to me three times in a dream lies here within." He then pulled the iron up out of the stone as easily as if it stood in sand, and he marveled greatly at that. He then put it back into the same hole and pressed it with his foot and it stood once more so firmly fixed that no one could pull it out of there.

Then the smith went away from there terrified and met Eadsige's servant in the marketplace and told him exactly what Swithun had commanded him and urgently begged him to announce it to him. He said that he was willing to

and ne dorste swaðeah hit secgan æt fruman,
80 ær þan ðe he beþohte þæt him ðearflic nære
þæt he ðæs halgan hæse forhule his hlaforde.
Sæde þa be ende-byrdnysse hwæt Swyðun him bebead.
Þa onscunode se Eadsige Aðelwold þone bisceop
and ealle ða munecas þe on ðam mynstre wæron,
85 for þære ut-dræfe þe he gedyde wið hi,
and nolde gehyran þæs halgan bebod,
þeah ðe se sanct wære gesib him for worulde.
He gebeah swaþeah binnan twam gearum
to þam ylcan mynstre and munuc wearð þurh God
90 and þær wunode oðþæt he gewat of life.
Geblætsod is se Ealmihtiga þe geeadmed þa modigan
and ða ead-modan ahæfð to healicum geðincþum
and gerihtlæcð þa synfullan and symle hylt ða godan
þe on hine hihtað forðan þe he hælend is.

95   Eft wæs sum earm ceorl, egeslice gehoferod
and ðearle gebiged þurh ðone bradan hofor:
þam wearð geswutelod on swefne gewislice
þæt he sceolde gefeccan æt Swyðunes byrgene
his lic-haman hæle and þære alefednysse.
100 He aras ða on mergen micclum fægnigende
and mid twam criccum creap him to Wynceastre
and gesohte ðone sanct, swa swa him gesæd wæs,
biddende his hæle gebigdum cneowum.
He wearð þa gehæled þurh þone halgan bisceop,
105 swa þæt næs gesyne syððan on his hricge
hwær se hofor stode, þe hine gehefegode oðþæt.
Þa nyston þa munecas be ðam mæran halgan
and wendon þæt sum oðer halga gehælde þone mann,

make it known to his lord, and yet he did not dare to say it at first, until he reflected that it would not be advantageous for him to conceal the saint's command from his lord. Then he told him point by point what Swithun had commanded him. At the time this Eadsige hated Æthelwold the bishop and all the monks who were in the monastery, on account of his having caused their expulsion, and he was not willing to obey the saint's command, even though the saint was related to him in this world. Within two years, however, he entered that same monastery and became a monk through the grace of God and lived there until he departed from this life. Blessed is the Almighty, who humbles the proud and exalts the humble to high offices and corrects the sinful and always protects the good who trust in him because he is the savior.

Likewise there was a miserable man, terribly hunch-backed and very bent over because of the large hump: it was clearly revealed to him in a dream that at Swithun's tomb he should obtain healing for his body and for his disability. Then he arose in the morning greatly rejoicing and with two crutches crept along to Winchester and went to the saint, just as he had been told, praying for healing on bended knees. He was then healed by the holy bishop, so that afterward it was not visible on his back where the hump had been, which had weighed him down until then. At that time the monks did not know about the glorious saint and thought that some other saint had healed the man, but the

ac se ceorl sæde þæt Swyðun hine gehælde,

110 forðan þe he sylf wiste gewissost be ðam.

Sum wer wæs geuntrumod swiðe yfelum broce,
swa þæt he earfoðlice þa eagan undyde
and uneaðe mihte ænig word gecweðan,
ac læg swa geancsumod, orwene his lifes.

115 Ða woldon his freond ealle hine ferian to Niwan Mynstre,
to þam halgan Iudoce, þæt he him hæle forgeafe,
ac him sæde sum man þæt him selra wære
þæt hi to Ealdan Mynstre þone adligan feredon,
to Swyðunes byrgene, and hi swa dydon sona.

120 Hi wacodon ða þa niht wið þa byrgene mid him,
biddende þone ælmihtigan God þæt he ðam adligan menn
his hæle forgeafe þurh þone halgan Swyðun.
Se untruma eac wacode oðþæt hit wolde dagian.
Þa wearð he on slæpe and seo wurðfulle byrgen,

125 þæs ðe him eallum þuhte, eall bifigende wæs,
and þam adlian þuhte swylce man his ænne sco
of ðam fet him atuge and he færlice awoc.
He wæs ða gehæled þurh ðone halgan Swyðun
and man sohte þone sco swyðe geornlice,

130 ac hine ne mihte nan man gemeten þær æfre,
and hi gewendan þa ham mid þam gehæledan menn.
Þær wurdon gehælede æt ðære halgan byrgene
eahta untrume menn, ær ðan þe he of ðære byrgene
up genumen wære, wundorlice þurh God.

135 Eadgar cyning þa, æfter ðysum tacnum,
wolde þæt se halga wer wurde up gedon
and spræc hit to Aðelwolde þam ar-wurðan bisceope
þæt he hine up adyde mid ar-wurðnysse.
Þa se bisceop Aðelwold, mid abbodum and munecum,

man said that Swithun had healed him, because he himself 110
knew about it with most certain knowledge.

One man was ill with a very harmful disease, so that he
could scarcely open his eyes and could hardly speak a single
word, but he lay tormented like this, despairing of his life.
Then all his friends wished to carry him to the New Minster, 115
to Saint Judoc, that he might grant him healing, but a man
told them that it would be better to carry the sick man to
the Old Minster, to Swithun's tomb, and they did so straightaway. They kept a vigil with him that night at the tomb, en- 120
treating the almighty God to grant healing to the sick man
through the holy Swithun. The sick man also kept watch until it was about to be day. Then he fell asleep and the glorious
tomb, as it seemed to them all, was all trembling, and it 125
seemed to the sick man as if one of his shoes was being
pulled off his foot and he suddenly woke up. He was then
healed by the holy Swithun, and they searched very diligently for the shoe, but no one was ever able to find it there, 130
and then they went home with the man who had been
healed. There at the holy tomb eight sick people were
healed miraculously by the grace of God, before he was
taken up from the grave.

Then King Edgar, after these miracles, wanted the holy 135
man to be exhumed and said to Æthelwold the honored
bishop that he should exhume him with honor. Then this
Bishop Æthelwold, with abbots and monks, exhumed the 140

140 dyde up þone sanct mid sange wurðlice
and bæron into cyrcan, Sancte Petres huse,
þær he stend mid wurð-mynte and wundra gefremað.
Þær wurdon gehælede þurh ðone halgan wer
feower wan-hale menn binnan ðrym dagum
145 and geond fif monþas feawa daga wæron
þæt ðær næron gehælede huru ðry untrume,
hwilon fif oððe syx, seofon oððe eahta,
tyn oððe twelf, syxtyne oððe eahtatyne.
Binnon tyn dagum þær wurdon twa hund manna gehælede
150 and swa fela binnan twelf monðum þæt man hi getellan ne
mihte.
Se lic-tun læg afylled mid alefedum mannum,
swa þæt man eaðe ne mihte þæt mynster gesecan
and þa ealle wurdon swa wundorlice gehælede
binnan feawa dagum þæt man þær findan ne mihte
155 fif unhale menn of þam micclan heape.
    On þam dagum wæron on Wihtlande þreo wif:
þa twa wæron blinde geond nigon geara fec
and þæt þrydde ne geseah þære sunnan leoht næfre.
Hi begeaton þa earfoðlice him ænne lat-teow,
160 ænne dumbne cnapan, and comon to þam halgan
and ane niht þær wacodon and wurdon gehælede,
ge ða blindan wif, ge se dumba lat-teow.
Þa sæde se cnapa þam cyrc-werde þæt
and cwæð þæt he næfre ær naht cweðan ne mihte,
165 and bæd þæt hi sungon þone gesettan lof-sang.
    On þære ylcan tide wæs sum wyln gehæft to swinglum
for swyðe lytlan gylte and læg on hæft-nedum
þæt heo hetelice wære þæs on mergen beswungen.
Þa wacode heo ealle ða niht and mid wope clypode

saint honorably to the accompaniment of singing and carried him into the church, Saint Peter's house, where he remains in glory and performs miracles. Four sick people were healed there by the holy man within three days, and over the 145 course of five months there were few days when at least three sick people were not healed, sometimes five or six, seven or eight, ten or twelve, sixteen or eighteen. Within ten days two hundred people were healed, and there were so 150 many within twelve months that they could not be counted. The cemetery was filled with disabled people, so that it was not easy to get to the minster, and then all were so miraculously healed within a few days that one could not find five 155 sick people out of that large crowd.

In those days there were three women on the Isle of Wight: two of them had been blind for the space of nine years and the third had never seen the light of the sun. With difficulty they obtained the services of a guide, a mute young 160 man, and they came to the saint and kept a vigil there for one night and were healed, both the blind women and the mute guide. Then the young man told this to the sacristan and said that he had never before been able to say anything, and asked that they should sing the designated hymn of 165 praise.

At the same time a female slave was imprisoned in order to be flogged for a very small offense, and she lay in custody so that she could be severely flogged for it in the morning. Then she lay awake all night and called out weeping

170 to ðam halgan Swyðune þæt he hulpe hire earmre
and fram þam reðum swinglum ahredde þurh God.
Mid þam þe hit dagode and man Drihtnes lof-sang ongan,
þa feollan ða fot-copsas færlice hire fram
and heo arn to cyrcan, to þam ar-wurðan halgan,
175 gebundenum handum, swa swa se halga wolde,
and se hlaford com æfter and alysde hire handa
and gefreode hi sona for Swyðunes wurð-mynte.
      Sum þegn læg alefed lange on paralisyn
and ne mihte of his bedde for manegum gearum.
180 Þa cwæð he þæt he wolde to Wynceastre syðian,
huru on his hors-bære, and biddan his hæle.
Mid þam þe he þis cwæð to his cnihtum and freondum,
þa wearð he gehæled and gewende swaþeah
to þam halgan sancte, siðigende on fotum,
185 fyrmest on þam flocce on ealre þære fare,
and ðancode þam halgan his hæle geornlice.
Fif and twentig manna myslice geuntrumode
comon to þam halgan, heora hæle biddende:
sume wæron blinde, sume wæron healte,
190 sume eac deafe, and dumbe eac sume,
and hi ealle wurdon anes dæges gehælede
þurh þæs halgan ðingunge and him ham gewendon.
      Sum þegn wæs on Englalande, on æhtum swyðe welig,
se wearð færlice blind. Þa ferde he to Rome:
195 wolde his hæle biddan æt þam halgum apostolum.
He wunode þa on Rome and ne wearð gehæled
feower gear fullice and gefran þa be Swyðune,
hwylce wundra he worhte syððan he gewende þanon.
He efste þa swyðe and to his earde gewende

to the holy Swithun to help her, a miserable woman, and to   170
rescue her with the aid of God from the cruel flogging.
When it was day and lauds began, the foot shackles suddenly fell off her and she ran to the church, to the honored
saint, with her hands still bound, as the saint wished, and   175
her master came after her and released her hands and immediately freed her in honor of Swithun.

One nobleman was disabled for a long time by paralysis,
and he could not get out of his bed for many years. Then he   180
said that he wished to travel to Winchester, at least in his
horse litter, and pray for healing. While he was saying this to
his servants and friends, he was healed and he went nevertheless to the holy saint, traveling on foot, at the forefront   185
of the company for the whole journey, and he fervently
thanked the saint for healing him. Twenty-five people with
various illnesses came to the saint, praying for healing: some
were blind, some were lame, some were deaf also, and some   190
mute too, and they were all healed in the one day through
the intercession of the saint and went home.

There was a nobleman in England, very rich in possessions, who suddenly became blind. Then he went to Rome:
he wished to pray to the apostles for healing. He stayed then   195
in Rome and was not healed for four full years, and then he
found out about Swithun, about what miracles he had
worked since he had left there. Then he made great haste

200 and com to þam halgan were and wearð gehæled þær
and ham gewende mid halre gesihðe.
   Sum wer wæs eac blind wel seofon gear fulle;
se hæfde ænne lat-teow þe hine lædde gehwider.
Ða sume dæg eode he, swa swa he oft dyde,
205 and se lat-teow wearð gebolgen and þone blindan forlet.
Arn him aweg and se oðer nyste
hu he ham come, ac clypode to Gode
mid innewerdre heortan and mid angsumnysse cwæð:
"Eala þu mihtiga Drihten manna and engla,
210 geseoh mine yrmðe! Ic geseon ne mæg
and min lyðra lat-teow forlet me þus ænne.
Gemiltsa me, Drihten, þurh ðone mæran Swyðun
and forgif me gesihðe for ðæs sanctes geearnungum."
Eft he clypode þus and cwæð to ðam halgan:
215 "Eala þu milda bisceop þe manega wundra of cumað
þurh þone lifigendan God—leof, ic þe bidde
þæt þu me geþingie to þam mihtigan hælende.
Ic gelyfe þæt he wille gewislice þe tiðian."
He wearð þa gehæled and hæfde his gesihðe
220 and ham eode blyðe butan lat-teowe ana,
se ðe lytle ær þanon wæs gelæd þurh ðone oþerne,
and his magas ðancodon mycclum ðæs Gode.
   Aþelwold þa, se ar-wurða and se eadiga bisceop,
þe on ðam dagum wæs on Winceastre bisceop,
225 bead his munecum eallum þe on ðam mynstre wunodon
þæt hi ealle eodon endemes to cyrcan
and mid sange heredon þæs sanctes mærða
and God mærsodon swa on þam mæran halgan,
swa oft swa ænig wan-hal mann wurde gehæled.
230 Þa dydon hi sona swa and sungon þone lof-sang,

and went back to his homeland and came to the holy man   200
and was healed there and went home with perfect sight.

One man was also blind for a full seven years; he had a
guide who led him everywhere. Then one day he went out,
as he often did, and the guide became enraged and aban-   205
doned the blind man. He ran away from him and the other
man did not know how he could get home, but he called to
God with his innermost heart and said with anguish: "You
mighty Lord of people and angels, see my misery! I cannot   210
see, and my wicked guide has abandoned me alone like this.
Have mercy on me, Lord, through the glorious Swithun and
grant me sight for the sake of the saint's merits." He called
out again thus and said to the saint: "You merciful bishop   215
from whom many miracles come through the grace of the
living God—I beseech you, lord, that you intercede for me
to the mighty savior. I believe that he will certainly be willing to grant your request." Then he was healed and received
his sight and joyfully went home alone without a guide, he   220
who a little while before had been led by the other man, and
his relatives thanked God very much for this.

Then Æthelwold, the honored and blessed bishop, who
was bishop of Winchester in those days, commanded all his   225
monks who lived in the minster to go one after the other to
the church and praise the glorious deeds of the saint with
song and in this way glorify God in the glorious saint, as often as any sick person was healed. Then they were doing this   230
without delay and singing the hymn, until they all hated that

oðþæt him laðode eallum þæt hi swa oft arisan,
hwilon þrywa on niht, hwilon feower syðum,
to singenne þone lof-sang, þonne hi slapan sceoldon,
and forleton þa ealle endemes þone sang,
235   forðam þe se bisceop wæs bysig mid þam cynincge
and nyste butan hi sungon þone lof-sang forð on.
Hwæt ða se halga Swyðun sylf com on swefne,
wundorlice geglencged, to sumum godan menn and cwæð:
"Gang nu to Ealdan Mynstre and þam munecum sege
240   þæt Gode swyðe oflicað heora ceorung and slæwð—
þæt hi dæghwamlice geseoð Drihtnes wundra mid him
and hi nellað herian þone hælend mid sange,
swa swa se bisceop bebead þam gebroðrum to donne.
And sege gif hi nellað þone sang gelæstan,
245   þonne geswicað eac sona ða wundra.
And gif hi þone lof-sang willað æt þam wundrum singan
swa oft swa wan-hale menn þær wurðað gerihte,
þonne wurðaþ mid him wundra swa fela
þæt nan man ne mæg gemunan on life
250   þæt ænig man gesawe swylce wundra ahwær."
Þa awæcnode se wer of þam wynsuman slæpe
and swyðe besargode þæt he geseon ne moste
ne nan læncg brucan þæs beorhtan leohtes
þe he mid Swiðune hæfde gesewen.
255   He aras swaðeah and swiðe hraðe ferde
to Aþelwolde bisceope and him eall þis sæde.
Aþelwold þa asende sona to þam munecum
of cyninges hyrede and cwæð þæt hi sceoldon
þone lof-sang singan, swa swa he geset hæfde,
260   and se þe hit forsawe sceolde hit mid fæstene
seofon niht on an swarlice gebetan.

they had to get up from sleep so often, sometimes three times in a night, sometimes four times, to sing the hymn, when they ought to be asleep, and then all together they neglected the singing, because the bishop was busy with the king and did not know anything except that they kept on singing the hymn. Well then, the holy Swithun himself came in a dream, wondrously adorned, to a good man and said: "Go now to the Old Minster and say to the monks that their complaining and sloth displease God greatly—in that they see the miracles of the Lord in their midst daily and they are not willing to praise the savior with singing, as the bishop commanded the brothers to do. And say that if they are not willing to carry out the singing, then the miracles will also cease straightaway. And if they are willing to sing the hymn at the miracles as often as sick people are cured there, then so many miracles will happen there among them that no living person will be able to recall that anyone saw such miracles anywhere." Then the man woke up from that delightful sleep and very much regretted that he was not permitted to see or enjoy any longer the bright light that he had seen accompanying Swithun. He arose nevertheless and went very quickly to Bishop Æthelwold and said all this to him. Then Æthelwold immediately sent word from the king's household to the monks and said that they must sing the hymn, as he had decreed, and whoever refused this would have to atone heavily for it by fasting continuously for seven days.

Hi hit heoldon þa syððan symle on gewunon,
swa swa we gesawon sylfe foroft,
and þone sang we sungon unseldon mid him.

265   Sum wer wæs betogen þæt he wære on stale
(wæs swaðeah unscyldig) and hine man sona gelæhte
and æfter woruld-dome dydon him ut þa eagan
and his earan forcurfon. Þa arn him þæt blod
into þam heafde þæt he gehyran ne mihte.

270   Þa wæs he seofon monðas wunigende swa blind
and his hlyst næfde, oþþæt he mid geleafan ferde
to þam halgan Swyðune and gesohte his ban,
biddende þone halgan þæt he his bene gehyrde
and him huru geearnode þæt he gehyran mihte

275   (forþan ðe he ne gelyfde þæt he onliht wurde)
and cwæð þæt he wurde wolice swa getucod.
Þa wearð Godes wundor geworht on þam menn
þurh Swyðunes þingunge þæt he geseah beorhte,
ansundum eagum, þeah ðe hi ær wæron ut aðyde

280   of þam eah-hringum and se oðer æppel mid ealle was
                                 geemtigod
and se oðer hangode gehal æt his hleore.
Him wæs eac forgifen þæt he wel mihte gehyran,
se ðe ær næfde ne eagan ne hlyst.

    Is swaðeah to witenne þæt we ne moton us gebiddan
285   swa to Godes halgum swa swa to Gode sylfum,
forðan þe he is ana God ofer ealle þincg.
Ac we sceolon biddan soðlice þa halgan
þæt hi us þingion to þam þrym-wealdendum Gode,
se þe is heora hlaford, þæt he helpe us.

290   Hwilon wacodon men, swa swa hit gewunelic is,
ofer an dead lic and ðær wæs sum dysig mann,

They always observed the custom after that, as we ourselves have seen very often, and not infrequently have we sung the song with them.

A man was accused of stealing (nevertheless he was inno- 265
cent) and straightaway he was seized and in accordance with the sentence of the secular court they put out his eyes and cut off his ears. The blood then ran into his head so that he could not hear. Then he remained blind like this for 270
seven months and did not have his hearing, until he made his way with faith to the holy Swithun and approached his bones, beseeching the saint to hear his prayer and bring it about that he could at least hear (because he did not be- 275
lieve that he would be given sight), and he said that he had been wrongly punished like this. Then God's wonderful power operated on the man through Swithun's intercession so that he saw clearly, with healthy eyes, though they had previously been forced out of their sockets and one eyeball 280
had been entirely removed and the second had hung down in one piece on his cheek. It was also granted to him that he could hear well, he who previously had neither eyes nor hearing. Let it also be known, however, that we may not pray to God's saints in the same way as to God himself, for 285
he alone is God over all things. But we must truly pray to the saints to intercede for us with the God who rules heaven, who is their lord, that he may help us.

Once people were holding a vigil, as is customary, over 290
a dead body, and a foolish man was there, immoderately

plegol ungemetlice, and to þam mannum cwæð,
swylce for plegan, þæt he Swyðun wære:
"Ge magon to soðum witan þæt ic Swyðun eom,
295 se ðe wundra wyrcð, and ic wille þæt ge beran
eower leoht to me and licgan on cneowum
and ic eow forgife þæt þæt ge gyrnende beoð."
He woffode ða swa lange mid wordum dyslice
oðþæt he feoll geswogen swylce he sawlleas wære
300 and hine man bær ham to his bædde sona
and he læg swa lange, his lifes orwene.
His magas ða æt nextan þone mann feredon
to þam halgan Swiþune and he sylf andette
his dyslican word þe he dyrstiglice spræc
305 and bæd him forgifnysse and he wearð þa gehæled,
swa þæt he hal eode ham mid his magum.
   Is eac to witenne þæt menn unwislice doð
þa ðe dwollice plegað æt deadra manna lice
and ælce fulnysse þær forð teoð mid plegan,
310 þonne hi sceoldon swyðor besargian þone deadan
and ondrædan him sylfum þæs deaðes tocyme
and biddan for his sawle butan gewede georne.
Sume menn eac drincað æt deadra manna lice
ofer ealle þa niht, swiðe unrihtlice,
315 and gremiað God mid heora gegaf-spræce,
þonne nan gebeorscype ne gebyrað æt lice,
ac halige gebedu þær gebyriað swiþor.
   Hwilon comon to ðam halgan hundtwelftig manna,
mislice geuntrumode mid manegum brocum,
320 and þa wurdon ealle wundorlice gehælde
binnan þrym wucum and hi wendon ham,
þancigende þam Ælmihtigan and þam ar-wurðan Swiþune.

fond of amusement, and he said to the people, as it were in jest, that he was Swithun: "You may truly know that I am Swithun, he who performs miracles, and I want you to bring your lights to me and to kneel down, and I will give you what you desire." Then he blasphemed in his utterances for a long time foolishly, until he fell down unconscious as if he were without a soul and he was carried home to his bed without delay, and he lay like this for a long time, despairing of his life. Finally then his relatives carried the man to the holy Swithun, and he himself confessed the foolish words that he had presumptuously spoken and asked him for forgiveness and then he was healed, so that he went home healthy with his relatives.

Let it also be known that those people act unwisely who foolishly amuse themselves near the bodies of dead people and utter every sort of filth in their play, when they ought rather to be sorry for the dead person and fear for themselves the coming of death and diligently pray for his soul without foolishness. Some people moreover drink beside the bodies of dead people throughout the night, very wickedly, and offend God with their idle talk, when no carousing is appropriate beside a body, but holy prayers are much more appropriate there.

Once a hundred and twelve people came to the saint, variously afflicted with many diseases, and then they were all miraculously healed within three weeks and they went home, thanking the Almighty and the honored Swithun.

Sumes þegnes cniht feoll færlice of horse
þæt him tobærst se earm and se oðer sceanca
325 and swiðe wearð gecwysed þæt hi sona wendon
þæt he þær-rihte sceolde sweltan him ætforan.
He wæs his hlaforde swyþe leof ær þan
and se hlaford þa besargode swyðe þone cniht
and bæd þone Ælmihtigan mid inwerdre heortan
330 þæt he þam menn geheolpe þurh ðone mæran Swiþun.
He clypode eac to Swiðune, þus secgende mid geomerunge:
"Eala ðu halga Swiðun, bide þone hælend
þæt he lif forgife þysum licgendum cnihte
and ic beo þæs þe geleaffulra þam lifigendan Gode
335 eallum minum dagum, gif he deð þis þurh þe."
Se cniht ða aras hal, gehæled þurh Swiþun,
and se hlaford þæs fægnode and mid geleafan God herede.

Sum eald þegn wæs eac on Wihtlande untrum,
swa þæt he læg bædd-ryda sume nigon gear,
340 and of ðam bedde ne mihte buton hine man bære.
Him comon þa on swefne to twegen scinende halgan
and heton hine yrnan ardlice mid him.
Þa cwæð se adliga: "Hu mæg ic yrnan mid eow,
þonne ic ne aras of þysum bedde ana
345 nu for nigon gearum butan oþres mannes fylste?"
Þa cwædon þa halgan: "Þu cymst to ðære stowe,
gif ðu færst mid us nu, ðær þær ðu underfehst þine hæle."
He wearð þa swyðe fægen and wolde faran mid him,
ac þa þa he ne mihte him mid syðian,
350 þa flugon hi geond þa lyft and feredon þone adligan
oðþæt hi becomon to sumum ænlicum felda fægre geblowen
and þær wæs an cyrce of scinendum golde

The servant of a nobleman fell suddenly from his horse in such a way that he broke his arm and his left leg and was so very crushed that they immediately thought that he would die straightaway in front of them. He had been very dear to his master before that, and the master felt very sorry for the servant and beseeched the Almighty with his innermost heart to help the man through the glorious Swithun. He cried out to Swithun also, saying with lamentation thus: "You holy Swithun, beseech the savior to grant life to this servant lying here, and I will be the more devoted to the living God all my days, if he does this through you." Then the servant arose healthy, healed through Swithun, and the master rejoiced at that and praised God with faith.

An old nobleman on the Isle of Wight was likewise sick, so that he lay bedridden for some nine years, and he could not get out of bed unless he was carried. Then two shining saints came to him in a dream and commanded him to run quickly with them. The sick man then said: "How can I run with you, when I have not got out of this bed on my own for nine years now without the help of another person?" Then the saints said: "If you go with us now, you will come to that place where you shall receive your health." Then he was very happy and wanted to go with them, but when he was not able to travel with them, they flew through the air and carried the sick man until they came to an incomparably lovely field beautifully flowering, and a church was standing there

and of gym-stanum standende on þam felde.
And se halga Swiðun on scinendum mæsse-reafe
355 stod æt ðam weofode, swylce he wolde mæssian.
Swyðun cwæð þa sona to þam seocan men:
"Ic secge ðe, broðor, þu ne scealt heonon-forð
nanon menn yfel don ne nanne man wyrigan
ne nænne man tælan ne teonful beon
360 ne ðu man-slagum ne geðwærlæce ne manfullum reaferum
ne ðeofum þu ne olæce ne yfel-dædum ne geðwærlæce,
ac swiðor gehelp, swa þu selost mæge,
wan-hafolum mannum mid þinum agenum spedum,
and þu swa þurh Godes mihte sylf bist gehæled."
365 Se adliga þa ðohte þæt he yfel nolde don
buton þam anum þe him ær yfel dyde
and ðam wolde don wel þe him wel dyde ær.
Þa wiste se halga Swiðun hu his heorte smeade
and cwæð bliðelice him to: "Broðor, ic þe secge,
370 ne do þu swa þu smeadest þæt ðu derige ænigum,
þeah ðe he derige ðe, ac þinum Drihtne geefenlæc,
se ðe nolde wyrian þa ðe hine wyrigdon,
and bæd for ða Iudeiscan þe hine dydon to cwale
and het his folgeras þæt hi for heora fyond gebædon.
375 Eac cwæð Paulus se apostol to eallum Cristenum mannum:
'Gif ðinum fynd hingrige, fed hine mid mettum,
oððe gif him þyrste, ðu do him drincan.'"
    Þa cwæð se bed-ryda to ðam bisceope eft:
"La leof, sege me hwæt þu sy manna,
380 nu ðu manna heortan miht swa asmeagen."
Þa cwæð se halga Swyðun: "Ic eom se þe nu niwan com,"
swylce he swa cwæde: "Ic wæs geswutelod nu niwan."

in the field made from shining gold and gemstones. And the
holy Swithun in shining Mass vestments stood at the altar, 355
as if he intended to say Mass. Then Swithun immediately
said to the sick man: "I tell you, brother, that from now on
you must not do evil to any person, nor curse anyone, nor
speak evil of anyone, nor be spiteful, nor be an accomplice 360
of murderers or wicked robbers, nor fawn upon thieves, nor
be an accomplice in evil deeds, but rather help, as best you
can, needy people with your own riches, and in this way you
yourself will be healed through the power of God." The sick 365
man was thinking then that he did not intend to do evil except to the person who had previously done evil to him and
that he intended to do well to those who had previously
done well to him. Then the holy Swithun knew what his
heart was contemplating and said gently to him: "Brother, I
say to you, do not, as you are contemplating, do harm to any- 370
one, though he should harm you, but imitate your Lord,
who was not willing to curse those who cursed him and
prayed for the Jews who put him to death and commanded
his followers to pray for their enemies. Likewise Paul the 375
apostle said to all Christian people: 'If your enemy be hun-
gry, feed him with foods, or if he be thirsty, give him to
drink.'"

Then the bedridden man spoke to the bishop again: "O
sir, tell me what kind of a man you are, since you are able to 380
comprehend people's hearts." Then the holy Swithun said:
"I am he who now recently came," as if he had said: "I was

Þa cwæð se bæd-ryda to ðam bisceope eft:
"Hu eart ðu gehaten?" And se halga him cwæð to:
385 "Þonne ðu cymst to Winceastre, þu wast minne naman."
Se man wearð þa gebroht to his bedde eft sona
and awoc of slæpe and sæde his wife
ealle ða gesihðe þe he gesewen hæfde.
Þa cwæð þæt wif him to þæt hit wære Swyðun
390 se ðe hine lærde mid þære halgan lare
and þone ðe he geseah on ðære cyrcan swa fægerne.
Heo cwæð ða to þam were: "Hit wære nu full good
þæt man ðe bære to cyrcan and þu bæde þone halgan
þæt he ðe gehælde þurh his halgan geearnunge."
395 Hine man bær ða sona of ðam bedde to cyrcan
binnan Wihtlande and he wearð gehæled sona
þurh þone ælmihtigan God, for Swyðunes geearnungum,
and eode him ða ham hal on his fotum,
se ðe ær wæs geboren on bære to cyrcan.
400 He ferde eac siððan to ceastre forraðe
and cydde Aðelwolde þam ar-wurþan bisceope
hu he wearð gehæled þurh þone halgan Swiþun
and Landferð se ofersæwisca hit gesette on Læden.
    Nu is us to witenne þæt we ne sceolan cepan ealles
405 to swyðe be swefnum, forðan þe hi ealle ne beoð of Gode.
Sume swefna syndon soðlice of Gode,
swa swa we on bocum rædað, and sume beoð of deofle
to sumum swicdome, hu he ða sawle forpære,
ac his gedwimor ne mæg derian þam godum,
410 gif hi hi bletsiaþ and hi gebiddað to Gode.
Þa swefna beoð wynsume þe gewurðaþ of Gode
and þa beoð egefulle ðe of þam deofle cumað

now recently revealed." Then the bedridden man spoke to the bishop again: "What are you called?" And the saint said to him: "When you come to Winchester, you will know my 385 name." Then the man was immediately brought back to his bed and awoke from sleep and told his wife all the vision that he had seen. Then the woman said to him that it was Swithun who had taught him with the holy teaching and 390 whom he had seen looking so beautiful in the church. She then said to the man: "It would be very good now if you were carried to the church and if you prayed to the saint to heal you through his holy merits." He was straightaway carried 395 from his bed to the church on the Isle of Wight, and he was immediately healed by the almighty God because of Swithun's merits, and he went home on his own feet, restored to health, he who had been carried to the church on a stretcher. Afterward he even went to the city very quickly and told 400 Æthelwold the honored bishop how he had been healed through the holy Swithun, and Lantfred the foreigner set it down in Latin.

Now we must note that we must not pay all too much attention to dreams, because they are not all from God. Some 405 dreams truly are from God, as we read in books, and some are from the devil as some kind of deception, as to how he may destroy the soul, but his delusion cannot harm good people, if they bless themselves and pray to God. Those 410 dreams that come from God are delightful and those that

and God sylf forbead þæt we swefnum ne folgion,
þe læs ðe se deofol us bedydrian mæge.

415   Sum man on Winceastre wearð yrre his ðeowan men
for sumere gymeleaste and gesette hine on fetera.
He sæt ða swa lange on þam laðum bendum,
oðþæt he bestæl ut, mid his stafe hoppende,
and gesohte ðone sanct Swyðun mid geomerunge.

420   Se scyttel ða asceat sona of þære fetere
and se ðeowa aras, ahred þurh ðone halgan.

Sum mann wæs gebunden onbutan þæt heafod
for his hefigum gylte. Se com to þam halgan
and his swara heafod-bend sona tobærst, swa he hine gebæd.

425   Ne mage we awritan, ne mid wordum asecgan,
ealle þa wundra þe se halga wer Swiðun
þurh God gefremode on ðæs folces gesihþe,
ge on gehæftum mannum, ge on unhalum mannum,
mannum to swutelunge þæt hi sylfe magon

430   Godes rice geearnian mid godum weorcum,
swa swa Swiþun dyde, þe nu scinð þurh wundra.
Seo ealde cyrce wæs eall behangen mid criccum
and mid creopera sceamelum fram ende oð oþerne,
on ægðrum wage, þe ðær wurdon gehælede,

435   and man ne mihte swaðeah macian hi healfe up.

Þyllice tacna cyþað þæt Crist is ælmihtig God,
þe his halgan geswutelode þurh swylce wel-dæda,
þeah ðe ða Iudeiscan, þurh deofol beswicene,
nellon gelyfan on þone lyfigendan God

440   ær ðan þe Antecrist ofslagen bið þurh God.
Þonne bugað þa earmingas on ende þysre worulde,
ðe þær to lafe beoð, mid geleafan to Criste
and ða ærran losiað þe ær noldon gelyfan.

come from the devil are terrifying, and God himself forbade us to be guided by dreams, for fear that the devil have the power to delude us.

A man in Winchester was angry with his slave on account 415 of some kind of negligence and put him into fetters. He sat there for a long time in those hateful bonds, until he stole out, hopping with his staff, and, groaning, sought out Swithun the saint. The bolt immediately sprang out of the fet- 420 ter and the slave stood up, having been set free by the saint.

A man was bound fast around his head because of his serious offense. He came to the saint, and the fetter around his head broke apart at once, as he was praying. We cannot 425 write down, nor say in words, all the miracles that this holy man Swithun performed through the power of God in this people's sight, both on imprisoned people and on sick people, in order to reveal to people that they themselves can earn God's kingdom with good works, just like Swithun did, 430 who now shines through his miracles. The old church was all hung round with crutches and with the stools of cripples who had been healed there, from one end to the other on both walls, and yet not even half of them could be put up. 435

Such signs show that Christ is almighty God, who made his saint known by means of such good deeds, even though the Jews, deceived by the devil, will refuse to believe in the living God until Antichrist will be slain by God. Then those 440 wretches, those who will be left, will submit to Christ with faith at the end of this world and the earlier ones, who had not been willing to believe, will perish.

We habbað nu gesæd be Swiðune þus sceortlice
445 and we secgað to soðan þæt se tima wæs gesælig
and wynsum on Angelcynne, þa ða Eadgar cynincg
þone Cristendom gefyrðrode and fela munuc-lifa arærde
and his cyne-rice wæs wunigende on sibbe,
swa þæt man ne gehyrde gif ænig scyp-here wære,
450 buton agenre leode þe ðis land heoldon.
And ealle ða cyningas þe on þysum ig-lande wæron,
Cumera and Scotta, comon to Eadgare
(hwilon anes dæges eahta cyningas)
and hi ealle gebugon to Eadgares wissunge.
455 Þær-toeacan wæron swilce wundra gefremode
þurh þone halgan Swyðun, swa swa we sædon ær,
and swa lange swa we leofodon, þær wurdon gelome wundra.
On ðam timan wæron eac wurðfulle bisceopas
(Dunstan se an-ræda æt ðam erce-stole,
460 and Aþelwold se ar-wurða, and oðre gehwylce)
ac Dunstan and Aþelwold wæron Drihtne gecorene
and hi swyðost manodon menn to Godes willan
and ælc god arærdon, Gode to gecwemednysse:
þæt geswuteliað þa wundra þe God wyrcð þurh hi.
465 Sy wuldor and lof þam wel-willendan scyppende
þe his halgan mærsað mihtiglice mid wundrum,
se ðe a rixað on ecnysse. Amen.

We have now thus briefly told about Swithun, and we say 445
truly that that time was blessed and delightful in England,
when King Edgar promoted the Christian faith and established many monasteries and his kingdom was living in
peace, so that no naval force was ever heard of, except that 450
of the people themselves who possessed this land. And all
the kings who were on this island, those of the Cumbrians
and the Scots, came to Edgar (once eight kings on the one
day), and they all submitted to Edgar's rule. In addition to 455
that, miracles such as those described were performed
through the holy Swithun, as we said previously, and as long
as we have lived, there have been frequent miracles there. At
that time there were also excellent bishops (the resolute
Dunstan in the archbishopric, and the honored Æthelwold, 460
and others like them), but Dunstan and Æthelwold were
chosen by the Lord, and they most of all exhorted people to
do God's will and promoted everything good, to the delight
of God: the miracles that God works through them reveal
that. Glory and praise be to the benevolent creator who 465
with his power glorifies his saints with miracles, who alone
reigns in eternity. Amen.

Item alia

Mannum is eac to witenne þæt manega dry-men maciað
menigfealde dydrunga þurh deofles cræft,
470 swa swa wischeras oft doð, and bedydriað menn
swylce hi soðlice swylc þincg don.
Ac hit is swaðeah dydrung mid deofles cræfte,
and gif hwa hit bletsað þonne ablynð seo dydrung.
Be ðam we magan secgan sume soðe bysne.
475 Macharius wæs gehaten sum halig fæder
on wæstene wunigende, fela wundra wyrcende,
munuc-lifes man. Ða wearð an mæden forbroden
þurh dry-manna dydrunge, gedwimorlice swaðeah.
Þæt mæden wæs swa forbroden swylce heo an myre wære
480 and eallum þam þuhte þe hire onlocodon
swilce heo myre wære, na mennisces gecyndes.
Þa leddon hire magas hi to Macharie
and he sona axode hwæt hi woldon mid þam.
Þa magas him cwædon to: "Þeos myre þe ðu gesihst
485 wæs ure dohtor, ar-wurðe mæden,
ac awyrigde dry-menn awendon hi to myran.
Nu bidde we ðe, leof, þæt ðu gebide for hi
and hi eft awende to þam ðe heo ær wæs."
Macharius þa cwæð to hire magum ðus:
490 "Ic geseo þis mæden on menniscum gecynde
and heo nis na awend swa swa ge wenað þæt heo sy
and heo nan þincg on hire næfð horses gecyndes,
ac on eowrum gesihþum hit is swa gehiwod

Another in the Same Manner
[Macarius and the Sorcerers]

People must also note that many sorcerers bring about many kinds of delusions through the devil's cunning, like wizards 470 often do, and delude people as if they were truly doing such things. But it is, however, a delusion by means of the devil's cunning, and if someone makes the sign of the cross over it, then the delusion comes to an end. Concerning that we can tell a true example. Macarius was the name of a holy father 475 living in the desert, performing many miracles, a man following the monastic life. Then a young woman was transformed by the delusions of sorcerers, but only as an illusion. The young woman was transformed in such a way as if she were a mare, and to all who looked at her it seemed as if she 480 were a mare, not of human kind. Then her relatives brought her to Macarius, and he at once asked what they wanted in regard to that. The relatives said to him: "This mare that you see was our daughter, an honorable young woman, but cursed 485 sorcerers have changed her into a mare. Now we beseech you, dear sir, to pray for her and change her back to what she previously was." Macarius then spoke to her relatives thus: "I see this young woman in her human nature, and she is not 490 changed as you think that she is, and she has nothing in her of a horse's nature, but in your sight she is transformed like

þurh ðæs deofles dydrunge and his dry-menn leaslice."
495 Macharius ða gebæd for þæt mæden God
and mid ele gesmyrode and mid ealle adræfde
þæs deofles gedwimor, þurh his Drihtnes naman,
swa þæt hi ealle gesawon þæt heo ansund wæs.
Swylce synd þa dydrunga þære dry-manna.

this by the devil's delusion and his sorcerers." Macarius then 495
prayed to God for that young woman and anointed her with
oil and completely drove away the devil's illusion, through
the name of his Lord, so that they all saw that she was perfect. Such are the delusions of sorcerers.

SAINT APOLLINARIS

Saint Apollinaris

X Kalendas Augusti: Natale sancti Apollonaris martyris

On ðæs caseres dagum ðe Claudius wæs gehaten,
com se eadiga Petrus fram Antiochian byrig
into Romebyrig mid manegum gebroðrum
and bodode geleafan bealdlice þam folce,
5 Romaniscum and Iudeiscum, swa swa Drihten him
                                        gewissode,
swa þæt ða Romaniscan and ða reðan Iudeiscan
manega gelyfdon on þone lyfigendan hælend
þurh Petres bodunge and gebugon to fulluhte,
behreowsigende heora synna mid soðre dæd-bote.
10 Hi underfengon þa Godes word mid gastlicre blysse:
þæt God wolde asendan his Sunu to man-cynne
and þurh hine geedniwigan ðisne ealdan middan-eard.

    Þa wæs ðær mid Petre sum ar-wurðe Godes man,
Apollonaris gehaten, þæs halgan apostoles folgere.
15 To ðam cwæð Petrus æfter sumum fyrste:
"Efne þu eart gelæred on eallum þingum be ðam hælende.
Aris nu and underfoh þone Halgan Gast
and haligne bisceophad on þæs hælendes naman

Saint Apollinaris

July 23: Feast of Saint Apollinaris the Martyr

In the days of the emperor who was called Claudius, the
blessed Peter came from the city of Antioch into the city of
Rome with many brothers and boldly preached the faith to
the people, to Romans and Jews, as the Lord had directed 5
him, so that many of the Romans and the cruel Jews believed in the living savior through Peter's preaching and submitted to baptism, repenting of their sins with true peni-
tence. They received the word of God with spiritual joy: 10
that God was willing to send his Son to mankind and renew
this old world through him.

With Peter there was a worthy man of God called Apollinaris, a disciple of the holy apostle. After a period of time 15
Peter said to him: "Truly you are educated in all things concerning the savior. Arise now and receive the Holy Spirit
and the holy office of bishop in the name of the savior and

and far to þære byrig þe is gehaten Rauenna.

20 Þær wunað micel folc on fulum hæðenscype;
boda him be þam hælende and ne beo ðu afyrht.
Swutollice ðu wast þæt se is soð Godes Sunu,
se ðe deadum forgeaf lif æfter deaðe
and wan-halum mannum mid his worde læcedom."

25 Æfter ðysum wordum se eadiga Petrus
gehadode Apollonarem and gehalgode to bisceope
and his handa sette ofer his heafod and cwæð:
"Asende ure hælend Crist his halgan engel mid þe,
se geforðige ðe and þine fare gewissige

30 and þe getiþige þæs ðe þu gewilnige."
And hine swa sende mid siblicum cosse.

Appollonaris ða ferde to ðære fore-sædan byrig
and sumne blindne gehælde ær þan þe he to ðære byrig
become
and manega gelyfdon þurh ðæs mannes hælþe

35 on ðone soðan God, and swa wurdon gefullode.
He com ða to Rauenna and hraðe þær geswutelode
þæs hælendes mihte on wann-halum mannum.
Þær wæs sum forð-þegen on þære fore-sædan byrig
se hæfde gehyred be ðam halgan were

40 and axode gif he cuðe aht on læce-cræfte.
Apollonaris him cwæð to: "Ne cann ic naht on lacnunge,
buton on þæs hælendes naman." And se þegen him cwæð to:
"Efne min wif is for manegum wintrum untrum;
þam wæs ælc læce-cræft wiðerræde oð þis.

45 Nu gif ænig miht is on ðe, geopena hi mid weorcum."
Apollonaris ða andwyrde and cwæð:
"Geopenige God ælmihtig eowre heortena eagan,

go to the city that is called Ravenna. A great many people 20
live there in foul heathenism; preach to them about the savior and do not be afraid. You know clearly that he is the true
Son of God, who gave life to the dead after death and healing to sick people with his word." After these words the 25
blessed Peter ordained Apollinaris and consecrated him as
bishop and placed his hands upon his head and said: "May
our savior Christ send his holy angel with you, who may help
you to succeed and may direct your journey and may grant 30
you what you wish." And in this way he sent him off with a
kiss of peace.

Apollinaris then made his way to the city already mentioned and before he arrived at the city healed a blind man,
and many people believed in the true God because of the 35
healing of the man, and so were baptized. Then he arrived at
Ravenna and there he quickly demonstrated the savior's
power on sick people. There was a high-ranking officer in
the city that we have mentioned who had heard about the
holy man and asked if he knew anything about the art of 40
healing. Apollinaris said to him: "I know nothing about
healing, except in the name of the savior." And the officer
said to him: "Truly my wife has been ill for many years; every
art of healing has been harmful to her until now. Now if 45
there is any power in you, reveal it in your actions." Apollinaris then answered and said: "May almighty God open the

þæt ge on þone hælend gelyfan þonne ge geseoð his
wundra."

He genam ða ðæs wifes hand, þas word clypigende:
50 "Aris nu on ðæs hælendes naman and on hine gelyf
and ne sege þu heonon-forð þæt ænig sy his gelica."
Heo aras þa sona andsund of þam bedde
and cwæð þæt nan God nære butan se hælend þe he embe
bodade.

Þa wundrode se þegn his wifes hælðe
55 and hi ealle sædon þæt se is soð God
þe swilce wundra macað and se mæg on gefeohte
þam sige forgifan þe hine soðlice lufiað.
He wearð þa gefullod mid his wife and cildum
and eall his hyred, on þæs hælendes naman,
60 and fela þære hæðenra fengon to geleafan.

Apollonaris þa ðær wunode mid him
on Rauenna byrig and bodode geleafan
and manega gefullode ðæs folces meniu.
Manega eac befæstan, syððan hi gefullode wæron,
65 heora cild to lare þam soðfæstan bydele
and Godes geleafa ðær weox and wanode se hæðenscype.

Hwæt se halga bisceop þa on ðære byrig wunode
ða twelf gear fullice and gefullode þa leode
and gelome him mæssode and mæsse-preostas gehadode
70 and diaconas and clericas and dæghwamlice mid him
Godes lof gefylde mid gastlicum sangum.

On ðære byrig wæs sum þegn Bonifacius gehaten
se wearð færlice dumb and his wif þa asende
to þam halgan bisceope and bæd his neosunge.
75 Efne ða se bisceop eode to his huse
and an wif-man wæs ðær wod on his huse

248

eyes of your hearts, so that you believe in the savior when
you see his miracles." Then he took the woman's hand, saying these words: "Arise now in the name of the savior and 50
believe in him and from now on do not say that anyone is his
equal." Then immediately she arose, healthy, from the bed
and said that there was no God except for the savior about
whom he preached. Then the officer marveled at the healing of his wife, and they all said that he is the true God who 55
performs such miracles and who in a battle can give victory
to those who truly love him. Then he was baptized with his
wife and children and all his household, in the name of the
savior, and many of the heathens accepted the faith. 60

Then Apollinaris lived there with him in the city of
Ravenna and preached the faith and baptized many of the
multitude of people. Many also, after they were baptized,
committed their children to the true preacher for instruc- 65
tion, and faith in God grew there and heathenism declined.

Well then, the holy bishop lived in the city for a full
twelve years and baptized the people and often celebrated
Mass for them and ordained priests and deacons and minor 70
clerics, and with them he performed God's praise with sacred songs daily.

In that city there was a nobleman called Boniface who
suddenly became dumb, and his wife then sent to the holy
bishop and implored him for a visit. Truly then the bishop 75
went to his house, and there was a woman who was insane

and se deofol clypode and cwæð þurh þone wodan
to ðam halgan bisceope: "Ic gedo þæt man gebint ðe
handum and fotum and heonon ðe swa tihð
80 of þysre byrig." And se bisceop andwyrde:
"Adumba ðu deofol and of hire gewit
and ne spræc þu næfre eft þurh ænigne mann!"
Þa gewat se deofol of ðam wodan sona
and se bisceop eode þær Bonifacius læg,
85 dumb on his bedde, and gebæd for hine ðus:
"Drihten hælend Crist, þu ðe beclysedest
þyses mannes muð þæt he ne moste leng
clypian to hæðen-gildum swylce him to fultume,
geopena nu his muð þæt he mærsige þinne naman,
90 and gelyfe þæt þu eart lifigende God on worulde."
Hi cwædon ða "Amen" and on ðære ylcan tide
wearð his tunge unbunden and he blyssigende cwæð:
"Nis nan oþer God on to gelyfenne,
butan se ana þe ðes eadiga bodað."
95 On þam ylcan dæge gelyfdon of þære leode on God
ma ðonne fif hund manna, micclum þancigende Gode
and þam halgan were, þurh þone þe hi wurdon onlihte.
     Rufus wæs gehaten sum hæðen mund-bora
þe ða burh bewiste. Ða wearð his dohtor seoc.
100 Þa sende se fæder sona to ðam bisceope
and sona swa he þyder com swa sawlode þæt mæden.
Hi weopon ða ealle ðe þær-inne wæron
and se halga wer cwæð to hire fæder ðus:
"Ongin nu wel, Rufe, and behat me mid aðe,
105 gif ðin dohtor nu hal bið, þæt þu hire geðafige
þæt heo folgie Criste and ðu oncnæwst nu his mihte."
Rufus him andwyrde: "Efne heo is nu dead,

there in his house, and the devil called out and spoke through the insane person to the holy bishop: "I will cause you to be bound hand and foot and dragged like that away from here out of this city." And the bishop answered: "Be si- 80 lent, you devil, and depart from her and never speak again through anyone!" Then the devil immediately departed from the insane person, and the bishop went to where Boni- face was lying, dumb in his bed, and prayed for him thus: 85 "Lord savior Christ, you who closed this man's mouth so that he might not any longer call upon the heathen idols as if to help him, open his mouth now so that he may glorify your name, and may believe that you are the living God for ever." 90 Then they said "Amen," and at the same time his tongue was unbound, and rejoicing he said: "There is no other God to believe in, save he alone of whom this blessed man preaches." On that same day more than five hundred of that 95 people believed in God, greatly thanking God and the holy man, through whom they had been enlightened.

A heathen protector who had charge over the city was called Rufus. Then his daughter became sick. The father 100 then sent immediately to the bishop, and as soon as he came there the young woman died. Then all who were inside there wept, and the holy man spoke to her father thus: "Act well now, Rufus, and promise me on oath that, if your daughter 105 is healed now, you will permit her to follow Christ and you will recognize his power." Rufus answered him: "Truly she is

ac gif ic geseo þæt heo eft gesund leofað,
ic herige þonne Godes mihte and heo hire hælende folgie."

110 Mid þam ðe hi ealle weopon, þa eode he to ðam lice
and clypode mid geleafan to Criste and cwæð:
"Min God, Drihten hælend, þe minum lareowe Petre
forgeafe his gewilnunga, swa hwæt swa he gewylnode æt ðe,
arær nu ðis mæden of ðysum reðum deaðe,

115 forðan þe heo is þin gesceaft and nis nan God buton ðu."
Heo aras þa sona and mid hreame clypode:
"Mære is se God þe ðes mann us bodað
and nis nan oðer God buton he ana!"
Þa blissodon þa Cristenan on Cristes herunge

120 and þæt mæden wearð gefullod, and hire modor samod,
and eall heora hired samod, sume þreo hund manna,
and fela ðæra hæðenra fengon to geleafan.
Se fæder swaðeah Rufus, for þæs caseres reðnysse,
ne dorste geopenian þæt he on Drihten gelyfde,

125 ac he digellice lufode þone geleaffullan bisceop
and mid wistum him þenode and his dohtor wearð gehadod
to Godes ðeowdome and þurhwunode mæden.

Appollonaris þa wearð gewreged to þam casere
and to witnunge gelæd and on þam witum geandette

130 þæs hælendes naman and sum hæðen mann,
þe him swyðost onwann, awedde ðær-rihte
and his lif geendode yfelum deaðe.
Þa woldon þa Cristenan bewerian þone halgan
and ofslogon þæra hæðenra sume twa hund manna.

135 Se dema þa het lædan þone geleaffullan bisceop
into blindum cweart-erne and on bendum healdan
and him ætes forwyrnan þæt he swa ateorode,
ac Godes engel com to þam Godes men nihtes

dead now, but if I see that she is alive again in good health, then I will praise God's power and she may follow her savior." While they were all weeping, he went to the corpse and called with faith to Christ and said: "My God, Lord savior, who granted my teacher Peter his desire, whatsoever he desired from you, raise this young woman now from this cruel death, because she is your creation and there is no God except for you." She arose immediately and proclaimed with a cry: "Great is the God of whom this man preaches to us, and there is no other God except for him alone!" Then the Christians rejoiced in the praise of Christ, and the young woman was baptized, along with her mother, and along with all of their household, some three hundred people, and many of the heathens accepted the faith. The father Rufus, however, because of the emperor's ferocity, did not dare to reveal that he believed in the Lord, but he secretly loved the devout bishop and he supplied him with provisions, and his daughter was consecrated to the service of God and remained a virgin.

Then an accusation was brought against Apollinaris to the emperor and he was taken to be tortured, and during the tortures he professed the savior's name and a heathen man, who was attacking him most fiercely, immediately became insane and ended his life with an evil death. Then the Christians wished to defend the saint and killed some two hundred of the heathens. The judge then ordered that the devout bishop be brought into a dark prison and be held in fetters and be denied food so that in this way he would become weak, but God's angel came to the man of God at

and hine gereordode and mid his ræde gehyrte
140 eallum onlocigendum, þe ðær on ymbhwyrfte wæron.
Hwæt ða on þone feorðan dæg het se fore-sæda dema
gelædan ðone halgan on heardre racen-teage
feorr on wræc-sið, ferigende on scipe.
   Þær wæs sum æðel-boren man, atelice hreoflig.
145 Þa axode se bisceop: "Wylt ðu beon hal?"
He cwæð: "Ic wylle." And him andwyrde se halga:
"Gelyf on hælend Crist." And se hæðena him andwyrde:
"Gif he me gehælð, he bið min hælend God."
Appollonaris ða hrepode þone untruman hreoflian
150 on ðæs hælendes naman and he wearð hal sona,
mid þam ðe he clypode Cristes naman him to fultume.
Þa awearp se gehæleda his hæðenscype him fram
and gelyfde on ðone hælend and mid geleafan wearð
                                        gefullod.
   Hit gelamp þa æfter fyrste þæt þa ungeleaffullan hæðenan
155 gebundon þone bisceop and to ðære byrig Rauenna
geleddon on bendum and beoton hine wodlice.
Ða gebæd hine se bisceop bealdlice to Gode
and heora deofol-gild wearð towend and heora templ
                                        toworpen.
Þa gesawon ða hæðenan þæs halgan weres mihte
160 and clypodon mid gehlyde, be ðam geleaffullan were:
"Beo se ealde arleasa ardlice ofslagen,
þurh þone synd toworpene ða wuldorfullan godas."
Þa blissodon þa Cristenan and cwædon mid geleafan
þæt se ana is soð God þe swylce wundra wyrcð.
165   Þa betæhton þa hæðenan þone halgan wer to slege
sumum arleasum cwellere, se wæs geciged Taurus.
And se Taurus gesamnode ða ceaster-gewaran him to

254

night and fed him and with his counsel encouraged all of the 140
onlookers who were round about. Well then, on the fourth
day the judge whom we have mentioned ordered that the
saint be taken under heavy restraint far into exile, conveyed
by ship.

There was a man of noble birth, horribly leprous. Then 145
the bishop asked: "Do you wish to be healed?" He said: "I
wish it." And the saint answered him: "Believe in the savior
Christ." And the heathen answered him: "If he heals me, he
will be my savior God." Apollinaris then touched the sick
leper in the savior's name, and he was immediately healed 150
while he was invoking Christ's name to help him. Then the
healed man renounced his heathenism and believed in the
savior and was baptized with faith.

Then it happened after a time that the unbelieving heathens bound the bishop and brought him in bonds to the 155
city of Ravenna and beat him furiously. Then the bishop
prayed confidently to God, and their idol was destroyed and
their temple torn down. Then the heathens saw the holy
man's power and called out loudly, with respect to that faith- 160
ful man: "Let that impious old man be killed quickly,
through whom the glorious gods have been overthrown."
Then the Christians rejoiced and said with faith that he
alone is the true God who works such miracles.

Then the heathens handed the holy man over for killing 165
to a wicked executioner, who was called Taurus. And this
Taurus gathered the citizens to him and asked the saint

and axode þone halgan þurh hwæs mihte he gefremode
þa wundorlican tacna, þæt swa micel werod him folgode.

170 Appollonaris him andwyrde: "Nis ðeos nan oðer miht
butan hælendes Cristes and we habbað Godes gife
on urum heortum." And þa betwux oþrum spræcum
cwæð se ylca Taurus to þam ar-wurðan were:
"Ic hæbbe ænne sunu þe ne geseah næfre dæges leoht.

175 Gedo þæt he geseo on þines Drihtnes naman
and we sona gelyfað þæt he is soðlice God;
elles we ðe forbærnað for ðinum deopum gyltum."
Ða cwæð se bisceop him to: "Cume se blinda to me."
Þa com se blinda him to and he cwæð mid geleafan:

180 "On þæs hælendes naman, geopena þin eagan
and geseoh þurh hine." And he sona wearð hal,
beorhte locigende, se ðe blind wæs geboren.
Hi wundrodon þa ealle and an-modlice cwædon
þæt se wære soð God þe swylce wundra worhte

185 and manega þa gelyfdon þurh ða mihte on God.

Taurus þa brohte þone bisceop digellice
of ðæs folces gehlyde to sumum his lande
and hine þær afedde feower gear mid wistum,
syx mila fram Rauenna. And hine sohton þa Cristenan

190 and his lare hlyston mid geleafan georne
and ealle ða untruman, þe him oft to comon,
wurdon gehælede and ham gesunde cyrdon.

Þa sendon ða hæðen-gildan mid hetelicum geðance
ærende to þam casere, þæt he acwellan hete

195 þone halgan bisceop, þæt heora biggencgas ne wurdon
mid ealle adwæscte þurh ðone Drihtnes bydel.
Ða sende se casere sona him þis gewrit:
"Gif ænig man gremige ure godas dyrstiglice,

through whose power he had performed those wondrous signs, so that such a large crowd followed him. Apollinaris 170 answered him: "This is no power other than that of the savior Christ, and we have God's grace in our hearts." And then, among other utterances, that same Taurus said to the worthy man: "I have one son who has never seen the light of day. Make him see in the name of your Lord, and we will imme- 175 diately believe that he is truly God; otherwise we will burn you on account of your heinous offenses." Then the bishop said to him: "Let the blind man come to me." Then the blind man came to him and he said with faith: "In the name of the 180 savior, open your eyes and see by means of him." And he was healed immediately, seeing clearly, who had been born blind. Then they were all amazed and unanimously said that he who worked such miracles was the true God, and many then 185 believed in God because of these powerful deeds.

Taurus then secretly brought the bishop away from the noise of the people to one of his estates and supported him there for four years with provisions, six miles from Ravenna. And the Christians sought him out and eagerly listened to 190 his teaching with faith, and all the sick people, who often came to him, were healed and returned home in good health.

Then, with hostile intent, the heathen priests sent a message to the emperor, that he should order that the holy 195 bishop be killed, so that their holy rites would not be completely destroyed by means of the Lord's preacher. Then the emperor immediately sent them this letter: "If any person should presumptuously anger our gods, let him make

gebete he wið hi oððe he beo adræfed
200 awæg of ðære byrig, forðan þe hit ne bið na rihtlic
þæt we wrecon ure godas, ac hi wrecað hi sylfe
gif hi beoð astyrode. Beoð ge gesunde."
Þa het se burh-ealdor þone bisceop him to gefeccan
and axode hine sona hwylcere eawfæstnysse he wære,
205 swylce he cwæde: "Cristen oððe hæðen?"
Se dema hatte Demosten and he wæs deofles biggencga.
Þa cwæð se halga wer to þam hæðenan deman:
"Ic eom soðlice Cristen and Sanctus Petrus me lærde
and he me hider asende to þissere gesæligan byrig,
210 þæt ðurh þæs hælendes naman eow hæl becume."
Demosten þa andwyrde ðam ar-wurðan halgan:
"Hwæt sceall hit swa langsum? Efne nu is se tima
þæt ðu forlæte þine ydelnysse and lac ðam godum geoffrige."
Appollonaris him andwyrde: "Ic offrige me sylfne
215 for minum gastlicum bearnum þe ic her Gode gestrynde.
And swa hwa swa hine ne gebit to þam heofonlican Gode,
se bið ecelice fordemed on þam ecan fyre,
and ða ðe on God gelyfað and mid geleafan beoð gefullode,
þa habbað þa ecan reste and unawendendlice welan."
220 Hwæt ða Demosten deoflice wearð gehat-hyrt
and betæhte þone halgan sumum hundredes ealdre
to healdenne on cweart-erne oðþæt he hine acwealde.
Se hundredes ealdor wæs ðam hæðenan bediglod
and wæs digellice Cristen and cwæð to þam bisceope:
225 "Min fæder, ic ðe bidde, ne beo þu swa hræd to deaðe,
forðan þe us is þin lif nyd-behefe git,
ac far þe nu digellice þær ðu frið hæbbe,
oþþæt ðises folces hat-heortnyss hwæthwega beo gestylled."
He eode ða nihtes þæt he his life geburge,

amends to them or let him be driven away from the city, be- 200
cause it is not right that we should avenge our gods, but they
will avenge themselves if they are provoked. Farewell." Then
the governor of the city ordered that the bishop be fetched
to him, and he asked him immediately to what religion he
belonged, as if he were saying: "Christian or heathen?" The 205
judge was called Demosthenes, and he was a worshipper of
the devil. Then the holy man said to the heathen judge: "I
am truly a Christian, and Saint Peter taught me, and he sent
me here to this fortunate city, so that salvation might come 210
to you through the savior's name." Demosthenes then answered the worthy saint: "What is the point of taking so
long? Truly now is the time for you to abandon your frivolity
and to offer a sacrifice to the gods." Apollinaris answered
him: "I am offering myself for my spiritual children whom I 215
gained for God here. And whoever does not pray to the
heavenly God, he will be eternally damned in the eternal
fire, and those who believe in God and are baptized with
faith will have eternal rest and immutable riches."

Well then, Demosthenes became diabolically enraged 220
and handed the saint over to a centurion to guard in prison
until he killed him. The centurion was hidden from the
heathen man and was secretly a Christian, and he said to
the bishop: "My father, I beg you, do not be so quick to 225
die, because your life is still necessary for us, but go now
secretly to where you will have security from harm, until
this people's rage has subsided somewhat." He left at night

230 ac ða hæðenan wurdon wære his fare
and hine gelæhton and hine swa lange beoton
oðþæt hi wendon þæt he wære dead.

He wearð swaþeah gebroht þurh his gebroðra þenunge
eft to ðam Cristenum and he anbidode on life
235 seofon niht fullice and hi fægre tihte
to þam ecan life and to geleafan georne.

He cwæð: "Ic secge eow þæt swara ehtnysse becumað
ofer þa Cristenan for Cristes naman,
ac æfter þære ehtnysse bið eft sybb forgifen
240 and ða caseras bugað to Cristes geleafan
and ælc deofol-gild bið adilegod mid ealle,
swa þæt man freolice mot mærsian þone Ælmihtigan
geond ealne middan-eard and him lac offrian.

And se ðe on geleafan þurhwunað, se leofað a on ecnysse."

245 Æfter ðyssere tihtinge and oðrum manegum spræcum
gewat se halga wer of worulde to Gode,
mid þam he a wunað on þam ecan wuldre,
and his leorning-cnihtes ledon his lic ar-wurðlice
on ane stænene þruh and seo stod wið þone weall.
250 Twam læs ðryttig geare he wæs heora bisceop
on manegum ehtnyssum, þam Ælmihtigan þeowigende,
and his edlean bið nu endeleas ðy
mid þam ælmihtigan Gode, þe on ecnysse rixað. Amen.

so that he might safeguard his life, but the heathens had 230
knowledge of his journey and seized him and beat him for a
long time until they thought that he was dead.

Nevertheless, through the ministrations of his brothers
he was brought back again to the Christians, and he continued to live for a full seven nights, and he urged them well to 235
the eternal life and eagerly to faith. He said: "I tell you that
severe persecutions will come upon the Christians for the
sake of Christ's name, but after the persecution peace will
be granted again and the emperors will submit to faith in 240
Christ and every idolatry will be destroyed completely, so
that the Almighty may be freely glorified throughout the
world and sacrifices may be offered to him. And he who perseveres in faith will live eternally."

After this exhortation and many other speeches, the holy 245
man departed from this world to God, with whom he lives
forever in eternal glory, and his disciples placed his body reverently in a stone tomb, and it stood near the wall. He was 250
their bishop for thirty years less two during many persecutions, serving the Almighty, and because of that his reward
will now be without end with the almighty God who reigns
in eternity. Amen.

SAINTS ABDON AND SENNES *AND* THE LETTER OF CHRIST TO ABGAR

Saints Abdon and Sennes *and*
The Letter of Christ to Abgar

III Kalendas Augusti: Natale sanctorum Abdon et Sennes

On Decies dagum ðæs deoflican caseres,
wæron twegen kyningas on Crist gelyfde,
Abdon and Sennes, mid soðum geleafan.
Ða asprang heora word to ðam wæl-hreowan casere
5 þe ða ana geweold ealles middan-eardes,
and ealle oðre cyningas to him cneowodon
and heora rice wunode swa swa he ana wolde.
Þa asende Decius to þam fore-sædum cyningum
and het hi gebringan on bendum to him:
10 wolde hi gebigan fram Godes biggencgum
to his gedwyldum and to his deofol-gildum.
    Hwæt þa cwelleras þa þa cynincgas gebundon
and on isenum racen-teagum to ðam arleasan gebrohton
for Cristes geleafan to cwealm-bærum witum.
15 Decius þa het þa halgan cyningas
his godum geoffrian, ac hi andwyrdon þus:
"We offriað ure lac þam lyfigendan Gode,
hælendum Criste, and we hopiað to him.

Saints Abdon and Sennes *and*
The Letter of Christ to Abgar

July 30: The Feast of Saints Abdon and Sennes

In the days of the diabolic emperor Decius, there were two
kings, Abdon and Sennes, who believed in Christ with true
faith. Then word of them reached the cruel emperor who
then alone ruled all the earth, and all other kings knelt before him and their power endured at his sole discretion.
Then Decius sent word to the kings of whom we have spoken and commanded that they be brought in chains to him:
he wished to convert them from the rituals of God to his
erroneous ways and to his idolatry.

Well then, the executioners bound the kings and brought
them in iron chains to the wicked emperor for deadly tortures because of their faith in Christ. Decius then ordered
the holy kings to offer sacrifices to his gods, but they answered him in this way: "We will offer our sacrifices to the
living God, the savior Christ, and we place our hope in him.

Geoffra ðu sylf þinum sceandlicum godum!"

20 Þa cwæð Decius, se deofles biggenga:
"Þysum is to gearcigenne þa reþestan wita!"
Abdon and Sennes him andwyrdon ðus:
"Hwæs abitst þu, casere? Cyð hwæt þu wylle,
þæt þu wite soðlice þæt we orsorge syndon

25 on urum hælende Criste, þe hæfð þa mihte
þæt he ðine geþohtas and þe sylfne mæg
mid ealle towurpon and on ecnysse fordon."

Þa on þam oðrum dæge, het Decius se casere
lætan leon and beran to þam geleaffullum cynegum

30 þæt hi hi abiton buton hi bugon to his godum,
and betæhte þa wican ðam wæl-hreowan Ualeriane.
Þa cwæð Ualerianus to þam cynegum þus:
"Beorgað eowrum gebyrdum and bugað to urum godum
and geoffriað him lac þæt ge lybban magon.

35 Gif ge þis ne doð, eow sceolon deor abitan!"
Abdon and Sennes sædon þam arleasan:
"We gebiddað us to Drihtne gebigdum limum,
and we næfre ne onbugað þam bysmorfullum anlicnyssum,
manna hand-geweorc, þe ge habbað for godas."

40 Þa het Ualerianus ða halgan unscrydan
and lædan swa nacode to ðære sunnan anlicnysse,
forðan ðe hi wurþodon ða sunnan for god,
and bebead his cempum þæt hi ða Cristenan cynegas
to þære offrunga geneadodon mid egeslicum witum.

45 Þa cwædon ða cynegas to þam cwellere ðus:
"Do þæt þu don wylt." And se dema het
beswingan þa halgan hetelice swyðe
mið leadenum swipum, and lædde hi syððan
to ðam wæfer-huse, þær ða deor wunodon,

Make offerings yourself to your shameful gods!" Then De- 20
cius, the devil worshipper, declared: "The most savage tortures are to be prepared for these men!" Abdon and Sennes
answered him like this: "What are you waiting for, emperor?
Say what you please, but you should know that we are totally
fearless because of our savior Christ, who has the power to 25
overthrow entirely and destroy forever your plans and you
yourself."

Then on the second day, the emperor Decius ordered
that lions and bears be let loose against the faithful kings to 30
devour them unless they submitted to his gods, and he en-
trusted this duty to the cruel Valerian. Then Valerian spoke
to the kings in this way: "Preserve your lineage and submit
to our gods and offer a sacrifice to them that you may live. If 35
you don't do this, wild animals will devour you!" Abdon and
Sennes said to the wicked Valerian: "We will pray to the
Lord upon bent knees, and we shall never bow down to your
shameful statues, the handiwork of men, which you consider to be gods."

Then Valerian ordered that the saints be stripped and 40
brought naked to the statue of the sun, because they worshiped the sun as a god, and he ordered his soldiers to force
the Christian kings with horrific tortures to offer the sacrifice. Then the kings said this to the executioner: "Do what 45
you intend to do." And the judge ordered that the saints
be beaten very violently with lead whips, and afterward
he brought them to the amphitheater, where the savage

50 beran and leon, þe hi abitan sceoldon.
And het lætan him to twegen leon
and feower beran binnan þam huse.
Þa urnon þa deor, egeslice grymetende,
to þære halgena fotum swylce hi fryðes bædon,
55 and noldon awæg gan, ac hi weredon hi swyðor
swa þæt nan man ne dorste for ðæra deora ware
þam halgum genealecan oððe into ðam huse gan.
Þa cwæð Ualerianus to ðam cempum þus:
"Heora dry-cræft is gesyne swutollice on ðysum!"
60 And he wearð swyðe gram for þære deora ware
and het ða æt nextan þa hæðenan cwelleras
ingan mid swurdum and ofslean þa halgan.
    Þa þa þis gedon wæs, þa het se dema teon
þæra halgena lic to ðam hæþen-gilde
65 þæt ða Cristenan sceoldon sceawian be him
and bysne niman and bugan to þam godum,
þe læs þe hi wurdon swa wæl-hreowlice acwealde.
Ða æfter þrym dagum com sum diacon þær to
Quirinus gehaten and he ða halgan lic
70 nihtes gelæhte and ledde to his huse
and lede hi digellice on ane lædene ðruh
mid mycele ar-wurðnysse. And hi mannum þær
bediglode lagon to langum fyrste,
oðþæt Constantinus, se Cristene casere, eft to rice feng,
75 and hi ða afundene wurdon þurh Cristes onwrygennysse.
    Ge habbað nu gehyrod hu ða halgan cyningas
heora cynedom forsawon for Cristes geleafan
and heora agen lif forleton for hine.
Nimað eow bysne be ðam, þæt ge ne bugon fram Criste
80 for ænigre earfoðnysse, þæt ge þæt ece lif habbon.

animals, the bears and lions who were to devour them, lived. 50
And he ordered them to release two lions and four bears
upon them within the amphitheater. Then, with terrifying
roars, the wild animals hurried to the feet of the saints as if
they sought peace, and refused to go away, but instead they 55
guarded them so that no one dared approach the saints or
enter the amphitheater because of the beasts' protection.
Then Valerian said this to the soldiers: "From these actions
their sorcery is clear to see!" And he became very angry be- 60
cause of the beasts' protection and finally commanded the
heathen executioners to go in with their swords and kill the
saints.

When this had been done, the judge ordered them to
drag the bodies of the saints to the heathen temple so that 65
the Christians would see them and take them as an example
and submit to the gods, so that they would not be so cruelly
killed. Then after three days a deacon who was called Quirinus came to that place and took the saints' bodies by night 70
and brought them to his house and secretly laid them in a
lead coffin with great honor. And they lay there hidden from
people for a long time, until Constantine, the Christian emperor, afterward took power, and then they were discovered 75
through Christ's revelation.

You have now heard how the holy kings renounced their
kingdom for the faith of Christ and gave up their own lives
for him. Take it as an example, so you do not turn from
Christ because of any hardship, so that you may have eternal 80
life.

Item alia

Nu we spræcon be cynegum, we willað þysne cwyde
gelencgan
and be sumum cynincge eow cyðan git. Abgarus wæs geciged
sum gesælig cynincg on Syrian lande,
and se læg bed-ryda on ðam timan
85 þe se hælend on þysum life wæs.
He hæfde geaxod be ðæs hælendes wundrum
and sende ða ardlice þis ærend-gewrit him to:
"Abgarus gret ead-modlice þone godan hælend,
þe becom to mannum mid Iudeiscum folce.
90 Ic hæbbe gehyred be ðe: hu ðu gehælst ða untruman,
blinde and healte, and bed-rydan arærst,
hreoflige þu geclænsast, and þa unclænan gastas afligst
of wodum mannum, and awrecst ða deadan.
Nu cwæð ic on minum mode þæt ðu eart ælmihtig God,
95 oððe Godes sunu ðe sylf come to mannum
þæt ðu ðas wundra wyrce, and ic wolde ðe biddan
þæt ðu gemedemige þe sylfne þæt þu siðige to me
and mine untrumnysse gehæle, forðan þe ic eom yfele
gehæfd.
Me is eac gesæd þæt ða Iudeiscan syrwiað
100 and runiað him betwynan hu hi þe berædan magon,
and ic hæbbe ane burh þe unc bam genihtsumað."
Þa awrat se hælend him sylf þis gewrit
and asende ðam cynincge ðus cwæðende him to:
"*Beatus es qui credidisti in me cum ipse me non videris.*
105 *Scriptum est enim de me quia hii qui me vident non credent in me,*

Another in the Same Manner
[The Letter of Christ to Abgar]

Now that we are talking about kings, we want to extend this account and tell you also about another king. There was a blessed king in Syria called Abgar, who lay bedridden at that time when the savior was alive on earth. He had learned 85 about the savior's miracles and then hastily sent this letter to him: "Abgar humbly greets the good savior, who has come to humankind among the Jewish people. I have learned 90 about you: how you heal the sick, the blind, and the lame, and restore the bedridden to good health, how you purify the leprous, and drive out unclean spirits from people possessed, and raise the dead. Now I said to myself that you are almighty God, or the Son of God, who has come himself to 95 humanity to perform these miracles, and I want to ask you to humble yourself to journey to me to heal my disease, because I am evilly afflicted. It is also reported to me that the Jews conspire and scheme among themselves how by 100 treachery they might seize you, and I have a city that will suffice for us both."

Then the savior himself wrote this letter and sent it to the king saying this to him: *"Blessed are you who have believed in me when you have not seen me. For it is written of me that those* 105

et qui non vident me ipsi credent et vivent.
De eo autem quod scripsisti mihi—ut veniam ad te—
oportet me omnia propter quae missus sum hic explere.
et postea quam complevero recipi me ad eum a quo missus sum.
110 *Cum ergo fuero assumptus, mittam tibi aliquem*
ex discipulis meis ut curet ægritudinem tuam
et vitam tibi atque his qui tecum sunt prestet."
Þæt is on Engliscum gereorde: "Eadig eart ðu, Abgar,
þu þe gelyfdest on me þonne ðu me ne gesawe.
115 Hit is awriten be me on witegung-bocum
þæt ða þe me geseoð hi ne gelyfað on me,
and þa þe me ne geseoð hi gelyfað and libbað.
Be þam þe ðu awrite to me—þæt ic come to þe—
ic sceal ærest afyllan þa þincg þe ic fore asend eom,
120 and ic sceal beon eft genumen to þam ylcan ðe me asende.
And ic asende to ðe, syððan ic genumen beo,
ænne minra learning-cnihta þe gelacnað þine untrumnysse
and þe lif gegearcað and þam þe gelyfað mid ðe."
Þis gewrit com þa to þam cyninge sona,
125 and se hælend foresceawode syððan he to heofonum astah
þæt he sende þam cyninge, swa swa he ær gecwæð,
ænne of ðam hundseofontigum þe he geceas to bodigenne,
se wæs Tatheus gehaten, þæt he gehælde ðone cynincg.
He com ða þurh Godes sande to þære fore-sædan byrig
130 and gehælde þone untrumne on þæs hælendes mihte
swa þæt ða ceaster-gewaran swyðe þæs wundrodon.
Þa gemunde se cyning hwæt Crist him ær behet
and het him to gefeccan þone fore-sædan Tatheum,
se wæs eac gehaten oþrum naman Iudas.
135 And mid ðam he ineode, þa aras se cyning
and feoll to his fotum ætforan his ðegnum

who see me will not believe in me, and those who do not see me will
believe and live. However, concerning that matter that you have
written to me about—that I should come to you—first I have to
fulfill all those things for which I was sent, and after I have ful-
filled this I will be taken up to him by whom I was sent. Therefore 110
when I have been taken up, I will send one of my disciples to you to
heal your sickness and grant life to you and those who are with
you." That is in English: "Blessed are you, Abgar, who believed in me when you had not seen me. It is written about 115
me in the books of prophecy that those who see me will not
believe in me, and those who do not see me will believe and
live. Concerning what you have written to me about—that
I should come to you—I must first fulfill those things for
which I am sent, and afterward I shall be taken up to the 120
one who sent me. And after I have been taken up, I will send
to you one of my disciples, who will heal your sickness and
grant life to you and to those who believe with you."

Immediately this letter came to the king, and the savior 125
made provision that after he had ascended to heaven, as he
had said previously, he would send one of the seventy that he
had chosen to preach, who was called Thaddeus, to heal the
king. He came on God's mission to the city about which we
spoke before, and healed the sick king through the power of 130
the savior, so that the city's inhabitants were greatly amazed
by it.

Then the king recalled what Christ had previously promised him and ordered them to bring him Thaddeus of whom
we spoke before, who was also called Judas by his other
name. And when he entered, the king got up and fell at his 135
feet in front of his nobles, because through God's revelation

forðan þe he geseah sume scinende beorhtnysse
on þæs Iudan andwlite þurh Godes onwrigennysse,
and cwæð þæt he wære soðlice Cristes discipulus
140   him to hæle asend, swa swa he sylf behet.

    Þa andwyrde se Tatheus ðam ar-wurðan cyninge þus:
"Forðan ðe þu rihtlice gelyfdest on þone ðe me asende,
forðam ic eom asend to þe þæt ðu gesund beo.
And gif ðu on his geleafan þurhwunast, he wile ðe getiðian
145   þinre heortan gewilnunga, toeacan þinre hæle."
Abgarus him andwyrde an-rædlice and cwæð:
"To þam swyðe ic gelyfe on þone lyfigendan hælend
þæt ic wolde ofslean gif hit swa mihte beon,
þa ðe hine gefæstnodon on rode-hencgene."

150   Þa cwæð Tatheus him to: "Crist ure hælend wolde
his Fæder willan gefyllan and eft faran to him."
Abgarus cwæð him eft to: "Ic wat eall be þam,
and ic on hine gelyfe and on his halgan Fæder."
Tatheus cwæð þa gyt to ðam wan-halan cyninge:
155   "Forþi ic sette mine hand on ðæs hælendes naman
ofer ðe, untrumne," and he swa dyde,
and se cyning wearð gehæled sona swa he hine hrepode
fram eallum his untrumnyssum þe he ær on þrowode.

    Abgarus þa wundrode þæt he wearð gehæled
160   butan læce-wyrtum þurh ðæs hælendes word,
swa swa he him ær behet þurh his ærend-gewrit.
Tatheus eac siððan sumne mann gehælde
fram þam micclan fot-adle, and fela oðre menn
on þære byrig gehælde and bodode him geleafan.

165   Ða cwæð Abgarus him to: "On Cristes mihte
þu wyrcst þas micclan wundra, and we ealle ðæs wundriað.
Sege me, ic þe bidde, soð be ðam hælende,

he saw a shining radiance on the face of Judas, and he said that he was truly a disciple of Christ sent to heal him, as he himself had promised. 140

Then this Thaddeus answered the honorable king in this way: "Because you rightly believed in him who sent me, therefore I am sent to you that you may be healed. And if you continue in his faith, he intends to grant you your heart's desire, in addition to your health." Abgar answered him resolutely and said: "I believe in the living savior so strongly that if it were possible, I would kill those who fastened him onto the cross." Then Thaddeus said to him: "Christ our savior wished to fulfill his Father's will and then return to him." Abgar said to him again: "I know all about that, and I believe in him and in his holy Father." In addition, Thaddeus said to the sick king: "Therefore I place my hand upon you, sick man, in the name of the savior," and he did so, and the king was healed from all illnesses from which he had previously suffered as soon as he touched him. 145 150 155

Abgar then marveled that he had been healed without medicine through the savior's word, just as he had promised him previously in his letter. Afterward Thaddeus also healed a person from a severe foot disease, and he healed many other people in the city and preached the faith to them. 160

Then Abgar said to him: "You perform these great miracles through the power of Christ, and we all marvel at them. Tell me, I pray, the truth about the savior, how he came to 165

hu he to mannum come and of middan-earde ferde."
Tatheus andwyrde Abgare and cwæð:
170 "Ic eom asend to bodigenne: hat þine burh-ware cuman
ealle tosomne on ærne-mergen
þæt ic him eallum cyðe Cristes tocyme
and be his wundrum þe he worhte on life."
Þa het se cynincg cuman his ceaster-gewaran
175 and Tatheus him bodade bealdlice be Criste
and him eallum sæde þone soðan geleafan
and man-cynnes alysednysse þurh ðone mildan hælend,
þæt he wolde hine sylfne syllan to deaðe
and to helle gecuman to gehelpene Adames
180 and eac his gecorenra of Adames cynne,
and hu he syþþan astah to his soðfæstan Fæder,
and cymð eft to demenne ælcum be his dædum.
Æfter ðyssere bodunge, bead se cyning þam bydele
goldes and seolfres godne dæl to lace,
185 ac he nolde niman nan ðingc to medes
his wunderlicre mihte oððe his mærlican bodunge.
And sæde ðam cyninge: "We forsawon ure æhta
and forleton ure agen, hwi sceole we oþres mannes niman?"
Þis wæs þus geworden, and þær wunode a syððan
190 se soða geleafa on þære land-leode,
þam hælende to lofe, þe leofað a on ecnysse. Amen.

humankind and departed from the world." Thaddeus answered Abgar and said: "I am sent to preach: order your citi-   170
zens to come all together early in the morning, so that I can
tell them all about Christ's coming and about the miracles
that he performed during his life." Then the king commanded the citizens to come, and Thaddeus preached   175
boldly to them about Christ and told them all about the true
faith and humanity's salvation through the merciful savior,
that he willingly offered himself up to death and descended
to hell to help Adam and also his chosen ones of Adam's kin,   180
and how he afterward ascended to his righteous Father, and
will come again to judge each according to his deeds. After
this preaching, the king offered the preacher a good deal of
gold and silver as a gift, but he refused to take anything as a   185
reward for his wondrous power or his glorious preaching.
And he said to the king: "We have abandoned our possessions and given up anything of our own, so why would we
take what is another person's?" This occurred in this way,
and forever after the true faith continued among the people   190
of that land, to the praise of the savior, who lives forever in
eternity. Amen.

THE MARTYRDOM OF
THE MACCABEES,
THEIR BATTLES, *AND*
THE THREE ORDERS
OF SOCIETY

23

The Martyrdom of the Maccabees,
Their Battles, *and*
The Three Orders of Society

Kalendas Augusti: Passio sanctorum Machabeorum

Æfter ðam ðe Alexander, se egefulla cyning,
todælde his rice his dyrlingum gehwilcum
on his forð-siðe, and hi fengon to rice,
gehwylc on his healfe, þa weoxon fela yfelu
5   wide geond eorðan for ðære cyninga gewinne.
An ðære cyninga wæs heora eallra forcuðost,
arleas and upp-ahafen, Antiochus gehaten.
Se feaht on Ægypta lande and afligde ðone cynincg,
and ferde syððan to Hierusalem mid mycelre fyrde
10 and bereafode Godes templ goldes and seolfres,
and fela gold-hordas forð mid him gelæhte,
and ða halgan maðm-fatu and þæt mære weofod,
and ofsloh þæs folces fela on ðære byrig,
and modelice spræc, on his mihta truwigende.
15   Eft æfter sumum fyrste, asende se cyning
on ærend-gewritum þæt ealle menn gebugon
to his hæðenscipe and to his gesetnyssum.

23

The Martyrdom of the Maccabees,
Their Battles, *and*
The Three Orders of Society

August 1: The Passion of the Holy Maccabees

After Alexander, the fearsome king, divided his kingdom at his death among all his favorites, and they took over the empire, each with his own portion, then many evils flourished widely throughout the world because of conflict among 5 these kings. One of these kings was the most wicked of them all, cruel and arrogant, and he was called Antiochus. He fought in Egypt and put the king to flight, and afterward advanced on Jerusalem with a great army and plundered 10 God's temple of gold and silver, and took many treasures away with him, both the holy treasure-vessels and the great altar, and slaughtered many of the people in the city, and spoke proudly, believing in his own power.

Again, after some time, the king sent letters declaring 15 that all men should submit to his heathen practices and to

And asende to Hierusalem, Iudeiscre byrig,
on þære wæs ða gewurðod se eall-wealdende God
20 æfter ðære ealdan æ, þe hi ana þa heoldon,
and het hi gebugan fram Gode and fram his biggengum,
and arærde þæt deofol-gild uppon Godes weofode
and het hi ealle offrian to ðære anlicnysse,
and ælcne acwellan þe wiðcwæde his hæsum.
25 Wearð þa mycel angsumnyss on eallum þam folce
þe on God gelyfdon for ðam gramlicum dædum,
and manega gebugon to ðam manfullan hæðen-gilde,
and eac fela wiðcwædon þæs cyninges hæsum
and woldon heora lif forlætan ær þan ðe heora geleafan,
30 and noldon hi fylan mid þam fulan hæðenscype,
ne Godes æ tobrecan, þe hi on bocum ræddon.
  Hwæt þa wearð gelæht sum geleafful bocere,
har-wencge and eald, se hatte Eleazarus,
and hi bestungon him on muþ mid mycelre ðreatunge
35 þone fulan mete þe Moyses forbead
Godes folce to þicgenne for þære gastlican getacnunge.
We moton nu secgan swutellicor be ðysum:
hwylce mettas wæron mannum forbodene
on ðære ealdan æ þe mann ett nu swaðeah.
40 Moyses forbead for mycelre getacnunge
on ðære ealdan æ, æfter Godes dihte,
þa nytenu to etanne þam ealdan folce
þe heora cude ne ceowað and het ða unclæne,
and þa þe synd gehofode on horses gelicnysse
45 untoclofenum clawum wæron unclæne eac.
Þa clænan nytenu þe heora cudu ceowað
getacniað þa men þe on heora mode smeagað
embe Godes willan, syððan hi his word gehyrað

his decrees. He sent them to Jerusalem, the city of the Jewish people, in which the all-ruling God was worshiped at that time according to the old law, which they alone then observed, and he ordered them to turn from God and from his rites, and he built a pagan shrine upon God's altar and ordered them all to offer sacrifices to the statue, and to kill anyone who opposed his command. There was then considerable distress because of these terrible actions among all the people who believed in God, and many converted to evil idolatry, but many also opposed the king's commands and were willing to relinquish their lives rather than their faith, and refused to defile themselves with these foul heathen practices, or to break God's law, which they read about in books.

Well then, a faithful scribe, gray haired and old, who was called Eleazar, was seized, and with terrible threats they stuck into his mouth the foul food which Moses had forbidden God's people to taste because of its spiritual significance. We must now speak more clearly about these things: which foods were forbidden to people under the old law that are nevertheless eaten now. Because of its great significance under the old law, according to God's decree, Moses forbade the people of old to eat those animals that do not chew the cud, and termed them unclean, and those that have hooves like a horse with uncloven hooves were unclean also. Those clean animals that chew the cud symbolize those people who, after hearing his word from the mouths of teachers, meditate upon God's will in their minds as if they

of lareowa muðum, swylce hi heora mete ceowan.

50 And ða synd unclæne þe heora cudu ne ceowað
forðan þe hi getacniað þa ðe tela nellað,
ne nellað leornian hwæt Gode leof sy,
ne on heora mode wealcan þæs hælendes beboda,
and syndon forðy unclæne swa swa ða forcuðan nytenu.

55 Þa nytenu synd clæne þe tocleofað heora clawa
and heora cudu ceowað. Hi getacniað þa geleaffullan
on Godes gelaðunge þe mid geleafan underfoð
þa ealdan gecyðnysse and Cristes gesetnysse,
þæt is seo ealde æ and seo niwe gecyðnyss,

60 and ceowað Godes beboda symle mid smeagunge.
Þa nytenu wæron unclæne gecwedene on þære æ,
þe ne tocleofað heora clawa þeah ðe hi cudu ceowan,
oððe gif hi tocleofað and ceowan nellað,
for ðære getacnunge, þe ða towerd wæs:

65 þæt we tocleofan ure clawa on þam twam gecyðnyssum,
þa ealdan and þa niwan, þæt is æ and god-spel,
and þæt we on mode smeagan þæs Ælmihtigan hæse,
and se ðe aþor forlæt se leofað unclæne.
Swa swa ða Iudeiscan þe urne Drihten forseoð

70 and his god-spel-bodunge to bysmre habbað
syndon unclæne and Criste andsæte
þeah ðe hi Moyses æ on heora muðe wealcon,
and nellað understanden butan þæt steaflice andgit.
Fela wæron forbodene Godes folce on ðære æ

75 þe nu syndon clæne æfter Cristes tocyme,
siððan Paulus cwæð to þam Cristenum ðus:
Omnia munda mundis.
"Ealle ðincg syndon clæne þam clænum mannum.
Þam ungeleaffullum and unclænum, nis nan þincg clæne."

were chewing their food. And those who do not chew the 50
cud are unclean because they symbolize those who do not
desire good, and refuse to learn what might be pleasing to
God, and do not turn the savior's commands over in their
minds, and are therefore unclean like the unclean beasts.
Those animals that split their hooves and chew their cud are 55
clean. They symbolize the believers in God's church who
with faith receive the old testament and Christ's command,
that is to say the old law and the new testament, and chew 60
upon God's commands continually through meditation. Under the law, those animals that do not divide their hooves
though they chew the cud, or if they divide them and will
not chew, were considered unclean, because of what they
signify, which was then yet to come: that we should divide 65
our hooves in those two testaments, the old and the new,
that is the law and the gospel, and that we should meditate
within our hearts upon the Almighty's command, for whoever abandons either one lives uncleanly. Likewise, the Jews
who scorn our Lord and hold his gospel teaching in con- 70
tempt are unclean and repugnant to Christ though they
chew the law of Moses in their mouths, but they refuse to
understand anything but the literal meaning. Many things
were forbidden to God's people under the law that are now 75
clean after Christ's coming, after Paul said this to the Christians: *All things are clean to the clean.* "All things are clean to
people who are clean. To the unbelievers and the unclean,

80 Hara wæs ða unclæne forðan ðe he is clifer-fete,
and swin wæs ða unclæne forðan þe hit ne ceow his cudu.
Sume wæron þa fule þe nu synd eac fule,
ac hit biþ to langsum eall her to logigenne
be ðam clænum nytenum oððe be þam unclænum
85 on ðære ealdan æ þe mann ett nu swaðeah.

Þa wolde Eleazarus werlice sweltan
ær ðan þe he Godes æ forgegan wolde,
and nolde forswelgan ðæs spices snæd
þe hi him on muð bestungon, forðan þe Moyses forbead
90 swyn to etenne, swa swa we ær sædon.

Þa bædon ða cwelleras, for heora eald cyððe,
þæt hi moston him beran unforboden flæsc
and dyde swilce he æte of ðam offrung-spice,
and swa mid ðære hiwunge him sylfum geburge.

95 Ða cwæð Eleazarus: "Ic eom eald to hiwigenne,
and wenað þa geongan þæt ic wille forgægan
Godes gesetnysse for ðisum sceortan life,
and bið þonne min hiwung him to forwyrde,
and ic sylf beo andsæte þurh swylce gebysnunge.

100 Ðeah ðe ic beo ahred fram manna reðnysse,
ic ne mæg þam Ælmihtigan ahwar ætberstan,
on life oþþe on deaðe. Ac ic læte bysne
þam iungum cnihtum gif ic cenlice swelte
ar-wurðum deaðe for ðære halgan æ."

105 Þa wurdon ða cwelleras, þe him cuðlice tospræcon,
swyðe geyrsode for ðære andsware
and tugon hine to þam witum þæt he wurde acweald,
and he ða mid geleafan his lif geendode.

Þær wurdon eac gelæhte and gelædde to ðam cynincge
110 seofon gebroðra, swyðe gelyfede,

nothing is clean." A hare was unclean at that time because it 80
has claws, and a pig was unclean then because it does not
chew its cud. Some things were unclean then that are also
unclean now, but it would take too long to record everything
here about the clean animals and the ones that are unclean
according to the old law that people nevertheless eat now. 85

Then Eleazar wished to die like a man rather than dis-
obey God's law, and he refused to swallow the piece of pork
that they forced into his mouth, because Moses forbade the 90
eating of pigs, as we said earlier. Then the executioners, for
old friendship's sake, begged him that they might bring
meat that was not forbidden and he should act as if he were
eating from the sacrificial pork, and by this deception save
himself.

Then Eleazar said: "I am too old to dissimulate, and the 95
young will think that I am willing to break God's commands
for the sake of this short life, and my deception will then be
their destruction, and I myself will be accursed for setting
such an example. Though I might be saved from human cru- 100
elty, I cannot escape the Almighty anywhere, in life or in
death. But I shall leave an example to young people if I
bravely die an honorable death for the holy law." Then the 105
executioners, who had spoken to him with familiarity, were
thoroughly enraged by this answer and dragged him to tortures so that he would be killed, and he then ended his life
with faith.

There were also seven brothers, devout believers, who 110
were seized and brought to the king, and with them their

and heora modor samod, and hi man mid swingle ðreade
þæt hi etan sceoldon, ongean Godes æ, spicc.
Þa cwæð se yldesta: "Hwæt axast ðu æt us?
We synd gearwe to sweltenne swyðor þonne to forgægenne
115 ures scyppendes æ, þe he gesette þurh Moyses."
Þa yrsode se cynincg and het forceorfan his tungan,
and hine behættian and his handa forceorfan,
and eac befotian, and het feccan ænne hwer
and hine þæron seoðan oðþæt he sawlode
120 ætforan his gebroþrum þæt hi abugan sceoldon.
    Hwæt þa six gebroþra hi sylfe þa tihton
and seo modor samod, secgende him betwynan
þæt hi sweltan woldon for Godes gesetnyssum:
"God sylf gefrefrað us, swa swa Moyses geswutelode
125 on ðære fiftan bec þæt God gefrefrað his ðeowan."
Þa gebundon ða cwelleras þone oþerne broðor,
and hine behættedon hetelice, and axodon
hwæðer he etan wolde ær ðan þe he behamelod wurde.
He cwæð þæt he nolde, and he ða gelice wita
130 swa swa his yldra broðor ardlice underfeng,
and cwæð to ðam cyninge þe hi acwellan het:
"Ðu, forscyldegodesta cynincg, ofslihst us and amyrst,
ac se ælmihtiga cyning us eft arærð
to þam ecan life, nu we for his æ sweltað."
135 Hi bundon ðone þryddan and mid bysmore hetan
his tungan forðræcan. And he hraðe swa dyde,
and his handa him ræhte and mid an-rædnysse cwæð:
"Ðas lima ic hæfde þurh ðone heofonlican cynincg,
ac ic hi nu forseo for his gesetnyssum,
140 forþan þe ic hopie to him þæt ic hi eft underfo æt him."

mother, and they were all tormented with beating to make them eat pork, contrary to God's law. Then the eldest said: "What are you asking of us? We are ready to die rather than break our creator's law, which he ordained through Moses." 115 Then the king became furious and ordered them to cut out his tongue, and to scalp him and to cut off his hands, and to cut off his feet also, and he ordered them to fetch a cauldron and to boil him in it until he died in front of his brothers 120 that they might yield.

Well then, the six brothers and the mother together encouraged each other, saying among themselves that they were willing to die for God's commands: "God himself will comfort us, as Moses revealed in the fifth book that God 125 comforts his servants." Then the executioners bound the second brother, and brutally scalped him, and asked whether he was willing to eat rather than be mutilated. He said that he was not willing, and quickly he received the same tor- 130 tures as his elder brother, and said to the king who had given the order to kill them: "You, most guilty king, are killing and destroying us, but the almighty king will raise us up again to the eternal life, because we are dying for his law."

They bound the third brother and with scorn com- 135 manded that he stick out his tongue. And he quickly did this, and reached out his hands to them and with resolve said: "I have these limbs from the heavenly king, but I now despise them for the sake of his commandments, because I 140 have hope in him that I will receive them from him again."

And se cynincg wundrode and þa þe mid him wæron
ðæs cnihtes an-rædnysse þæt he ða cwylmincge forseah.
   Æfter ðyses forð-siðe, hi gefengon ðone feorðan
and eallswa getintregedon, ac he an-rædlice cwæð:

145 "Selre us is to sweltenne and soðlice anbidian
þæs ecan æristes æt ðam ælmihtigan Gode,
ac ðe ne bið nan ærist to ðam ecan life!"
Se ða geendode mid an-rædum geleafan,
and hi gefengon to dreccenne þone fiftan broðor.

150 He beseah ða to ðam cynincge and cwæð him þus to:
"Nu ðu mihte hæfst betwux mannum sume hwile,
þu dest swa swa ðu wylt, ac ne wen ðu swaðeah
þæt se God us forlæte þe we on gelyfað.
Þu afindst his mihte ungefyrn on ðe sylfum,

155 hu he þe tintregað teartlice on witum."
   Se geendode ða, and hi ardlice gelæhton
þone sixtan broðor, and he sweltende cwæð:
"Ne dwela ðu on idel, þeah ðe Drihten ðe geþafige
þæt we for urum synnum to swylcere wæfer-syne synd,

160 and ne wen ðu na be þe þæt þu ungewitnod beo
nu ðu winst ongean God!" And se gewat þa swa sona.
   Þa wundrode heora modor þæt hi swa wel ongunnon,
and heo mid bliþum mode hyre bearn æfre tihte,
ælcne onsundron, and sæde him eallum:

165 "Ne fegde ic eowre lima, ne ic eow lif ne forgeaf,
ac middan-eardes scyppend eow sealde gast and lif,
and he eft eow forgifð þæt ece lif mid him
swa swa ge nu syllað eow sylfe for his æ."
   Hwæt ða Antiochus se arleasa cynincg

170 behet þam anum cnapan þe þær cucu wæs þa git
mycele woruld-æhta gif he wolde him abugan,

And the king and those who were with him were amazed at the young man's resolve as he scorned these torments.

After the death of this one, they took the fourth brother and tortured him in a similar way, but he resolutely said: "It 145 is better for us to die and in truth await the eternal resurrection through almighty God, but for you there will be no resurrection to the eternal life!" He then died with constant faith, and they brought the fifth brother out to torment. He 150 then looked toward the king and said this to him: "Now that you have power over people for a brief period, you do as you will, but nevertheless do not think that the God in whom we believe forsakes us. Before long you will discover his power over you, and how he will punish you severely in tor- 155 ments."

Then he died, and they quickly seized the sixth brother, and dying he said: "Do not err without cause, although the Lord may be allowing you to make such a spectacle of us because of our sins, and do not think of yourself that you 160 will go unpunished when you contend against God!" And he then died in this way immediately.

Then their mother marveled that they had acted so fittingly, and with a happy heart she continually encouraged her sons, each one individually, and said to them all: "I did 165 not assemble your limbs, nor did I give you life, but the creator of the world gave you spirit and life, and he will again give you that eternal life with him as you are now giving yourselves for his law."

Well then, Antiochus the dishonorable king promised 170 the one young man who was still alive great worldly wealth if

and bæd eac ða modor þæt heo hire bearn tihte,
þæt he huru ana abuge, þeah þe his gebroðra noldon.
And seo modor behet him þæt heo wolde hine læran.
175 Þa abeah seo modor to hire bearne and cwæð:
"Gemiltsa me, min sunu, ic ðe to men gebær.
Beseoh nu to heofonum, and besceawa þas eorðan
and ealle ða gesceafta þe him on synd nu,
and understand be ðam hu se ælmihtiga God
180 hi ealle gesceop butan an-timbre of nahte,
and ne forhta ðu ana for ðysum feondlican cwellere,
ac underfoh þone deað swa swa ðine gebroðra dydon,
þæt ic ðe eft underfo on eadignysse mid him."
    Þa clypode se iungling to ðam cwellerum þus and cwæð:
185 "Hwæs andbidige ge? Ne beo ic
na gehyrsum þæs cyninges hæsum,
ac Godes bebodum þe he bebead þurh Moysen.
And þu, manfulla cyning, þinre modignysse scealt
soðlice on Godes dome susle ðrowian.
190 Ic sylle min agen lif and minne lic-haman samod
for Godes gesetnyssum, swa swa mine six gebroðra.
And ic clypige to Gode þæt he urum cynne gemiltsige,
and þæt he do mid witum þæt ðu wite þæt he is ana God."
    Þa wearð se cynincg wæl-hreow þam cnihte,
195 ofer ealle þa oðre þa he ær acwealde,
for ðære forsewennysse, and se gesæliga cniht
on þam teartum witum gewat þa of life
mid fullum geleafan. And seo geleaffulle modor
wearð eac acweald ætforan þam cyninge,
200 æfter hire seofon sunum, gesæliglice for Gode.
    Þyssera martyra gemynd is on Hlaf-mæssan dæg,
swa wide swa Godes þeowas Godes þenunge gymað.

he would yield to him, and asked the mother also that she encourage her son, that he alone might submit at least, even though his brothers had refused. And the mother promised him that she would instruct him. Then the mother bent down to her son and said: "Have mercy on me, my son, I who bore you as a man. Gaze now upon the heavens, and look upon the earth and all the creatures that are now upon it, and understand from them how the almighty God created them all without material from nothing, and do not be the only one afraid of this fiendish murderer, but accept death as your brothers did, that I may receive you again with them in blessedness." 175 180

Then the young man called to the executioners in this way and said: "What are you waiting for? I will not be obedient to the king's orders, but to God's commandments that he commanded through Moses. And truly you, evil king, will suffer torments at God's judgment for your pride. I will give my own life and my body together for God's decrees, as my six brothers did. And I call upon God to have mercy on our people, and to make you realize through torments that he alone is God." Then the king became furious with this young man, more than all the others whom he had already killed, because of his scorn, and the blessed young man then died from bitter tortures with true faith. And the faithful mother was also killed before the king, following her seven sons, blissfully for the sake of God. 185 190 195 200

The commemoration of these martyrs takes place on Lammas day, wherever God's servants observe God's rites.

Manega halgan wæron under Moyses æ,
ac we nabbað heora gemynd mid nanum mæsse-dæge,
205   butan þyssere gebroðra þe swa bealdlice ðrowodon.

Item

We wyllað eac awritan hu þæt gewinn geendode,
and hu se ælmihtiga God þa arleasan afligde
mid mycelre sceame, swa swa us sægð seo racu:
      Mathathias wæs gehaten sum heah Godes þægn,
210   se hæfde fif suna ful cene mid him.
An hatte Iohannes, oðer Symon,
ðridde Iudas, feorða Eleazarus,
fifta Ionathas, binnan Hierusalem.
Þas bemændan sarlice mid swyðlicre heofunge
215   þæt hi swylce yrmðe gesawon on heora life,
and noldon abugan to ðam bysmorfullan hæðenscipe.
      Þa asende se cynincg to ðam fore-sædan ðegene,
and het hi ealle bugan to his blindum godum
and him lac offrian and forlætan Godes æ.
220   Ac Mathathias nolde þam manfullan gehyran
ne Godes æ forgægan for his gramlican ðreate.
Efne þa eode, on heora eallra gesihðe,
an Iudeisc mann to þam deofol-gilde
and geoffrode his lac swa swa Antiochus het.
225   Hwæt ða Mathathias on mode wearð geangsumod,
and ræsde to ðam were þe ðær wolde offrian
and ofsloh hine sona and siððan þone oþerne,

There were many saints under Moses's law, but we do not commemorate them with any Mass day, with the exception 205 of these brothers who so boldly suffered.

In the Same Manner
[On the Battles of the Maccabees]

We wish also to record how that conflict ended, and how the almighty God put the wicked ones to flight with great shame, as the story tells us.

There was a high-ranking servant of God called Mathathias, and he had five very brave sons. One was called John, the 210 second Simon, the third Judas, the fourth Eleazar, the fifth Jonathan, all within Jerusalem. These young men complained bitterly with loud lamentation that they saw such 215 misery in their lifetime, and refused to submit to shameful heathen practices.

Then the king sent word to Mathathias, whom we have already mentioned, and commanded them all to submit to his blind gods and offer them sacrifices and abandon God's law. But Mathathias refused to obey the wicked man or 220 transgress God's law because of his angry threat. Just then, in the sight of them all, a Jewish man approached the heathen shrine and was making his offering as Antiochus had commanded. Well then, Mathathias became troubled in his 225 heart, and rushed at the man who intended to make an offering there and immediately killed him and afterward a

þæs cynincges ðegn þe hine ðærto neadode,
and towearp þæt deofol-gild and wearð him awege.

230 Clypode þa hlude: "Ælc þe geleafan hæbbe
and Godes æ recce gange him to me!"
He fleah ða to westene, and fela manna mid him,
mid an-rædum mode, and ða manfullan forsawon.
Þa asende se cynincg him sona æfter

235 mycele meniu to ðam wid-gillum muntum,
þær hi floc-mælum ferdon mid heora hiwum.
Þa wearð þær ofslagen sum dæl þæs folces
þe on fyrlene wæs fram Mathathian,
forðan þe hi noldon feohton on þam freols-dæge

240 ac leton hi ofslean on unscæððignysse.
Þæt werod weox ða swyðe þe wæs mid Mathathian,
and hi an-rædlice fuhton and afligdon ða hæðenan,
mid mycelre strængðe, þe modegodon ongean God.
Mathathias þa ferde mid his maga fultume

245 and ehte þæra hæþenra, and mid ealle adræfde,
and Godes æ arærde, and him eac God fylste.

He ealdode þa and his ende genealæhte,
and lærde his suna mid geleafan and cwæð:
"Onginnað nu þegenlice, nu eow þearf mycel is,

250 and syllað eower agen lif for ðære soðfæstan æ
and for ura fædera cyðnysse, hit cymð eow to wuldre.
Beoð gemyndige nu, mine bearn,
hu se mæra Abraham on mycelre costnunge
Gode wæs getrywe, and him com þæt to rihtwysnysse.

255 Eallswa Ioseph and Hiesus Naue,
Dauid and Danihel, and ealle ða þe on God truwodon
wurdon æfre getrymde for heora trywðe wið hine.
Beoð nu gehyrte, and gehihtað on God,

second man, the king's official who was compelling him to it, and he overthrew the heathen shrine and went away.

Then he cried out loudly: "Let everyone who has faith 230 and heeds God's law come to me!" Then he fled to the desert, and many people with him, with a resolute mind, and they despised the wicked people. Then immediately the king sent a great force after them to the vast mountains, 235 where they went in droves with their families. Then part of the people who were at a distance from Mathathias were killed, because they refused to fight on the Sabbath but al- 240 lowed themselves to be slaughtered in innocence. Then the company that was with Mathathias greatly increased, and they fought resolutely and put the heathens, who exalted themselves against God, to flight with great strength. Mathathias then went with the support of his relatives and 245 pursued the heathens, and drove them away completely, and established God's law, and God helped them also.

He grew old then and his end neared, and he taught his sons with faith and said: "Act valiantly now, now that your need is great, and give your own lives for the true law and for 250 our fathers' covenant, for it will result in glory for you. Be mindful now, my sons, of how the great Abraham was true to God in the midst of great tribulation, and that justified him. Also Joseph and Joshua son of Nun, David and Daniel, and 255 all those who believed in God were always strengthened because of their trust in him. Be encouraged now, and trust in

and healdað mid ðegenscipe ða halgan Godes æ,
260 forðan þe ge beoð wuldorfulle on hire.
Ne forhtige ge, ic bidde, for ðæs fyrnfullan þreatum,
forðan þe his wuldor is wyrms and meox.
Nu, todæg, he modegað, and tomergen he ne bið,
he awent to eorðan, and his geðoht forwyrð.
265 Eower broðor Symon is snotor and rædfæst;
he bið eow for fæder: folgiað his rædum.
Iudas Machabeus is mihtig and strang;
beo he eower ealdor on ælcum gefeohte,
and gaderiað eow to þa þe Godes æ lufiað,
270 and wrecað eower folc on ðam fulum hæðenum,
and healdað Godes æ on godum biggencgum."
He bletsode ða his suna, and swa gewat of life,
and his lic wæs bebyriged on his agenre byrig,
and Israhel hine beweop on þa ealdan wisan.
275 Hwæt ða Iudas Machabeus mihtiglice aras
on his fæder stede and wiðstod his feondum,
and his feower gebroðra him fylston an-rædlice
and ealle ða þe wæron wunigende mid his fæder
and fuhton ða mid blisse and afligdon þa hæþenan.
280 Iudas ða hine gescrydde mid his scinendan byrnan,
swa swa ormæte ent, and hine ealne gewæpnode
and his fyrde bewerode wið fynd mid his swurde.
He wearð þa leon gelic on his gewinnum and dædum,
and todræfde þa arleasan, and his eðel gerymde.
285 His fynd þa flugon afyrhte for him,
and ealle ða yfel-wyrcendan wurdon gedræfde.
And se hæl wearð gesped on Iudan handum ða,
and he geblissode his cynn, þe wæs gecweden Iacob,
and his hlisa þa asprang to þam ytemestan lande.

God, and keep the holy law of God valiantly, because you 260
will be glorified by it. Do not fear, I pray, the threats of the
sinful man, because his glory is decayed flesh and dung.
Now, today, he exalts himself, but tomorrow he will be no
more, he will return to the dust, and his thought will perish.
Your brother Simon is wise and prudent; he will be a father 265
to you: follow his advice. Judas Machabeus is mighty and
strong; let him be your leader in every battle, and gather to
yourselves those who love God's law, and avenge your people 270
on the foul heathens, and observe God's law with good practices." Then he blessed his sons, and so he died, and his body
was buried in his own city, and Israel mourned him in the
old traditions.

Well then, Judas Machabeus rose up powerfully in his fa- 275
ther's place and withstood his enemies, and his four brothers and all those who had been living with his father supported him steadfastly and fought joyfully then and put the
heathens to flight. Judas then clothed himself in his shining 280
mail shirt, like a huge giant, and armed himself fully and defended his army against enemies with his sword. He became
like a lion in his conflicts and actions, and scattered the
wicked, and enlarged his homeland. His enemies then fled 285
in fear of him, and all the evildoers were driven away. And
salvation prospered in the hands of Judas then, and he made
his people, who were called Jacob, joyful, and his fame
spread to the furthest land.

290   Ða gegaderode Appollonius, sum gramlic here-toga,
of Samarian byrig swyðlice fyrde,
and of manegum ðeodum menn to gefeohte
togeanes Israel and Iudan mægðe.
Ac Iudas him com to and acwealde hine sona
295   and fela his folces, and ða oðre ætflugon.
Iudas ða gelæhte þæs Appollonies swurd,
þæt wæs mærlic wæpn, and he wann mid þam
on ælcum gefeohte on eallum his life.
     Eft ða wæs sum here-toga gehaten Seron
300   on Syrian lande se cwæð to his leode:
"Ic wille wyrcan me naman and oferwinnan Iudan
and þa ðe him mid synd þe forsawon ðone cyning."
He gesamnode þa his fyrde, and ferde mid prasse
to Iudea lande, and fela leoda mid him.
305   Iudas þa him com to, and his geferan cwædon:
"Hu mage we, þus feawa, feohtan ongean ðas meniu,
nu we synd gewæhte mid gewinne and meteleaste?"
Iudas him andwyrde an-rædlice and cwæð:
"Nis nan earfoðnyss ðam ælmihtigan Gode,
310   on feawum mannum oððe on micclum werode,
to helpenne on gefeohte and healdan þa ðe he wile,
forðan þe se sige bið symle of heofonum.
Ðas cumað to us swylce hi cenran syndon
and willað us fordon and awestan ure land.
315   We soðlice feohtað for us sylfe wið hi,
and for Godes æ, and God hi eac fordeð
ætforan ure gesihðe, ne forhtige ge nateshwon."
     Æfter ðyssere spræce hi eodon togædere,
and Iudas ða afligde þone fore-sædan Seron,
320   and his here samod, mid swyðlicre bylde,

Then Apollonius, a fierce leader, gathered a great army 290
from the city of Samaria, and brought men from many tribes
to the battle against Israel and Judas's people. But Judas advanced upon him and killed him immediately and many of 295
his people, and the rest fled. Judas then seized Apollonius's
sword, which was a glorious weapon, and he fought with it
in every battle for the rest of his life.

Now there was a leader in Syria called Seron who said to 300
his people: "I wish to make a name for myself and conquer
Judas and those who are with him who despised the king."
Then he gathered his army, and many peoples with him, and
went with pomp to Judea. Judas then approached him, and 305
his companions said: "How can we, who are so few, fight
against this multitude, now that we are weakened by conflict and hunger?" Judas resolutely answered them and said:
"It is no obstacle for the almighty God to help in battle and 310
to protect those whom he wishes, with a few men or a great
army, because the victory is always from heaven. These men
advance upon us as if they were braver and intend to destroy
us and lay waste to our land. Truly, we will fight against them 315
for ourselves and for God's law, and before our eyes God will
destroy them also, so have no fear at all."

After this speech they engaged in battle, and with great
courage Judas then put to flight Seron, whom we mentioned 320
before, together with his army, and eight hundred men were

and þær wurdon ofslagene eahta hund wera,
and ða oðre ætflugon to Philistea lande.
Iudan ege ða asprang wide geond land
and his gebroðra oga ofer ealle ða hæðenan,

325 and ealle þeoda spræcon hu ðegenlice hi fuhton.
Iudea land wæs ða lange butan cyninge,
on eallum þysum gewinnum, ac hi werode Iudas,
and eft his gebroðra æfter his geendunge.

Hwæt ða wearð gecydd þam cyninge Antioche

330 embe Iudan sige, and he geswarc ða on mode,
and sende ða his here mid anum heah-þegne
Lisias gehaten to Iudea lande.
On ðære fyrde wæron feowertig þusenda,
and seofon þusenda swyðe gewæpnode,

335 and comon ða mid þrymme to Iudeiscum cynne.
Iudas þa gehyrte his geferan mid wordum,
and fæston ænne dæg, fultumes biddende
æt þam ælmihtigan Gode, þæt he hi gemundian sceolde
and his halige templ healdan wið þa hæðenan.

340 Hi ferdon ða gehyrte to þam gefeohte werd,
and Iudas eft ða spræc to eallum his geferum:
"Beoð ymbgyrde stranglice to þysum stiðan gewinne,
forðan þe us is selre þæt we sweltan on gefeohte
þonne þas yrmðe geseon on urum cynne ðus

345 and on urum haligdome. Ac swa swa se heofonlica God
wylle don be us, gewurðe hit swa.
Beoð gemyndige hu mihtiglice he ahredde
ure fæderas iu wið Pharao þone kyning
on ðære Readan Sæ, on þære ðe he besanc to grunde.

350 Uton clypian to heofonum þæt God ure helpe

killed there, and the rest fled to Palestine. Fear of Judas and terror of his brothers then spread widely throughout the land among all the heathens, and all peoples said how val- 325 iantly they had fought. Judea was then without a king for a long period, throughout all these conflicts, but Judas protected them, as did his brothers later after his death.

Well then, news about Judas's victory was announced to 330 king Antiochus, and his mood darkened, and then he sent his army to Judea under a high-ranking noble called Lisias. There were in that army forty thousand men, with seven thousand heavily armed, and they then advanced upon the 335 Jewish people with military force. Judas then encouraged his companions with his words, and they fasted for a day, praying to the almighty God for help, that he might protect them and defend his holy temple against the heathens. Thus 340 encouraged, they went toward the battle, and Judas spoke again to all his companions: "Be boldly equipped for this tough conflict, because it is better for us to die in the battle than to see this misery inflicted upon our people and upon 345 our sanctuary in this way. But as the heavenly God intends to act concerning us, so shall it be. Remember how powerfully he rescued our fathers long ago from Pharaoh the king in the Red Sea, in which he sank to the bottom. Let us call 350 out to the heavens that God may help us and destroy this

and tobryte þisne here, þæt þa hæðenan tocnawon
þæt nis nan oðer God þe Israhel alyse."
    Machabeus þa genealæhte mid lytlum werode
þæt wæron ðreo þusend þe him ða gelæstan wolde.
355 Hi bleowan þa heora byman and bealdlice fuhton
oðþæt þa hæðenan flugon to fyrlenum landum,
and Iudas hi todræfde swa swa deor to wuda.
Þær wurdon ofslagene sume þreo þusend,
and Iudas þa funde, þa ða he fram fyrde gecyrde,
360 gold and seolfor, gode-web and purpuran,
and fela oðre here-reaf on þam fyrd-wicum,
and hi þancodon ða Gode eallre his godnysse.
Eft on ðam oþrum geare, geanlæhte Lisias
fif and sixtig þusende fyrdendra þegena
365 and wolde oferfeohtan þæt Iudeisce folc.
Iudas ða Machabeus micclum on God truwode
and ferde him togeanes mid þam folce þe he hæfde
(þæt wæron twelf þusend wigendra manna).
And Iudas hine gebæd þa and bletsode his scyppend:
370 "Gebletsod eart ðu, ælmihtig Israhela hælend,
þu ðe tobryttest iu þone breman here
on Dauides handum. Tobryt nu ðas hæðenan
on þines folces handum and mid fyrhte geegse.
Alege hi mid swurdum ðe lufigendra,
375 þæt ealle þe herian þe gehyrað þinne naman."
Hi slogon þa togædere unslawe mid wæpnum,
and þær feollon ða hæþenan fif ðusend ofslagene,
and Lisias fleah mid þære fyrd-lafe.
    Þa cwæð Iudas to his geferum þæt he ða fylðe wolde adon
380 of þam Godes temple þe se gramlica Antiochus
þær aræran het on hæðene wisan.

army, so that the heathens will recognize that there is no other god who can save Israel."

Machabeus then advanced with a small troop that consisted of three thousand who wished to follow him. Then they sounded their trumpets and fought bravely until the heathens fled to distant lands, and Judas drove them away like beasts to the woods. There were some three thousand killed there and, when he returned from the expedition, then Judas found gold and silver, fine cloth and purple cloth, and many other spoils within the camps, and they then thanked God for all his goodness. Again, in the next year, Lisias gathered sixty-five thousand military men and intended to conquer the Jewish people. Then Judas Machabeus trusted greatly in God and marched against him together with the people that he had (that was twelve thousand fighting men). And then Judas prayed to and praised his creator: "Blessed are you, almighty savior of Israel, you who destroyed the violent army long ago by the hands of David. Destroy these heathens now by the hands of your people and terrify them with fright. Overthrow them with the swords of those who love you, that all who hear your name may praise you." Then they struck at one another, those quick men with their weapons, and five thousand of the heathens fell slaughtered there, and Lisias fled with the remains of the army.

Then Judas told his companions that he intended to remove from God's temple the abominations that the cruel Antiochus had commanded be erected there in the heathen

355

360

365

370

375

380

And hi ferdon ða to and þa fylðe adydon ut
of ðam Godes huse and Godes lof aræerdon
æfter Moyses æ mid mycelre blysse,
385 and offrodon Gode lac mid geleafan and sange.
Iudas ða hine bewende and wan wið ða hæðenan,
forðan ðe hi woldon awestan þa Iudeiscan.
Ac Iudas hi oferfeaht and aflymde hi æfre,
and heora burga forbernde and hi to bysmore tawode.
390   Efne ða on sumum dæge, sende man to Iudan
ærend-gewritu fram Israhela ðeode,
and cyddon þæt þa hæþenan hæfdon hi besetene
and ofslagen hæfdon sum þusend manna.
Eac on oðre healfe him comon ærend-racan to
395 of Galileiscum lande, heora lifes orwene,
and cyddon þæt ða hæðenan him comon to gehwanon,
and woldon hi fordon and adilegian heora eard.
Iudas ða befran his geferan rædes,
and cwæð to Simone, his gescead-wisan breþer:
400 "Geceos ðe nu fultum and far to Galilea
and gehelp ðinum magum, ðe ða manfullan besittað.
Ic and Ionathas, min gingra broðor,
farað to Galaað to afligenne þa hæðenan."
He gesette ða heafod-menn to gehealdenne þæt folc
405 and bead þæt hi ne ferdon to nanum gefeohte
ongean ða hæðenan oðþæt he ham come.
Simon ða genam þreo ðusend mid him,
and Iudas and Ionathas eahta þusenda.
And Symon feaht gelome and aflymde ða hæðenan
410 and his magas ahredde wið heora reðnysse
and to lande gebrohte mid mycelre blisse.

fashion. And they went there then and removed the abominations from the house of God and offered up praise to God according to the law of Moses with great joy, and offered 385 their sacrifices to God with faith and song. Judas then turned around and fought against the heathen, because they intended to destroy the Jewish people. But Judas conquered them and put them to flight forever, and burned their towns and treated them with contempt.

Now on a certain day, written messages were sent to Ju- 390 das from the people of Israel, and they said that the heathens had besieged them and had killed a thousand men. Also, from the other side, messengers came to him from 395 Galilee, despairing of their lives, saying that the heathens had come against them on all sides, and that they intended to kill them and destroy their land. Judas then sought his companions' advice, and said to Simon, his prudent brother: "Choose a troop for yourself now and go to Galilee and help 400 your people, whom the wicked ones are attacking. Jonathan, my younger brother, and I will go to Galaad to expel the heathens." Then he appointed leaders to take charge of the people and ordered them not to enter into any battle 405 against the heathen until he came home. Simon then took three thousand men with him, and Judas and Jonathan took eight thousand. And Simon fought often and put the heathens to flight and rescued his people from their cruelty 410 and brought them back to the land with great rejoicing.

Iudas eac ferde ofer Iordanen ða ea,
geond þæt wid-gille wæsten, and gewylde ða hæðenan.
He com þa to anre byrig Bosor gehaten,
on ðære wæron ða hæðenan þe hyndon his magas.
Þa he ealle ofsloh mid swurdes ecge,
and ontende ða burh and tencgde him forð syððan.
Efne ðæs on mergen him com swa mycel mennisc to
þæt nan mann ne mihte ða meniu geriman,
and begunnon to feohtenne fæstlice mid cræfte,
and nyston þæt Machabeus mid þam mannum wæs.
Þa ða Iudas gehyrde þæra hæðenra gehlyd
and þæs feohtes hream, þa ferde he him hindan to
mid ðrym scyld-truman and sloh ða hæðenan
oðþæt hi oncneowon þæt se cena Iudas
him wiðfeohtende wæs, and wendon ða to horsum:
wiston þæt hi ne mihton Machabeo wiðstandan.
On þam gefeohte wurdon eahta ðusend wera
ofslagene þæs hæðenan folces, and ða oþre ætflugon.
Iudas ða ferde, feohtende wið þa hæðenan,
and heora burga forbærnde and hi bysmorlice ofsloh.
    Þa com Timotheus, sum cene here-toga,
mid ormætre fyrde and gesæt æt anum forda.
Ac Iudas him com to caflice mid wæpnum,
and oferferdon ðone ford and fuhton wið þa hæðenan,
swa swa his gewuna wæs, oðþæt hi wendon him fram
and heora wæpna awurpon and gewendon to anre byrig.
Ac Iudas hi forbærnde and þa burh samod.
He genam ða his magas of ðam manfullan,
mid wifum and mid cildrum, and gewendon him ham.
Þa wæs þær an mycel burh on heora wege middan,
and næs nanes mannes fær on naþre healfe þære byrig

Judas also traveled over the river Jordan, across the vast desert, and subdued the heathens.

Then he came to a city called Bosor, in which there were heathens who were oppressing his people. Then he killed them all with the edge of his sword, and he burned the city and hastened away afterward. First thing in the morning a crowd came against him, so great that no one could count the multitude, and they began to fight steadfastly and with skill, and they did not know that Machabeus was among the men. When Judas heard the clamor of the heathens and the noise of the battle, then he went behind them with three companies and was killing the heathens until they realized that Judas the brave was fighting against them, and then they turned to their horses: they knew that they could not withstand Machabeus. In that battle eight thousand men from the heathen tribes were killed, and the others fled. Judas then advanced, fighting against the heathen, and burned their cities and killed them all ignominiously.

Then Timothy, a brave leader, came with a huge army and took up quarters at a ford. But Judas came to him boldly with weapons, and they crossed the ford and fought against the heathen, as was his custom, until they turned away and threw away their weapons and retreated to a city. But Judas burned them and the city together. Then he took his people from among the wicked ones, with women and children, and they returned home. A great city was in the middle of their path there, with no passage for anybody on either side

buton ðurh þæt port, and hi bædon ða georne
þæt hi mid friðe moston faran þurh ða burh
445 þe hi forbugan ne mihton. Ac ða burh-ware noldon
þæs færes him getyðian, ac betyndon þa gata
mid micclum weorc-stanum and truwodon to þam wealle.
Þa ne mihte Iudas meteleas þær abidan,
ac het abrecan þone weall, þeah þe he brad wære.
450 Eodon ða ealle inn and ofslogon ealle ða hæðenan
and awestan ða burh, and wendon him hamwerd
oþþæt hi comon ansunde to lande,
and geoffrodon heora lac þam lifigendan Gode,
þancigende his gescyldnysse, þæt hi ealle gesunde
455 comon eft to heora earde of swa micelre frecednysse.
Ac heora geferan æt ham fuhton unwærlice
wið þa hæðenan leoda ofer Iudan leafe
þa hwile ðe he ute wæs, and wurdon ða ofslagene
wel fela manna ða ða hi fuhton buton wisdome.
460   Seo æftre boc us sægð þæt hi on sumne sæl fuhton,
þa wurdon hi sume beswicene mid gitsunge
swa þæt hi feoh naman and fracodlice behyddan
on heora bosmum of ðam deofollicum biggencgum
ongean Godes æ, and hi ealle ðær feollon,
465 þe þæt feoh behyddon, on ðam gefeohte ofslagene.
And heora geferan fundon þæt feoh on heora bosmum
and cwædon þæt God sylf geswutelode heora unriht,
and heredon Godes dom, þe heora digle geopenode.
Iudas gegaderode ða godne dæl feos
470 (þæt wæron twelf þusend scyllinga, eall hwites seolfres)
and sende to Hierusalem for heora synnum to offrigenne,
heora sawle to alysednysse þe ðær ofslagene wæron,
æwfæstlice understandende be ure ealre æriste.

of the city except through the fortified town, and so they earnestly entreated that they might travel in peace through the city they could not detour around. But the citizens re- 445 fused to grant them passage and secured the gates with huge blocks of stone and put their faith in the wall. Then Judas could not remain there without food, but ordered that the wall be broken down, though it was large. Then they all en- 450 tered the city and killed all the heathens and laid waste to the city, then turned homeward until they came safe to their land, and offered sacrifices to the living God, thanking him for his protection, that they had all returned to their land 455 unhurt out of such great danger. But their comrades at home had foolishly fought against the heathen tribes while he was away without Judas's permission, and very many men who had unwisely fought were killed.

The second book tells us that on one occasion when they 460 were fighting, some of them were seduced by greed and took money from among the diabolical heathen offerings and sinfully hid it in the folds of their tunics contrary to God's law, and all those who had hidden the money fell there, 465 slaughtered in the battle. And their companions found the money in the folds of their tunics and said that God himself had revealed their sin, and they praised the judgment of God, who had revealed their secret. Judas then gathered a good portion of the money (there were twelve thousand 470 shillings, all white silver) and sent it to Jerusalem as an offering for their sins, to redeem the souls of those who had been killed, piously understanding about the resurrection of us all.

Buton he gelyfde þæt hi æfter langum fyrste
475   of deaðe arisan sceoldon þe ðær ofslagene wæron,
elles he offrode on idel his lac.

Ac he soðlice besceawode þæt ða ðe mid soðre arfæstnysse
on deaþe geendiað þæt hi mid Drihtne habbað
þa selestan gife on þam soðan life.
480   Hit is halig geðoht and halwende to gebiddenne
for ðam forð-farendum þæt hi fram synnum beon alysede.

Hit sægð on þære æftran bec Machabeorum þus:
þæt Timotheus, ðe ær fleah æt ðam forda fram Iudan,
þæt he eft gegaderode oþerne here him to,
485   and wolde mid wæpnum gewyldan þa Iudeiscan,
and com ða mid fyrde to gefeohte gearu.

And Machabeus se cena clypode to Gode,
and his geferan eac, swa fultumes biddende.

Eodon þa of ðære byrig, gebylde þurh God,
490   and hi fengon togadere fæstlice mid wæpnum.

Hwæt ða færlice comon fif englas of heofonum
ridende on horsum mid gyldenum gerædum,
and twægen þære engla on twa healfe Iudan,
feohtende wæron and hine eac bewerodon.

495   And hi ealle fif fuhton mid Iudan,
sceotende heora flan and fyrene ligettas
on ða hæðenan leoda oðþæt hi licgende swulton,
twentig þusend manna and six hund ofslagene.

Timotheus þa fleah, mid fyrhte fornumen,
500   into anre byrig, and him æfter ferde
Iudas mid fultume, and fuhton wiðutan
oðþæt hi oferwunnon and gewyldon þa burh
and Timotheum acwealdon þær ðær he becropen wæs,
and his broðor samod, mid swurdes ecge.

Unless he believed that after a long period those who had 475
been killed there would rise from the dead, he made his offering in vain. But he truly perceived that those who die in
true piety will have the greatest gift in true life with the
Lord. It is a blessed intention and it is salutary to pray for 480
the dead to be redeemed from their sins.

In the second book of the Maccabees it says this: that
Timothy, who previously had fled from Judas at the ford,
again gathered a second army around himself, and intended 485
to subdue the Jewish people with weapons, and advanced
with the army eager to the fight. And Machabeus the brave,
and his companions also, called out to God, praying for help
in this way. Then they left the city, emboldened by God, and 490
they fought vigorously with weapons. Well then, suddenly
five angels descended from heaven riding on horses with
golden trappings, and two angels were on either side of Judas, fighting and also guarding him. And all five of them 495
fought along with Judas, shooting their arrows and fiery
lightning bolts into the heathen people until they lay dead,
with twenty thousand and six hundred people killed. Overcome with fear, Timothy then fled into a city, and Judas came 500
after him with a troop, and fought outside the walls until
they overcame them and seized the city and killed Timothy
with the edge of the sword where he had crept away to hide,

505 Æfter þysum dædum hi þancodon Drihtne
mid lof-sangum and andetnyssum eallra þæra mærða
þe he ðam Iudeiscum gedyde foroft
and him sige forgeaf, and siðedon ða ham.

Gif hwa nu wundrige hu hit gewurþan mihte
510 þæt englas sceoldon ridan on gerædedum horsum,
þonne wite he to soþan þæt us secgað gehwær
ða halgan Godes bec, þe ne magon beon lease,
þæt englas oft comon cuðlice to mannum
swilce on horse ridende, swa swa we her rehton.

515 Þa Iudeiscan wæron ða dyreste Gode
on ðære ealdan æ, forðan þe hi ana wurðodon
þone ælmihtigan God mid biggencgum symle
oþþæt Crist, Godes sunu, sylf wearð acenned
of menniscum gecynde of þam Iudeiscum cynne
520 of Marian þam mædene butan menniscum fæder.
Þa noldon hi sume gelyfan þæt he soð God wære
ac syrwdon embe his lif, swa swa he sylf geðafode.
Wæron swaþeah manega of þam mancynne gode
ge on ðære ealdan æ ge eac on þære niwan,
525 heah-fæderas and witegan and halige apostolas,
and fela ðusenda þe folgiað Criste,
þeah þe hi sume wunian wiðerwerde oþ þis.
Hi sceolon swaðeah ealle on ende gelyfan,
ac ðær losiað to fela on þam fyrste betwux
530 for heora heard-heortnysse wið þone heofonlican hælend.

Betwux þysum ferde se fore-sæda Antiochus
to Persiscre ðeode mid micclum þrymme:
wolde þær oferwinnan sume welige burh.
Ac he wearð þanon afliged and fracodlice ætbærst,
535 and mid micelre angsumnysse of þam earde gewende

and his brother with him. After these deeds, they thanked 505
the Lord with songs of praise and thanksgiving for all the
glorious things that he had achieved on many occasions for
the Jewish people and for giving them victory, and then they
traveled home.

If anyone now wonders how it could come to pass that 510
angels should ride on horses in trappings, then let that person know that truly God's holy books, which cannot be
false, report everywhere that angels often appeared clearly
to people as if riding on horses, as we have recorded here.
The Jewish people were the dearest to God under the old 515
law, for they alone always worshiped almighty God with
their rites until Christ himself, the Son of God, was born of
human nature among the Jewish people to the virgin Mary 520
without a human father. Then some of them refused to believe that he was the true God but conspired against his life,
as he himself permitted. Nevertheless, many of those people were virtuous both under the old law and also under the
new, patriarchs and prophets and holy apostles, and many 525
thousands who follow Christ, although some remain resis-
tant up to now. Nevertheless, they shall all believe in the
end, but too many will perish in the interval because of their 530
hard-heartedness toward the heavenly savior.

Meanwhile, Antiochus, of whom we spoke before, advanced upon the Persian people with a large military force:
he intended to conquer a wealthy city there. But he was
chased from there and shamefully escaped, and in great 535

.

to Babilonian werd, and him wearð þa gecydd
hu Iudas oferfeaht his fynd mid wæpnum,
and hu he geclænsod hæfde þæt halige Godes templ
fram eallum þam fylðum þe he fyrnlice þær arærde.

540 Wearð þa geangsumod and eac geuntrumod
forðam þe him God gram wæs, and he grimetode egeslice,
secgende and seðende þæt him swa gelumpen wæs
forðan ðe he Godes templ tawode to bysmore
and ða geleaffullan wolde of heora lande adylegian.

545 Him weollon þa wurmas of ðam gewitnodon lic-haman,
and he stanc swa fule þæt man hine ferian ne mihte,
and he ða yfele and earmlice geendode
on ælfremede earde, to þam ecum witum.
And his sunu Eupator æfter him rixode.

550 Se wearð eac ongebroht þæt he ofslean wolde
þa geleaffullan Iudei, þe gelyfdon ða on God.
Hi gelyfdon þa on þa ealdan wisan on þone ælmihtigan God,
þeah ðe hi sume wiðsocon siðþan þone hælend
and eac swa ofslogon, swa swa he sylf wolde.

555 Hwæt ða Eupator, Antioches sunu,
gegaderode his fyrde fyrran and nean
and sende hundteontig þusenda gangendra manna
and twentig þusenda gehorsedra manna
and þrittig ylpas, ealle getemode

560 and to wige gewenode mid wundorlicum cræfte.
Fif hund gehorsedra manna ferdon mid ælcum ylpe,
and on ælcum ylpe wæs an wig-hus getimbrod,
and on ælcum wig-huse wæron þrittig wera,
feohtende mid cræfte and mid gecneordnysse farende.

565 Sumum menn wile þincan syllic þis to gehyrenne
forþan þe ylpas ne comon næfre on Englalande.

316

distress turned from that land toward Babylon, and it was then revealed to him how Judas had conquered his enemies by force, and how he had cleansed the holy temple of God from all the abominations that he had established there previously. Then he became troubled and also sick because God was angry with him, and he roared terrifyingly, speaking and testifying that this had happened to him because he had treated God's temple contemptuously and had intended to expel the faithful from that country. Then worms surged out of his tormented body, and he stank so foully that no one could carry him, and he then died evilly and miserably in a foreign country, going to eternal torments. And his son Eupator reigned after him. He was also so inclined that he intended to kill the faithful Jewish people, who then believed in God. They then believed in the almighty God in the old fashion, though some of them later denied the savior and even killed him, as he himself intended.

Well then, Eupator, Antiochus's son, gathered his army from far and near and sent a hundred thousand marching men and twenty thousand cavalry and thirty elephants, all tamed and trained for war with marvelous skill. Five hundred horsemen traveled with each elephant, and on each of the elephants a war house had been built, and in each war house were thirty men, fighting with skill and traveling with zeal. To some people this will seem strange to hear because elephants have never come to England. An elephant is a

Ylp is ormæte nyten, mare þonne sum hus,
eall mid banum befangen binnan þam felle,
butan æt ðam nauelan, and he næfre ne lið.

570 Feower and twentig monða gæð seo modor mid folan,
and þreo hund geara hi libbað gif hi alefede ne beoð,
and hi man mæg wenian wundorlice to gefeohte.
Hwæl is ealre fixa mæst, and ylp is eallra nytena mæst,
ac swaþeah mannes gescead hi mæg gewyldan.

575 Þa hæðenan ða ferdon to ðam gefeohte swyðe
and mid morberium gebyldon þa ylpas,
forðan þe morberian him is mette leofost.
Þær wæs swyðe egeslic here þæra hæðenra manna,
ac swaðeah Iudas him eode to mid wige

580 and ofsloh þær sona six hund wera.
And an his geferena, Eleazarus hatte,
arn to anum ylpe þe ðær enlicost wæs:
wende þæt se cyning wære on ðam wig-huse ðe he bær.
He arn mid atogenum swurde betwux þam eorode middan

585 and sloh æfre on twa healfe þæt hi sweltende feollon
oðþæt he to þam ylpe com, and eode him on under.
Stang ða æt ðam nauelan þæt hi lagon ðær begen,
heora egðer oðres slaga, and Iudas siððan gewende
into Hierusalem mid ealre his fyrde,

590 and weredon hi cenlice wið þone onwinnendan here,
oðþæt se cynincg feng to friðe wið hi
be his witena ræde, ac he hit hraðe tobræc.
He cyrde ða hamwerd mid his here-lafe,
and hine ofsloh sona sum sigefæst þegen,

595 Demetrius gehaten, and hæfde his rice
on Antiochian byrig and þær abutan gehwær.

massive beast, bigger than a house, all encased in bones beneath the skin, except at the navel, and it never lies down. A 570 mother is with foal for twenty-four months, and they live three hundred years if they are not injured, and people can tame them amazingly for battle. The whale is the biggest of all the fish, and the elephant is the biggest of all animals, but nevertheless a person's reason can subdue them.

The heathens then advanced into battle quickly and en- 575 couraged the elephants with mulberries, because mulberries are their favorite food. It was a truly terrible army of heathen men there, but nevertheless Judas advanced against them in battle and immediately killed six hundred men 580 there. And one of his companions called Eleazar ran to the greatest elephant: he thought that the king was in the war house that it was carrying. He ran with a drawn sword through the middle of the troop and killed continuously on 585 both sides so that they fell dying until he came to the elephant, and then he ran beneath it. Then he pierced it at the navel so that they both lay there, each of them the other's killer, and Judas afterward returned to Jerusalem with all his army, and they defended themselves bravely against the at- 590 tacking army, until the king made peace with them at the advice of his counselors, but he soon broke it. Eupator then turned homeward with the remains of his army, and immediately a victorious official called Demetrius killed him and 595 took possession of his kingdom in the city of Antioch and everywhere around.

Hwæt þa Alchimus se arleasa sacerd
wrehte mid leasungum his leode to þam cyninge.
And se cyning Demetrius þam manfullan gelyfde
600 and geswencte ða Iudeiscan, oðþæt he sende him to
Nicanor his ealdor-man þæt he hi ealle fordyde.
Nicanor þa ferde mid fyrde to Hierusalem
and sende to Iudan mid swicdome and cwæð:
"Ne com ic for nanum gefeohte, ac for freondscipe to eow,"
605 and cyste ða Iudan, and his cempan wæron
gearwe to genimenne Iudan on bendum.
Iudas þa undergeat heora wæl-hreowan swicdom,
and wende him fram sona and nolde hine geseon.
Nicanor þa oncneow þæt his facn cuð wæs:
610 began ða to feohtenne færlice wið Iudan,
oðþæt þær feollon of his fyrde fif ðusend manna
and þa oðre ætflugon, afyrhte for Iudan.
Nicanor þa sceawode Salomones templ
and swor þurh his godas þæt he þæt Godes hus
615 wolde mid fyre forbærnan, butan him man betæhte
Iudan, gebundene, to bismorlicum deaðe.
Wende him swa awæg, wodlice geyrsod.
  Hwæt ða sacerdas ða mid swyðlicre heofunge
bædon þone ælmihtigan God þæt he his agen hus gescylde
620 wið þone arleasan and hine ardlice fordyde.
Nicanor þa eft genam oðre fyrde of Sirian:
wolde his gebeot mid weorcum gefremman.
And Iudas him com to mid þrim ðusend cempum
and gebæd hine to Gode gebigedum limum þus:
625 "Drihten, þu þe asendest þinne scinende engel
þa ða Syrian kynincg sende þurh his here-togan
on ærend-gewritum þe tallice word,

Well then, Alcimus the wicked priest accused his people before the king with falsehoods. And the king Demetrius believed the wicked priest and oppressed the Jewish people, 600 until he sent them his commander Nicanor to destroy them all completely. Nicanor then advanced with an army toward Jerusalem and sent a message to Judas full of deceit and said: "I am not coming to you for a fight, but for friendship," and 605 then he kissed Judas, and his soldiers were ready to take Judas in chains. Judas then realized their cruel deceit, and he turned away from them immediately and refused to see them. Nicanor then realized that his treachery was uncovered: then he began to fight suddenly against Judas, until 610 five thousand of his army fell there and the rest fled, terrified of Judas. Nicanor then saw Solomon's temple and swore by his gods that he would burn that house of God with fire, 615 unless someone delivered Judas to him, bound, for a shameful death. And so he turned away, enraged with fury.

Well then, the priests prayed to almighty God with great lamentation that he should protect his own house against 620 the impious leader and quickly destroy him. Nicanor then took a second army from Syria again: he intended to follow up his threat with actions. And Judas met him with three thousand soldiers and prayed to God upon bent knees in this way: "Lord, you who sent your shining angel when the 625 Syrian king sent abusive words to you in messages through

and se engel ofsloh þa on anre nihte of him
hundteontig þusenda and hundeahtatig þusenda,
630   tobryt nu, swa ic bidde, þisne breman here
ætforan urum gesihðum, þæt men magon geseon þine
mihte on him."

Hi fengon þa togædere fæstlice mid wæpnum
and Nicanor æt fruman feoll þær ofslagen,
and his here awearp heora wæpna and flugon,
635   ac Iudas him folgode fæstlice mid wæpnum
and bicnode gehwanon mid blawunge him fultum,
oðþæt hi man gynde ongean eft to Iudan,
and hi ealle ofslogon, þæt ðær an ne belaf.
Namon þa heora wæpna and heora gewæda mid him,
640   and Nicanores heafod and his swyðran hand,
and setton þa to tacne for his teon-rædene,
and þancodon þa Gode þearle mid wurð-mynte.

     Wunodon ða on sibbe sume hwile æfter ðam,
and Iudas þa sende mid sibbe to Rome
645   gecorene ærend-racan: wolde cuðlæcen wið hi,
forðan þe Romanisce witan wæron ða mihtige
and rædfæste on weorcum and oferwunnan heora fynd.
Hit wearð gecydd syððan þam cynincge Demetrio
þæt Nicanor feol and eall his folc mid him.
650   Þa wolde he git sendan and ofslean þa Iudeiscan,
and funde ða Bachidem, se wæs mid bealuwe afylled,
and Alchimum mid him, þone arleasan sacerd,
and sende hi mid gefylce to Iudeiscum folce.
Hi comon ða færlice mid gefeohte to Iudan,
655   and his geferan eargodon butan eahta hund mannum
þe him mid fuhton wið þone feondlican here.
Þa cwædon his geferan þæt hi fleon woldon

his leaders, and the angel killed one hundred and eighty thousand people in one night, destroy this fierce army now, 630 I pray you, before our eyes, that men might see your power over them." They then engaged together vigorously in battle and at the start Nicanor fell there killed, and his army threw down their weapons and fled, but Judas followed 635 them closely with weapons and summoned help from everywhere with blowing trumpets, until they were driven back again to Judas, and they killed them all, so that not one survived. Then they took their weapons and their clothes with them, and Nicanor's head and his right hand, and displayed 640 them as a symbol of the wrong he had done to them, and thanked God profusely with honor.

They lived in peace for some time after that, and Judas then sent chosen messengers to Rome in peace: he intended 645 to get to know them better, because the Roman senators were powerful then and prudent in works and conquered their enemies. Afterward, it was reported to the king Demetrius that Nicanor had fallen and all his people with him. Then he still wanted to send an army and kill the Jewish 650 people, and then he found Bacchides, who was filled with malice, and with him Alcimus, the impious priest, and he sent them with an army to the Jewish people. They advanced suddenly into battle against Judas, and his companions 655 turned coward except for eight hundred men who fought with him against the hostile army. Then his companions said

323

forðan þe heora werod wæs gewanod mid þam fleame,
and woldon him beorgan wið þone breman here.

660 Þa andwyrde Iudas, swa swa he eall cene wæs:
"Ne gewurðe hit na on life þæt we alecgan ure wuldor
mid earhlicum fleame, ac uton feohtan wið hi,
and gif God swa foresceawað, we sweltað on mihte
for urum gebroðrum, butan bysmorlicum fleame."

665 Hi comon þa togædere and begunnon to feohtenne
on twam gefylcum forð eallne ðone dæg,
and Iudas þa beseah to þære swyðran healfe
þæt þa wæron strængran, and stop ðyder sona
mid ðam an-rædystum mannum þe him mid fuhton,

670 and todrifon þone ende, ac him æfter eode
þæt oðer gefylce, mid gefeohte hindan.
And feollon ða on twa healfe on þam gefeohte manega,
and Iudas eac feoll, and þa oðre ætflugon.
Þa gelæhton his gebroðra his lic of ðam wæle

675 and bebyrigdon on Modin, to Mathathian his fæder,
and eall folc hine beweop on ða ealdan wisan.

    Ne synd swaþeah awritene, þæs ðe wyrd-writeras sæcgaþ,
ealle Iudan gefeoht for his freonda ware
and ealle ða mihte þe he mærlice gefremode

680 his folce to gebeorge, swa swa us bec secgað.
Menigfealde wæron his micclan gefeoht,
and he is eall swa halig on ðære ealdan gecyðnysse
swa swa Godes gecorenan on ðære god-spel-bodunge,
forðan þe he æfre wan for willan þæs Ælmihtigan.

685 On þam dagum wæs alyfed to alecgenne his fynd,
and swiþost ða hæðenan þe him hetole wæron,
and se wæs Godes ðegen þe ða swiðost feaht
wið heora onwinnendan to ware heora leode.

that they intended to flee because their troop was reduced
by the flight of the others, and they wished to protect themselves against that celebrated army. Then Judas answered, 660
totally brave as he was: "Let it never come to pass in our life-
times that we lay aside our glory with cowardly flight, but let
us fight against them, and if God so ordains, we shall die for
our brothers bravely, without shameful flight." Then they 665
came together and began to fight in two companies the
whole day through, and then Judas saw that they were stron-
ger to the right side, and immediately advanced there with
the most resolute of the men who fought with him, and they 670
drove that end of the army apart, but the other flank went
after him, bringing the battle from behind. And many from
the two sides fell in the battle there, and Judas also fell, and
the rest fled. Then his brothers brought his body from the
carnage and buried him in the city of Modin, with Mathath- 675
ias his father, and all the people mourned him in the old way.

Nevertheless, not all of Judas's battles for the defense of
his kin, as historians tell us, are recorded, nor all the mighty
deeds that he performed illustriously for the defense of his 680
people, as books tell us. His great battles were numerous,
and he is as holy in the old testament as God's chosen are in
the new dispensation, because he always fought for the sake
of the Almighty. In those days he was permitted to defeat 685
his enemies, and especially the heathen who were hostile toward him, and he was the servant of God who most often
fought against their attackers to defend their people. But at

Ac Crist on his tocyme us cydde oðre ðincg,
690   and het us healdan sibbe and soðfæstnysse æfre.
And we sceolon winnan wið þa wæl-hreowan fynd
þæt synd ða ungesewenlican and þa swicolan deofla
þe willað ofslean ure sawla mid leahtrum.
Wið ða we sceolon winnan mid gastlicum wæpnum
695   and biddan us gescyldnysse simle æt Criste,
þæt we moton oferwinnan þa wæl-hreowan leahtras
and þæs deofles tihtinge þæt he us derian ne mæge.
Þonne beoð we Godes cempan on ðam gastlican gefeohte,
gif we ðone deofol forseoþ þurh soðne geleafan
700   and þa heafod-leahtras þurh gehealtsumnysse,
and gif we Godes willan mid weorcum gefremmað.
Þæt ealde folc sceolde feohtan þa mid wæpnum,
and heora gewinn hæfde haligra manna getacnunge
þe todræfað þa leahtras and deofla him fram
705   on ðære niwan gecyðnysse, þe Crist sylf astealde.

    Secgað swaþeah lareowas þæt synd feower cynne gefeoht:
iustum, þæt is rihtlic; *iniustum,* unrihtlic;
civile, betwux ceastergewarum; *plusquam civile,* betwux
                                        siblingum.
Iustum bellum is rihtlic gefeoht wið ða reðan flot-menn
710   oþþe wið oðre þeoda þe eard willað fordon.
Unrihtlic gefeoht is þe of yrre cymð.
Þæt þridde gefeoht, þe of geflite cymð
betwux ceaster-gewarum, is swyðe pleolic.
And þæt feorðe gefeoht, þe betwux freondum bið,
715   is swiðe earmlic and endeleas sorh.

    Israhela folc þa an-modlice geceas
Ionathan his broþor, biddende þæt he wære
heora heafod and here-toga wið þa hæþenan þeoda.

326

his coming Christ revealed another way to us, and ordered 690
us to keep peace and truth forever. And we must fight
against the cruel enemies that are the invisible and the deceitful devils who desire to destroy our souls with vices. We
must fight against them with spiritual weapons and pray to 695
Christ continually for protection for ourselves, that we may
conquer the cruel vices and the devil's enticements so that
he cannot harm us. Then we will be God's soldiers in the
spiritual battle, if we despise the devil by means of true faith
and the cardinal sins by means of self-control, and if we ful- 700
fill God's will by our deeds. That ancient people had to fight
with weapons then, and their battle prefigured that of the
holy men who drive vices and the devil from them in the 705
new testament, which Christ himself established.

Yet teachers tell us that there are four kinds of war: *just,*
that is just; *unjust,* unjust; *civil,* between citizens; *more than
civil,* between relatives. *Just war* is just war against the fierce
seamen or against other peoples who intend to destroy our 710
land. Unjust war is that which derives from anger. The third
war, that arises from dispute between citizens, is very dan-
gerous. And the fourth war, which is between kinsmen, is 715
the cause of great misery and endless sorrow.

The people of Israel then unanimously chose Jonathan
his brother, asking him to be their chief and leader against

And he feng ða to ealdordome, swa swa hi ealle bædon,
720 and werode hi manega gear wið þone onwinnendan here,
and wiþ Bachidem feaht, þe his broþor ofsloh,
and þær sige gefor, and ofsloh þær an þusend.
Þa wolde Alchimus, se arleasa sacerd,
tobrecan Godes templ mid teonfullum graman,
725 ac hine sloh God sona mid swyðlicum paralisyn,
swa þæt he dumb wæs and to deaðe gebroht,
and mid mycclum tintregum his teonfullan gast
of ðam lic-haman forlet to langsumum witum.
Ionathas wunode on wurð-mynte ða lange,
730 and cynegas hine wurðodon mid wordum and gifum,
and he sige geferde on manegum gefeohtum,
and æfre wæs winnende embe Godes willan,
and eac his lif forlet for his leode ware.
    Symon þa syððan snoterlice geheold
735 þone Iudeiscan eard æfter Ionathan his breðer,
and on eallum his dagum ne derode him nan man,
ac wunodon æfre on sibbe on Symones dæge,
oþþæt he on ende eac wearð ofslagen,
swa swa his gebroðra, for soðfæstum biggencgum
740 and for heora leoda ware. Ac hi lybbað on ecnysse
mid þam heah-fæderum for heora hylde wið God.
Iohannes wæs geciged þæs Symones sunu,
se wæs æfter his fæder ðæs folces here-toga,
and hi hlysfullice geheold wið þa hæðenan ðeoda
745 on eallum his life and þæt land bewerode.
    We habbað forlæten, for þysre langsuman race,
an wundorlic ðincg, þe we willaþ secgan nu.
On ðam dagum þe Hierusalem and eall Iudea land
wunode on sibbe, þa wæs þær sum sacerd,

the heathen tribes. And he succeeded to power then, as they
had all requested, and for many years defended them against 720
the attacking army, and fought against Bacchides, who had
killed his brother, and seized victory there, and killed a
thousand men. Then Alcimus, the impious priest, intended
to destroy God's temple with spiteful anger, but God struck 725
him with severe paralysis immediately, so that he was mute
and eventually died, and with many torments he released his
spiteful soul from his body to enduring punishments. Jonathan lived in honor for a long time, and kings honored him 730
with words and gifts, and he obtained victory in many battles, and he was always laboring for God's will, and even gave
up his life for the defense of his people.

Afterward, Simon then wisely protected the Jewish land 735
after Jonathan his brother, and in all his days no one harmed
them, but in Simon's time they lived continually in peace,
until in the end he too was killed as his brothers had been,
for the defense of true worship and their people. But they 740
live in eternity with the patriarchs for their loyalty to God.
Simon's son was called John, who after his father was the
leader of the people, and he protected them against the heathen peoples gloriously throughout his life and defended 745
the land.

We have neglected a wondrous thing, on account of this
long story, that we wish to tell now. In the days when Jerusalem and all the land of Judea dwelt in peace, there was a
priest called Onias, a man of holy life. And the king Seleucus 750

750 Onias gehaten, haliges lifes mann.
And Seleucus cynincg sende fela laca
on golde and on seolfre to þam Godes temple
of Asian lande, þæs easternan rices,
and wide of middan-earde man wurðode þæt templ.

755 And Onias se ar-wurða wolde mid ðam lacum
widewan and steop-bearn bewerian wið hunger.
Þa ferde sum leogore and belæwde þæt feoh:
sæde þam ealdor-menn Appollonius geciged
þæt þæt feoh mihte becuman ðam cyninge to handa,

760 and se ealdor-mann sona hit sæde þam cyninge.
    Hwæt ða se cynincg sende sona ænne þegen,
Heliodorus gehaten, to ðam halgan temple
þæt he feccan sceolde þæt feoh mid reaflace.
He com þa mid werode and wolde þæt feoh habban,

765 and se sacerd Onias sæde þæt hit wære
widewena bigleofa and wan-hafolra manna,
of goddra manna ælmyssan ðam Ælmihtigan to lofe.
And þa sacerdas feollon ætforan þam weofode,
biddende þone ælmihtigan God þæt he gehulpe his
                                                    ðeowum.

770 Heliodorus ða gemynte þa maðmas to genimenne,
ac þær wearð gesewen swutol Godes wundor,
swa þæt his geferan feollon geunmihte
and mid fyrhte fornumene færlice þurh God.
And ðær com ridende sum egeful ridda,

775 and him mid siðedon twægen scinende englas
mid wundorlicre wlite, swa he sylf wæs geglenged.
And þæt heofonlice hors þe se heah-engel on sæt
wearp sona adune þone dyrstigan Heliodorum,
and þa twegen ænglas hine teartlice beoton,

sent many offerings in gold and in silver to God's temple from Asia, the eastern kingdom, and throughout the world people honored the temple. And the honorable Onias 755 wished to protect widows and orphans against hunger with the offerings. Then a liar came and disclosed the existence of that wealth: he suggested to the governor called Apollonius that that wealth should come into the hands of the king, and the governor immediately reported this to the 760 king.

Well then, the king immediately sent a nobleman called Heliodorus to the holy temple to fetch that wealth by theft. Then he came with a troop and intended to have the treasure, but the priest Onias said that it was the livelihood of 765 widows and destitute people, from the alms of good people given in praise to the Almighty. And the priests fell before the altar, praying to almighty God that he might help his servants. Heliodorus intended to take the treasures then, 770 but a visible miracle from God was seen there, so that his companions fell down deprived of their strength and were suddenly overcome with fear through the power of God. And a terrifying rider came riding there, and two shining an- 775 gels of wonderful beauty traveled with him, as he himself was adorned. And the heavenly horse that the archangel sat on threw down the presumptuous Heliodorus immediately, and, standing on either side of him, the two angels

780 on twa healfe him standende, oðþæt he stille læg,
orwene his lifes, se ðe ær mid gebeote
and mid micclum þrymme þrang into ðam temple.
He læg ða dumb, swa oð deaþ beswungen,
and his frynd bædon þa þone fore-sædan Onian
785 þæt he his life geðingode æt þam lifigendan Gode,
on þære frecednysse þe he on befeallen wæs.
Onias þa eode and offrode him lac
fore þam ælmihtigan Gode on þa ealdan wisan,
and bæd þæt he miltsode þæs mannes nytennysse.
790 And þa englas þa hwile Heliodorum gespræcon:
sædon þæt he sceolde þam sacerde Onian
micclum þancian þæt he moste lybban,
and heton hine cyðan on his cyððe æt ham
Godes wundor on him, and wendon þa him fram.
795   Heliodorus þa geedcucode and geoffrode his lac
þam ælmihtigan Gode mid incundre heortan
þæt he cucu beon moste, and þancode Onian,
and þanon ferde swa mid ealre his fyrde,
and þæs Ælmihtigan mihte his hlaforde cydde and his
                                        leodum eallum,
800 swa swa he sylf geseah, and hu he beswungen wæs.
Eft ða se cynincg axode Heliodorum and cwæð:
"Hwæne mage we sendan to þam fore-sædan feo?"
Þa cwæð Heliodorus: "Gif ðu hæfst ænigne feond, send
                                        þone to þam feo,
and he bið wel beswungen, oððe gewisslice dead,
805 forðan ðe se ælmihtiga God mundað þa stowe
and þa slihð and gescynt þe þær sceaðian willað."
Oft is geswutelod hu God gescylde þæt folc
wið heora wiþer-sacan gif hi wurðodon hine.

beat him severely, until he who had previously stormed into   780
the temple with threats and great pomp lay still, despairing
of his life. He lay there silent, as if beaten to death, and his
friends then asked Onias of whom we spoke before to inter-   785
cede with the living God for his life, because of the danger
into which he had fallen. Onias then went and offered a sacrifice on his behalf in the sight of almighty God in the old
fashion, and prayed that he might have mercy on the man's
ignorance. And meanwhile the angels spoke to Heliodorus: 790
they told him that he should give great thanks to the priest
Onias that he was allowed to live, and ordered him to tell of
God's miracle upon him in his native land, and then they left
him.

Heliodorus then revived and offered his sacrifice to al-   795
mighty God with his inner heart because he had been allowed to live, and thanked Onias, and so departed from
there with all his army, and told his lord and all his people of
the power of the Almighty, as he himself had seen, and how   800
he had been beaten. Afterward the king questioned Heliodorus and said: "Who can we send for the wealth about
which we spoke before?" Then Heliodorus said: "If you have
any enemy, send him for the wealth, and he will be well
beaten, if not certainly dead, because almighty God pro-   805
tects that place and strikes and puts to shame those who intend to do it harm." It is often revealed how God protected
that people against their enemies if they worshiped him.

And swa oft swa hi gebugon fram his biggengcum ahwar,
810 þonne wurdon hi gescynde and swyðe gewitnode.
Sy wuldor and lof þam wel-willendan Gode,
a on ecnysse, we cwæþað. Amen.

De tribus ordinibus saeculi

Is swaðeah to witenne þæt on þysre worulde
synd þreo ende-byrdnysse, on annysse gesette.
815 Þæt synd *laboratores, oratores, bellatores.*
Laboratores synd þa þe urne bigleafan beswincað,
oratores synd þa ðe us to Gode geðingiað,
bellatores synd þa ðe ure burga healdað
and urne eard beweriað wið onwinnendne here.
820 Nu swincð se yrðlincg embe urne bigleofan,
and se woruld-cempa sceall winnan wið ure fynd,
and se Godes þeowa sceall symle for us gebiddan
and feohtan gastlice wið þa ungesewenlican fynd.
    Is nu forþy mare þæra muneca gewinn
825 wið þa ungesewenlican deofla þe syrwiað embe us
þonne sy þæra woruld-manna þe winnað wiþ ða flæsclican
and wið þa gesewenlican gesewenlice feohtað.
Nu ne sceolon þa woruld-cempan to þam woruldlicum
                                                gefeohte
þa Godes þeowan neadian fram þam gastlican gewinne,
830 forðan þe him fremað swiðor þæt þa ungesewenlican fynd
beon oferswyðde þonne ða gesewenlican,
and hit bið swyðe derigendlic þæt hi Drihtnes þeowdom
                                                forlætan
and to woruld-gewinne bugan, þe him naht to ne gebyriað.

334

And as often as they turned from worship of him in any way, then they were shamed and severely punished. May there be 810 praise and glory to the benevolent God, forever and ever, we say. Amen.

On the Three Orders of Society

Nevertheless let it be known that in this world there are three orders, established together. They are *workers, those* 815 *that pray,* and *warriors. Workers* are those who labor for our food; *those that pray* are those who intercede with God for us; *warriors* are those who protect our towns and defend our land against an attacking army. Now the plowman works to 820 produce our food, and the worldly warrior must fight against our enemies, and the servant of God must pray for us always and fight spiritually against invisible enemies.

The fight of the monks against the invisible devils who 825 lay traps around us is greater now, therefore, than that of the men of the world who fight against human enemies and fight visibly against the visible. Now worldly soldiers should not force the servants of God away from the spiritual battle to the worldly battle, because it will serve them better that 830 invisible enemies are overcome rather than the visible, and it would be very harmful for them to neglect their service of the Lord and to turn to the worldly fight, which in no way

Iulianus, se wiðer-saca and se wæl-hreowa casere,

835 wolde neadian preostas to woruldlicum gecampe,

and eac þa halgan munecas, and het hi on cweart-erne
gebringan.

Þa wearð Appollonius, se Egiptisca abbod,

on þam cweart-erne belocen mid his geleaffullum
gebroðrum,

ac Godes engel him com to to þam cweart-erne nihtes,

840 mid heofonlicum leohte, and unlæc þæt cweart-ern.

Eac, se hundredes ealdor þe hi þærinne beleac

com on ærne-mergen mid mycclum þrymme,

and sæde þæt his hus feolle færlice mid eorð-styrunge

swa þæt his leofestan menn þær lagon ofhrorene,

845 and he bæd þa halgan þa þæt hi þanon ferdon.

And hi ða mid lof-sangum siþedon eft to þam westene.

    Godes þeowas sceolon unscæððignysse healdan,

swa swa Crist astealde þurh hine sylfne þa bysne

þa þa he het Petrum behydan his swurd

850 and gehælde þurh his mihte þæs mannes eare,

þe Petrus of asloh, and geswutelode his godnysse.

Nu se munuc þe bihð to Benedictes regole

and forlæt ealle woruld-ðingc, hwi wile he eft gecyrran

to woruldlicum wæpnum and awurpan his gewinn

855 wið þa ungesewenlican fynd his scyppende to teonan?

Se Godes þeowa ne mæg mid woruld-mannum feohtan

gif he on þam gastlican gefeohte forð-gang habban sceall.

Næs nan halig Godes þeowa æfter þæs hælendes þrowunga

þe æfre on gefeohte his handa wolde afylan.

860 Ac hi forbæron ehtnysse arleasra cwellera

and heora lif sealdon mid unscæþþignysse

for Godes geleafan, and hi mid Gode nu lybbað,

forðan þe hi furþon noldon ænne fugel acwellan.

concerns them. Julian, the apostate and the cruel emperor, intended to force priests, and even holy monks, into worldly 835 conflict and ordered them to be put into prison. Then Apollonius, the Egyptian abbot, was locked in a prison with his faithful brothers, but an angel of God came to him in the prison during the night, surrounded by heavenly light, and 840 unlocked the prison. Also, the centurion who had locked them in came early in the morning with a great force, and said that his house had fallen suddenly in an earthquake so that those dearest to him lay buried, and he begged the holy 845 men to depart from that place. And they traveled back to the desert singing hymns.

The servants of God must preserve their innocence, as Christ himself established through his own example when he ordered Peter to sheathe his sword and through his 850 power healed the man's ear, which Peter had cut off, and thus revealed his goodness. Now the monk who submits to the rule of Benedict and abandons all worldly things, why would he return to worldly weapons and abandon his struggle against the invisible enemies to anger his creator? The 855 servant of God cannot fight with men of the world if he is to have any success in the spiritual fight. There has been no holy servant of God since the savior's passion who would ever wish to defile his hands in battle. But they bore the per- 860 secution of their impious executioners and gave their lives with innocence for their faith in God, and they now live with God, because they refused to kill even a bird.

Abbreviations

AS = J. Bollandus et al., ed., *Acta Sanctorum,* 68 vols. (1643–1940): Ian.–
Oct, 60 vols. (repr., Brussels, 1965–1970); Auctaria Oct. (Paris, 1875);
Propylaeum ad Nov. (Brussels, 1902); Nov. vol. 1 (Paris, 1887); Nov. vol.
2, pt. 1 (Brussels, 1894); Nov. vol. 2, pt. 2 (Brussels, 1931); Nov. vol. 3
(Brussels, 1910); Nov. vol. 4 (Brussels, 1925); and Propylaeum ad Dec.
(Brussels, 1940)

Belfour = A. O. Belfour, ed., *Twelfth-Century Homilies in MS Bodley 343.
Part I, Text and Translation,* EETS os. 137 (London, 1909)

BHL = *Bibliotheca Hagiographica Latina,* 2 vols., Subsidia hagiographica 6 (Brussels, 1898–1901); *Supplementi editio altera,* Subsidia hagiographica 12 (Brussels, 1911); *Novum supplementum,* Subsidia hagiographica 70 (Brussels, 1986)

BL = London, British Library

BT = J. Bosworth and T. N. Toller, *An Anglo-Saxon Dictionary* (London, 1898); T. N. Toller, *Supplement* (Oxford, 1921); with *Revised and Enlarged Addenda* by A. Campbell (Oxford, 1972); the digital Bosworth Toller online, http://bosworth.ff.cuni.cz/

CCCC = Cambridge, Corpus Christi College

CH I = Peter Clemoes, ed., *Ælfric's Catholic Homilies: The First Series,*
EETS ss. 17 (Oxford, 1997)

CH II = Malcolm Godden, ed., *Ælfric's Catholic Homilies: The Second
Series,* EETS ss. 5 (Oxford, 1979)

CH III = Malcolm Godden, ed., *Ælfric's Catholic Homilies: Introduction, Commentary and Glossary,* EETS ss. 18 (Oxford, 2000)

CSEL = Corpus Scriptorum Ecclesiasticorum Latinorum

CUL = Cambridge University Library

DOE = *The Dictionary of Old English: A to H,* http://tapor.library.utoronto.ca.ucd.idm.oclc.org/doe/

EETS = Early English Text Society: os. = Original series; ss. = supplementary series

Fontes = *Fontes Anglo-Saxonici,* http://fontes.english.ox.ac.uk/

HE = Bede's *Historia Ecclesiastica gentis Anglorum,* in *Bede's Ecclesiastical History of the English People,* ed. Bertram Colgrave and R. A. B. Mynors (Oxford, 1969)

Irvine = Susan Irvine, ed., *Old English Homilies from MS. Bodley 343,* EETS os. 302 (London, 1993)

Jackson and Lapidge = Peter Jackson and Michael Lapidge, "The Contents of the Cotton-Corpus Legendary," in *Holy Men and Holy Women: Old English Prose Saints' Lives and Their Contexts,* ed. Paul E. Szarmach (Albany, 1996), 131–46

Ker = *Ker, N. R. Catalogue of Manuscripts Containing Anglo-Saxon* (Oxford, 1957)

LS = Ælfric's *Lives of Saints*

Moloney = Bernadette Moloney, ed., "A Critical Edition of Ælfric's Virgin-Martyr Stories" (PhD diss. University of Exeter, 1980)

Mombritius = B. Mombritius, ed., *Sanctuarium seu Vitae sanctorum,* 2 vols. (Paris, 1910; repr., Hildesheim and New York, 1978)

OED = Oxford English Dictionary, http://www.oed.com.ucd.idm.oclc.org/

PL = J.-P. Migne, ed., *Patrologia Latina,* 221 vols. (Paris, 1844–1864)

Pope = John C. Pope, ed., *Homilies of Ælfric: A Supplementary Collection,* 2 vols., EETS os. 259, 260 (London, 1967–1968)

Skeat = W. W. Skeat, ed., *Ælfric's Lives of Saints,* EETS os. 76, 82, 94, 114, reprinted in 2 vols. (London, 1966)

Wanley = Humfrey Wanley, *Librorum Veterum Septentrionalium,* in vol. 2 of George Hickes, *Linguarum Septentrionalium Thesaurus* (Oxford, 1705)

Zettel = Patrick H. Zettel, "Ælfric's Hagiographic Sources and the Latin Legendary Preserved in B.L. MS Cotton Nero E.i + CCC MS 9 and Other Manuscripts" (D.Phil. diss., Oxford University, 1979)

Note on the Text

LIVES OF SAINTS MANUSCRIPTS

The sigla in this list are those commonly used for Ælfric studies; it should be noted, however, that they were devised for his *Catholic Homilies,* and the order of sigla is relevant for those texts, not for the *Lives of Saints.* We have adopted the sigla in Aaron Kleist's forthcoming *The Chronology and Canon of Ælfric of Eynsham* for the last two manuscripts in the list.

B = Oxford, Bodleian Library, Bodley 343 (second half of the 12th century)

C = Cambridge, Corpus Christi College 303 (first half of the 12th century)

E = Cambridge, Corpus Christi College 198 (LS items from the first half of the 11th century)

F = Cambridge, Corpus Christi College 162, Part I, pp. 1–138 and 161–564 (beginning of the 11th century)

G = London, British Library, Cotton Vespasian D. xiv (middle of the 12th century)

J = London, Lambeth Palace Library 489 (third quarter of the 11th century)

K = Cambridge, University Library Gg.3.28 (end of the 10th or beginning of the 11th century)

L = Cambridge, University Library Ii.1.33 (second half of the 12th century)

M = Cambridge, University Library Ii.4.6 (middle of the 11th century)

N = London, British Library, Cotton Faustina A. ix (first half of the 12th century)

O = Cambridge, Corpus Christi College 302 (end of the 11th or beginning of the 12th century)

P = Oxford, Bodleian Library, Hatton 115 (LS items from the second half of the 11th century)

R = Cambridge, Corpus Christi College 178, Part I, pp. 1–270 (first half of the 11th century)

S = Oxford, Bodleian Library, Hatton 116 (first half of the 12th century)

T = Oxford, Bodleian Library, Hatton 114 and Oxford, Bodleian Library, Junius 121 (third quarter of the 11th century)

V = Cambridge, Corpus Christi College 419 (first half of the 11th century)

W = London, British Library, Cotton Julius E. vii (beginning of the 11th century)

f^a = Cambridge, Corpus Christi College 367 (LS item from the middle of the 12th century)

f^c = Cambridge, Queens' College, Horne 75 and Bloomington, Indiana University, Lilly Library, Poole 10 (beginning of the 11th century)

f^d = Gloucester, Cathedral Library 35 (LS item from the first half of the 11th century)

f^i = London, British Library, Cotton Otho B. x and Oxford, Bodleian Library, Rawlinson Q.e.20 (first half of the 11th century)

f^k = London, British Library, Cotton Vitellius D. xvii, fols. 4–92 (formerly fols. 23–234) (middle of the 11th century)

X[i] = London, Lambeth Palace 487 (end of the 12th or beginning of the 13th century)

Y12 = London, British Library, Cotton Caligula A. xiv, fols. 93–130 (middle of the 11th century)

Y20 = London, British Library, Royal 8 C. vii, fols. 1–2 (beginning of the 11th century)

Ælfric's *Lives of Saints* is found as a series in only one manuscript, London, British Library, Cotton Julius E. vii (W), written at the beginning of the eleventh century in a scriptorium that was certainly not Ælfric's. It is the base text for our edition. It was at Bury Saint Edmund's by the thirteenth century and may have come there at the time of or shortly after the refoundation of Bury as a Benedictine house ca. 1020.[1]

Although written in southern England within a decade of Ælfric's composition of the texts, the spelling system of the scribe who copied all of the Ælfric texts in W is quite different from what we know to have been Ælfric's. As Mechthild Gretsch says, "We may assume that the saints' *uitae* left Ælfric's scriptorium in a linguistic form very close to the *Catholic Homilies*."[2] However, the texts must have been considerably altered by transmission before and/or when W was copied. The W scribe, to quote Gretsch again, "clearly had not been trained by someone thoroughly imbued with Ælfric's ideas of writing correct English" and "is noted for quite a number of orthographic peculiarities."[3] Some of the scribe's spellings are typical of late Old English, while others may be his own rather idiosyncratic practice.[4] The scribe's practice changes to some extent over the course of the manuscript; for example, the distinction between *þone* and *þonne* becomes much more consistently observed. Some features are more typical of the early texts in W, which suggests that he corrected the manuscript as he worked on it.[5] The principal scribe corrected the text by comparison with the exemplar, signaling superscript insertions, usually of missing letters, with a comma-like caret (referred to as a comma in the Notes to the Text). He also occasionally used a *punctum* under erroneous letters and corrected them superscript; we have reserved the word *punctum* for instances where we think the original scribe was responsible.

Another corrector, a little later, then went over the manuscript and made many more corrections, as well as some independent insertions.[6] The thirteen Ælfric texts on which he worked are, according to the numbering of this edition, LS 2, 10, 11, 12, 15, 17, 18, 19, 20, 21, 23, 24, and 29. He also corrected two anonymous texts not included in this volume. Four of the fifteen are the Lives of English saints (*Æthelthryth, Swithun, Oswald,* and *Edmund*), one British (*Alban*), and five from elsewhere (*Eugenia, Forty Soldiers, Apollinaris,* and the anonymous texts the *Seven Sleepers* and *Eustace*). Four are sermons (*Shrove Sunday, Prayer of Moses, Memory of Saints,* and *Kings*), and *Maccabees* is a combination of saint's Life and sermon. We do not know exactly when this corrector worked, but N. R. Ker dates his hand to the middle of the first half of the eleventh century.[7] G. I. Needham suggested, on the basis of the corrections to the *Life of Edmund* (LS 29), line 2.244, that he might have worked at Bury St. Edmunds.[8] The points corrector usually put a point under letters he wished to change and put his correction superscript. He generally signaled longer corrections (a word or more) by two points, often arranged like a colon, and also used them to signal his insertions. When the double points signal a longer insertion, the superscript insertion is often also preceded by double points. He occasionally also erased what the W scribe wrote and then wrote over the erasure.

The points corrector's numerous corrections show that he was much more fastidious about inflectional endings than the W scribe and altered many of them. As Needham, Michael Lapidge, and Michèle Bussières all point out, he does not seem to have worked from an exemplar, but was correcting according to what seemed right to him, and he also made additions, often quite pedantic.[9] Many of his corrections are in accordance with what we think of as correct OE grammar in the treatment of vowels in inflectional endings. He also systematically distinguished between the dative singular and plural of *he* in a way that Ælfric himself did not, by correcting the dative plural *him* to *heom,* reserving *him* for dative singular.[10] The points corrector has his own linguistic peculiarities. For example, he frequently inserted an *e* in forms like *ecan,* to give *ecean,* and on occasion attempted to rectify deficiencies in the text in front of him. At other times he made insertions with lexical alternatives (e.g., *sceande* for *hætse* in LS 17, line 350). As Needham has pointed out, the points corrector was particularly interested in doxologies, or the lack of them, and he made alterations to the conclusions of six out of the fifteen homilies that he corrected.[11] Bussières has tabulated all of the corrections and insertions in the manuscript, distinguishing those of the W scribe, the points corrector, and those that cannot be attributed on the basis of script or points;[12] those corrections involving inflectional endings are, however, more numerous in the texts on which the points corrector was active, suggesting that he was primarily responsible for them. Bussières's work is an excellent guide to the activities of the points corrector, and to all of the corrections in the manuscript, and we are much indebted to it.

In addition to these two correcting hands, there is a very large number of corrections by erasure in the manuscript. Erasures by their nature are not attributable, but there are some indications that both correctors used erasure, although it is impossible to be certain. These corrections are found in the majority of texts, almost to the end of the manuscript, but they become much less frequent.

W, therefore, is a complex manuscript because of the two layers of correction, with erasures making it impossible to recover all of the original readings, and it presents editorial challenges. But it is not the only manuscript for most of the texts that it contains. Many of the individual texts in W, or parts of them, are also found elsewhere. Altogether, twenty-six manuscripts (counting T as two) preserve parts of the series, though some of these are binding fragments containing only parts of texts. These manuscripts range in date from the beginning of the eleventh century to the second half of the twelfth. The two manuscripts other than W that had the biggest selection of texts from the LS were both victims of the Cotton Library fire of 1731, f^i and f^k; they are now in a fragmentary state, with some texts in both entirely destroyed. Fortunately, both were catalogued by Humfrey Wanley before the fire, and he recorded the titles and opening lines of all the texts in both manuscripts, but for some texts that is all that we now have. Because the individual texts in LS have such different transmission histories, they present very different editorial challenges, depending on how and where they have been transmitted. The simplest to edit are texts now extant only in W, such as LS 6 or LS 10. Others have a more complicated transmission: LS 12, for example, is now extant in W, C, F, M, and O, and in addition to the complete text in M, was also excerpted for another text in M.

The only other edition of the series as a whole is that of W. W. Skeat, who published it in parts from 1881 to 1900; facing translations were provided partly by him but largely by two assistants, Catherine Gunning and J. E. Wilkinson.[13] Skeat's text is in general accurate; some minor transcription errors have been silently corrected in this edition. The basis on which he edited the series has, however, been much criticized in recent years, which makes a new edition all the more necessary.[14] There have been other editions of individual Lives or small groups, including Needham's *Three English Saints,* Lapidge's edition of the *Life of Swithun,* Gabriella Corona's of the *Life of Basil*, Robert Upchurch's of the Lives of the virgin spouses, as well as editions in PhD dissertations, such as that of Moloney. These are noted in the Notes to the Text.

Editorial Procedures

As the only complete manuscript, W is the obvious choice of base manuscript, but we have collated all known manuscripts for each text in the series. Our aim has been to present the texts in what we hope is as close to Ælfric's wording as possible. We have not, however, attempted to restore Ælfric's orthography. Lapidge's edition of the *Life of Swithun* and Corona's of the *Life of Basil* normalize the W text by systematically correcting the W scribe's spelling according to Ælfric's usual practice, without signaling each instance of departure from W. This produces a much more normal-looking text (similar to the *Catholic Homilies*) but does not correspond to any medieval manuscript, and the apparatus in their editions does not allow one to work out the original manuscript readings. We have been more cautious and have preserved the W scribe's orthography, unusual though it may be. Punctuation is modern and abbreviations have been silently expanded. The numbering of the texts is editorial, and, as we not have included the four anonymous Lives, differs from that of Skeat's edition.

Where texts survive in other manuscripts, we can see that the W scribe made errors, usually minor ones that we cannot detect without these other manuscripts. Where W is obviously in error, we have corrected it from other witnesses, or occasionally without manuscript authority where the error appears clear to us. Very occasionally, even where we suspect or know that the points corrector erased and corrected, we have had to keep the correction in the edited text because what is erased is not recoverable. Where the points corrector interfered with the text on a larger scale, we have attempted to undo his work with the help of other manuscripts.

Departures from W's reading and the principal scribe's corrections are given in the Notes to the Text, but the notes do not record every correction or erasure. Among the features not recorded are the numerous corrections, especially in the first five texts, made by erasure of part of *æ* to yield *e;* letters written over erasures; the frequent corrections, especially in the first five texts, of *seo* and *heo* forms to *se* and *he* (although any editorial correction of such forms is noted); the points corrector's alterations of individual words, except on those rare occasions when they supply a missing word or correct an obvious error. His larger additions have, however, been included in the Notes to the Text, as have erasures of more than roughly four letters.

When collating the other manuscripts, we have not included variations in spelling or minor scribal errors, or the presence or absence of the *ge-* prefix. *Selþe* and *seo/þeo* variations in B and in L are not included in the notes. Where the manuscripts have conflicting readings, we have taken each case on its merits and have accepted some readings from another manuscript or manuscripts that we think are superior (where they are supported by the source, where they make better sense, where they improve the alliterative pattern, or where they agree better with Ælfric's normal usage).

The names of people and places that are familiar to a general audience have been modernized in the translations and accompanying notes; those that are less familiar have been left in their original form. The Dumbarton Oaks Medieval Library's Vulgate supplies the translations of Ælfric's Latin Vulgate quotations as well as other quotations from the Bible. Classical Latin orthography has been silently adopted in the titles of the texts.

Following series practice, hyphens have been added to compound nouns and adjectives and their derivatives, and also to some other words (excluding personal names) where the meaning of the separate constituents is particularly transparent.

Notes

1 See Lapidge, *Cult of St Swithun*, 581.
2 "In Search of Standard Old English," 42.
3 "In Search of Standard Old English," 45. These peculiarities include

much vowel confusion and much leveling of inflectional endings. The scribe frequently does not preserve the distinction between -*a* and -*e* endings in nouns of various types. There are sporadic -*as* for -*es* endings, and vice versa. See Needham, "Additions and Alterations," 163; Gretsch, "In Search of Standard Old English," 49.

4 Gretsch, "In Search of Standard Old English," 49.

5 Michèle Bussières points out that the number of *æ* for *e* spellings, very common at the beginning of the manuscript, decreases dramatically after the first five texts, but they never disappear ("The Controversy about Scribe C in British Library, Cotton MS Julius E. vii," *Leeds Studies in English* n.s. 38 [2007]: 67). Many of these instances were corrected in the manuscript by erasure. At the beginning of the manuscript, in the first three texts, the scribe confuses masculine and feminine definite articles and pronouns rather frequently, in an odd series of errors. These errors virtually disappear after the first three texts. It is hard to explain how a scribe would make a whole series of such fundamental errors. See Bussières, "Étude," 181.

6 We call this corrector the points corrector; G. I. Needham calls him the point corrector, Michael Lapidge calls him W[1] or the "dotting hand," and Bussières calls him D.

7 Ker, 207.

8 Needham, "Additions and Alterations," 160.

9 Needham, *Three English Saints,* 112; Lapidge, *Cult of St Swithun,* 584; and Bussières, "Etude," 178.

10 On this, see Donald G. Scragg, "Ælfric's Scribes," *Leeds Studies in English* 37 (2006): 179–90, at 182.

11 "Additions and Alterations," 162n3.

12 "Étude," 365–87.

13 As he explains, Skeat, vol. 2, liv–lv.

14 See Alexander, "W. W. Skeat and Ælfric"; and Schipper, "W. W. Skeat's Edition of Ælfric's *Lives of Saints,*" 229–36.

Notes to the Text

Manuscripts: Five manuscripts contain this text in its entirety, W, C, F, M, and O. The W text is on fols. 63v–67v, and the points corrector worked on it. C's text is on pp. 327–33, F's on pp. 194–206, and O's on pp. 104–12. M, fols. 47r–55v, has the full text, and there are also extracts from this text in the composite homily, *Feria IIIa in letania maiore,* on fols. 228r–38r. Readings from these extracts are designated Ma in the notes. This composite homily is discussed in detail in Malcolm R. Godden, "Old English Composite Homilies from Winchester," *Anglo-Saxon England* 4 (1975): 57–65, and is edited as homily 7 in *Eleven Old English Rogationtide Homilies,* ed. Joyce Bazire and James E. Cross, Toronto Old English Series 7 (Toronto, 1982), 90–100. It is likely that N also once contained this text, as Ker, 190, suggests. In parts of this text, Ælfric recycles material that he had already written. Prior forms of section 2.8–11 are not included in these notes.

Previously edited and translated by Skeat, vol. 1, 261–83, and edited by Leinbaugh, "The Liturgical Homilies in Ælfric's Lives of Saints."

title   Þis spel gebyrað seofon niht ær lenctene: *W only*   IN CAPUT IEIUNII: Dominica in quinquagesima *C*; Alia narratio doctrina populi *F*; Feria .IIII. in capite ieiunii *M*; Larspel. In capite ieiunii *O*   IEIUNII: *corrected from* ieiunium *by erasure W*

1.2   lenctenes: lencten *F*

1.6   dæð: a *of* æ *subpuncted W*

1.12   þær foran to: þær beforan to *M*; þar to foran *O*

1.14   eow nu secgan: nu eow secgeon *C*

1.17   lecgað: lecgan *O*

1.18   uppan: *C F M O*; uppa *W*   þæt: to þi þæt *M O*

1.22   leofast: -e- *on erasure and* -o- *superscript with two vertical points be-*
       neath W   þu: þu ær *F*

2.2   þa swa: swa þa *O*   his sceaft: se sceft *C*   þæs ðe he: þæs he *O*

2.3   lenctenes: lengtenlices *F*   began to: began him to *C*   ear-
       foðlice: -r- *superscript with comma beneath W*   þæt feorh ear-
       foðlice: earðfoðlice þæt feorh *C*; þæt feorh swiðe earfoðlice
       F   hine lyste: him lyste *C*   he nolde: and he nolde *O*   eode
       him: him eode *C*   fearr: *with* ea *over erasure and* rr *added*
       in margin, all by points corrector W   drenc: n *with comma be-*
       neath W

2.4   se ne: and se ne *F*   þe: *omitted F*   þe he: *omitted C*   oþþe un-
       trum: untruma *C*   oððe his feoh: oðð his feoh *W*   life him:
       life *F*   deaðes: deað *C M O*   and sare: *omitted F*   ealra ge-
       swencednyssa: eallum geswæncednessum *C*; eallre geswenced-
       nyssa, *with* -r- *of* eallre *superscript F*; eallum geswencednyssum
       M O   gesceop: geworhte *C*   God: an god *M*

2.5   mycelne scet and ungerim feos syllan: *W C*; mycelne scet syllan
       and ungerim feos *F*; micelne scet syllan *M O*   her: *omitted C*
       for worulde: on worulde *F O*   gelumpon: gelumpe *O*   þe
       geliccre þære ecan myrhðe: þære ecan myrhþe þe gelicre *F*
       þonne: þe ma þe, *with second* þe *superscript F*   þam menn þe
       færð frig geond land: *omitted O*   hu: ne *O*   þe: *omitted M*
       O   ðe: *omitted C M O*

2.6   bið nu micel: nu byð forði micel *Ma*   þam: þam men *O*   þencst:
       with -n- *superscript and comma beneath W*   cwiðst: cwycst *M*
       onscunie: ascunige *Ma*   onscunað: ascunað *Ma*   ascunað:
       onscunað *C F*   and lufað: and he lufað *F*   swicol: swica *O*
       beo: beo ðu *O*   se soðfæsta god his: *C F M O*; ðæs untreowan
       God, *with* ðæs *written over an erasure by the points corrector W*

2.7   cepe: and kepe *Ma*

2.8   geswicennyssum: geswicennysse *F*   us: ut *F*   urum synnum: *C*
       M O; þam synnum *F*; his synnum *W*   fremfulle: fremfullice
       C   nis na: *C F M O*; nis *W*   buge: gecyrre *F*

2.9   synfullan: synfullan mannes *C*   gecyrre: gecyrron *C*; cyrre *M*
       se synfulla: se *superscript with comma beneath W*   hylt: hylt

ealle *F*   mæge: *F*; mage *C O M*; mæg *W*   lareowa: *written over erasure by points corrector* *W*

2.10   æfter his: æfter *F*   and he bið: *C F*; he bið *M*; þæt he bið *O*; swa þæt he bið (swa *added by points corrector*) *W*   behet: *omitted* *F*   behet nanum: behet na nanum *F*   elciendum: elciendum men *M O*   anum: anum menn *C*   forðan þe: for ðan *F*   se þe: se *O*

2.11   for sceame his gyltas: his gyltas for sceame *F* þone sceamian: sceamian þonne *F*   and be his dome gebete: *omitted C*

2.12   forlætan: alætan *C*

3.2   forlicgan: *in margin by original scribe with signe de renvoi* *W*

3.5   swyðlice: swiðe *C*

3.6   wæs gewunelic: gewunelic wæs *C*

3.11   anðræcum: anwræcum *O*

3.13   ðu þe: þu þu *F*

3.15   sylfe: sylfne *F O*

3.16   þæt ic wið þe ne syngie gif ic me sylfe: *omitted C*   sylfe: sylfne *F O*

3.20   unsceðþignysse: unscildignysse *F*

3.21   se: *in margin W (original scribe)*

3.22   an-rædnysse: andrædnysse *O*

3.25   hi: him *M*   hi man: man hi *F*   buta: butan *O*

3.27   cwellere: c- *superscript with comma beneath* *W*

3.28   læg: læg þær *C*

3.31   þa to: þa *M O*

3.33   ceorfan: forceorfan *O*

3.39   hit þe: hit *F*

3.41   belifian: *glossed by* vel heafdian *(points corrector)* *W*

3.43   gelette: gelahte *C*

3.45   þwyres: swyres *O*

3.47   ne: *C F M O*; and ne *W*

3.49   swencan hi: *C M O*; *with* hi *superscript W (probably points corrector)*; hi swencan *F*

3.50   wæpne: wæpnum *C M O*

3.60   se: *omitted C M O*

3.62   þe: *omitted C*

3.65   *second* þe: *omitted C M O*

3.68   eac: -a- *superscript with comma beneath W*

3.71   dead wæs: wæs dead *C*

4   don þonne: þonne don *F*

       him: hine *F*

       his god-spelle: his þam halgan godspelle *C*

       cunnan his: cunnan *C*

5.4   to gode don: *M O*; to gode gedon *C F Ma*; don to gode *W*

5.5   her: her on life *Ma*

5.9   þæt he: þe he *C F*

5.14   we nu: we *C M O*

5.16   habban huru ead-modnysse: huru eadmodnesse habban *C*

5.17   is us: us is *C*   smeagenne: smeagenne hure *M*

5.21   þe ælmihtig God is: þe is ælmihtig god *C*; þe is ælmihti god *M O*

5.22   Sy him a wuldor on ecnysse. Amen: *after* wuldor *in W the points
       corrector has written over an erasure* "ðe leofað and rixað on ec-
       nys" *with superscript continuation* "se ece drihten. Amen" *and has
       used two barred h's as signes de renvoi to signal that this should come
       after the next lines, which were originally intended as a note to follow
       the text of the sermon.*

6   Wodnes-dæg: *followed by superscript* ðonne nu to dæg beoð. *with
       two vertical points at beginning and at point of insertion W*

       gebyrað: gebyrod *C*

       ðære: þissere *C*

12. On The Prayer of Moses for Mid-Lent Sunday

Manuscripts: Six manuscripts contain this text in its entirety, W, C, F, M, N, and T. In W the text is on fols. 67v–72r, and the points corrector worked on it. In C it is on pp. 333–38; in F, on pp. 66–79; in N, on fols. 85v–91v; and in T (Hatton 114), on fols. 68r–75v. In M the text as a whole is on fols. 109r–17v, and there is also a brief extract in the composite homily, *Feria IIIa in letania maiore* (fols. 228r–38r; the extract, which contains no variant readings, consists of lines 116–19, on fol. 236v). There is also an extract, consisting of lines 75–86, in J, fol. 41r–v, where it is part of a composite homily, *In dedicatione aecclesiae.* Lines 68–83 are incorporated in Ælfric's *Pastoral Letter for Wulfsige* in T (Junius 121) and in K (lines 68–80 only, due to the loss of a folio). Another part, lines 98–101, is incorporated in the composite *De octo vitiis et de duodecim abusivis* in R, S, and X [i].

Previously edited and translated by Skeat, vol. 1, 282–307, and edited by Leinbaugh, "The Liturgical Homilies in Ælfric's Lives of Saints."

title	DE ORATIONE MOYSI: IN MEDIO QUADRAGESIMAE: De oratione Moysi in media quadragesima *C*; De oratione Moysi in medio .xl. uel quando uolueris *F*; De oratione Moysi *M*; De oratione Moysi in media quadragesima *N*; De oratione Moysi in media quadragessima *T*
2	Aegypta: AEgyfta *W*
3	fotum: drium fotum *C*
4	becomon: becom *F*
5	feohtende: swiðe feohtende *C*
7–8	wæras and gewend tomergen togeanes: weras tomerien and gewend togeanes *N*
13	Aarone: aarone his breðer *C* Ælmihtigan: ælmihtigan god *F*
24	alede: lede *F*
30	Cristene: cristene menn *C*
34	hit: *omitted M N*
36	geswican þære bene: þære bene geswican *C M N*
43	þonne: *omitted F*
45	deofol: feond *T*
47	swa swa: swa *C M N*
49	Ælmihtigan: ælmihtigan gode *F*
51	swa þæt hine man: swa þæt þæt mann hine, *with second* þæt *added in margin F*
52	þe: *omitted C* se: *C F M F*; *omitted N T W*
56	mæge: magen *M*
57	of þam weorce þurh þæt: þurh þæt of þam weorce *F*
58	geameleaste huru: gemeaste *C*
63	to us: us to *C*
65	þe: *omitted N*
66	Drihten: drihtenes naman *C*

67   þær þær: þær *C*

68   Man sceal swaþeah: cristene men sceolon *K T*

69   spræce drifan: drifan spræca *C*

70   is gebed-hus: *C F K M N T (Hatton 114 and Junius 121)*; gebedhus is *W*

77   bysmorlice: bismerlicean *C*

82   wacie: wacian *C T (Junius 121)*   wyrce: *C F M N T (Hatton 114)*; wyrcan *W*

83   swa: swa swa *F*

84   hlydan: libban *C*

85   drince: drincan *N*   na: and na *F*

90   sceal seo sawl: seo sawul sceal *F*   lare: larum *C*

95   we: ge *F*

96   fæston eac: eac fæstan *C*

98   ac: swa swa *R S X^i*   sume: sume men *R S X^i*

99   hi sylfe forðearle: swiðe heomseolfe *X^i*

100   næfdon: næfdon æt gode *F*   þæs mycclan geswinces: for þa michele iswinche *X^i*

101   ac: and *S*   fram: *C F M N R S T (Hatton 114) X^i*; *omitted W*   miltsunge: milce *X^i*

105   ofermæst: *C F M N T*; oferfæt *W*

110   nis: nis nan *F*

112   swa swa: swa *C M N*

117   ealde: ealda mann *F*

120   wif-men: wifmann *C*

124   þæt: þæt se *F*

125   eac: eac hit *F*

126   þæt: þæt þæt *F*

129   witena: a *over subpuncted* e *(probably original scribe) W*   ma witena: witena ma *C*

131   þe: se ðe *F*   unwislice: unrihtlice *F*

134   gesettan: asettan *F T*

135   and: *omitted C*

136   we: ge *C*

142   forsewennysse: sewennysse *M*

143   hungre: hungre oððe mid hergunge *F T*

144   forsewennysse: sewennysse *M*

149   munuc-lif: *F*; munuclif *with letter erased after* f *W*; munuclifa *C M*
          N T

152   wæs: wæs hit, *with* hit *superscript with two vertical points beneath* *W*
          towearp: *C W*; towearp þa *F M N T*

156   swilcum: *C F M N T*; þysum *W*

159   eow: forð *C*

160   and ic forgife sibbe and gesehtnysse eow: *omitted F*

162   ða yfelan deor eow fram: eow þa yfelan deor fram *C*

165   seo: se *M*   bið swa heard eow: beoð eow swa heard *C*; bið eow
          swa heard *M N*

179   ælmihtig: *C M T*; *followed by superscript* god *with two vertical*
          points beneath *W*; ælmihtig god *F N*   menn: mannum *C T*

187   sende: asende *F*

198   to eft: eft to *C*

203   getiþode: *C F M N T*; tiþode *W*   began: began þa *F*

204   becom: com *F T*   ða God: *C F M N T*; god ða *W*

206   ða: *omitted N*; þa sona *F*

207   God: and god *N*

210   ma: ma manna *F*

226   hi: hi hi *C*   mid cyldum: *F W*; cildum *C M N T*

227   ða suncon: suncon þa *C*; þa besuncon *F*

228   ofrorene: ofhrorene, *with* -h- *superscript and two vertical points be-*
          neath *W*

236   ungeðwære and þwyre him betwynan: *C F T W*; unþwære him
          betwynan *M N*

238   nane: *superscript with comma beneath* *W*

239   and: *C F M N T*; for *with* ðam ðe *added superscript by points correc-*
          tor *W*   soðfæstnysse: soðnysse *F*

240   gecweme were Gode: gode gecweme were *C*

241   agylte: he agylte *N T*   God him: him god *F*

244   ðreo: ðreora *with* -ra *superscript and two vertical points beneath* *W*
          (*F has an erasure of two letters after* þreo)

247   swaðeah: þis swaþeah *C*

250   God sende ða sona sumne encgel him to: god þa sona sumne en-
          gel him to asende *N*

252   ealle wæp-menn: wæpmen ealle *F*

257   sylf: *omitted C*

258   clypode: he clypode *F*

259   eom: eom sylf *F*

259–60   unrihtlice dyde: dyde unrihtlice *C*

260   þas: þa *F M*

261   bidde: bidde þe *F*

262   hired: hired awend *F*

272   ða: ealle ða *F*   wæron: syndon *F T*   gehealdene: gehealdene mid gode *F*

275   Niniueiscan: niniuitiscan *with* -itis- *by points corrector on erasure W*

276   to: *omitted C*

278   sceoldon: sceolde *N*

279   sona: sona to gode *C*

280   to ðam ælmihtigan Gode: *F T*; *omitted C M N W*

282   areccan: gereccan *F T*

284–86   on scyldigum mannum ... mid andetnysse: *omitted C*

286   þa: þam *M N*

288   ðe: *omitted C M N*   getime: getiman *T*

289   swyðe: *omitted C*

292   emlice: ænlice *C*

293   syngie: -y- *superscript over subpunct*ed -i-, *probably by original scribe W*

294   and: *omitted N*

297   wið: on *C*

303   suos: *followed by* þæt is on Englisc; *superscript by points corrector W*

304   facn: fac *N*

305   hi: *omitted N*

312   ende: heora ende *C F*

316   hi: *C F M N T*; *superscript with two vertical points beneath W*

319   truwan: truwa *W*   of: on *N*   ðinre: *omitted C*

320   swyðe: to swiðe *F M N*

326   se: *omitted F*

328   on: to *N*   life: life. AMEN *C*, life *followed by* mid þam þe leofað and rixað a buton ænde Amen *superscript in a different hand F*

329   *line omitted C F*

13. Saint George

Manuscripts: Two manuscripts now contain this text, W and L. In W it is on fols. 72r–74r, and the points corrector did not work on it. In L it is on fols. 144r–47r. We know that the text was in f ^{i} (fols. 190r–93r) and f ^{k} (fols. 142v–44r) before the Cotton fire, but it was entirely destroyed in both manuscripts. The title and the first two lines of f ^{i} are recorded by Wanley, 192, and the title and the first line of f ^{k}, Wanley, 207.

Previously edited by and translated by Skeat, vol. 1, 306–19, and the text in L was edited and translated by Hardwick, *An Anglo-Saxon Passion of St George*.

title	VIIII KALENDAS MAII: *omitted f ^{i}* VIIII: VIII *L*; IX *f ^{k}*
	NATALE: passio *L* MARTYRIS: *omitted f ^{k}*
7	þe wæs Datianus geciged: datianus *L*
14	unforht: *L*; unforh *W*
17	autem: *superscript in margin with signe de renvoi to correct place in line W (original scribe)*
21	stænene and treowene: stæne and treowe *L*
29	earde: gearde *L*
33	Geori: georius *L*
39	worulda: *L*; woruldra *W*
44	blysan: blasan *L*
45	het: and het *L*
57	beo ic: ic beo *L*
64	fordo þe: þe fordo *L*
74	þam: *L*; omitted W*
91	God: þæt is god *L* nu: *omitted L*
92	þa: *omitted L*
110	Drihtnes: godes *L*
112	nu: *omitted L*
115	Cristes: godes *W*
124	mycelne wurð-mynt miht: miht micelne wurðmunt *L*
133	godum: stanum *L*
144	æteowdon: æteowdon næfre *L*
157	syþþan: *omitted L*

159   him gediht hæfde: het *L*

166   Cristen: godes *L*

176   sona: *L; omitted W*

182   and: ac *L*   his: *omitted L*

14. Saint Mark *and* The Four Evangelists

Manuscripts: There are four manuscripts of this text, W, E, L, and f^k. In W the *Life of Saint Mark* is on fols. 74r–75v, and the *Item alia* on the four evangelists is on fols. 75v–77r; the points corrector did not work on it. E, fols. 295r–98v, and L, fols. 110r–14r, also include both parts of the text. In f^k what was fols. 48r–50r, now fols. 22r–24r, contain the *Life of Mark,* and what was fols. 50r–52r, now fols. 24r–26r, contain the discussion of the evangelists, there headed *De quatuor euangelistarum.* Wanley, 206, records the title and the first line and a half of the first part and the title and the first line of the second part.

Previously edited and translated by Skeat, vol. 1, 320–47.

title   VII KALENDAS MAII: PASSIO SANCTI MARCI EVAN-
           GELISTAE: *W*; De quarta evuangelistas. matheus. marcus. lu-
           cas. iohannes. *E*; VII kalendas mai passio sancti marci ewange-
           liste *L*; VII kalendas Mai. Natale Sancti Marci Evangelista f^k

4   eall: *omitted L*

7   gewitte: *E L*; witte *W*; gewitte he f^k

8   derodon: deredon þam *E L*   mannum: mancynne *E*

9   ða: *superscript with comma beneath W*

12   Gast þa: *E L* f^k; gast *W*

23   Sum: *preceded by superscript* hit gelamp æt sume sæle þæt *L*

27   wæs gehaten: hatte f^k

29   þære: and þære *E*

30   eac þa: þa eac *E*

32   syrwdon: wurdon *E, with superscript* þohtan *L*   and: *with super-*
           script þæt hi *L*

33   þe: *omitted E*

41   on geleafan: on gode f^k

42   þancode Gode: gode þancode *E*

43	aræred on hrædincge: on hrædince aræred *E*
44	Godes: -s *superscript with comma beneath W*
48	hæðenan: *followed by superscript* þa *L*
53	swuran sona mid rape: his sweoran mid anum rape *E*
54	ða: þas f^k
58	Þa: þæs *L* f^k
62	and awræhte þone god-spellere, and ðas word: and þam god-spellere þas word *E* ðas word: þus f^k
67	on worulde: *omitted E*
72	þu: *omitted E* ascired: astyred *L*
78	cwæð to: to cwæþ *E*
79	sona: ða f^k
81	rape: rapon *E*
84	þæs: *omitted L*
89	mid ðam: mid *with* him *superscript* f^k
90	woldon þa hæðenan: ... nan þa woldon f^k
91	mycel: micelne f^k adwæsced: acwenced *E L*
92	mycelne: *E L* f^k; mycel *W*
97	þa: *omitted L*
100	ar-wurðnysse: eadmodnysse *E*
title	ITEM ALIA: *W*; *omitted E L*; DE QVATTVOR EVANGE-LISTARUM f^k
106	halga: snotera *E L*
110	Læden-spræce: ledenre spræce *E L*; [.]ædene spræce f^k ðe: *omitted* f^k
114	and: *omitted* f^k
115	þam: of þam f^k
118	ne: *omitted E*
124	stane: stanum *E*
125	ne: eac ne f^k underfehð: underfehð he *E*
127	is: *E L* f^k; *omitted W*
129	gastlicum: *omitted* f^k
130	Cristes: godes *W*
131	he: þe *W*
133	mannum: *omitted L*
134	Criste: crist *E*

135   gewrite: gewritum *E*

138   leodum: ðeodum f^k

139–40   on ær his agenre leode þæt god-spell awritan: an ær ða godspel
          awritan hys agenre leode *E*

141   is: *W* f^k; *omitted E L*   se: *E L* f^k; þe *W*

143   wæs: . . . eac f^k gestrynde: getrymde *E*

146   oðre: on þære *E*

151   wunode: wunigende *E*

152   Ælmihtigan: ælmihtigan gode *E*   leahtre: læhtrum f^k

157   gewat: gewat þær *E*

159   moddrian: *first* -d- *superscript with comma beneath W*

161   eal: *E L* f^k; *omitted W*

163   awrat: *omitted* f^k wundorlicre: *L*; wundorlice *E*; wundor . . cere
         f^k; wundorlicor *W*

169   þas: þa *W*

170   awrat: wrat *E L*

171   lange: *omitted L*

175   ealne: ealle f^k

176   neorxne-wange: *first* -e- *superscript with comma beneath W*

178   and: *omitted E*

181   nytena: *E L* f^k; feower nytena *W*

182   and þæt: *E L*; þæt *W*   gelic: *E L* f^k; lic *W*   anre leon hiwe:
         anum leo *E*

183   stod anum styrce gelic: anum cealfe gelic *E*

184   fagum: anum *E*

185   Mathee: Matheę *W*

187   seo: *E L* f^k; se *W*

188   hlud-swege: hludswige *E*; on swege f^k

191   clypiende: clypiendes *L*

193   god-spell: spel *E*

200   driht-wurða: *W*; dyrwurþa *E*; rihtwurða *L*; drihtwurð . f^k

202   mærlicost: gleawlicost *E*

209   ðisum: *E L* f^k; ðis *W*

211   on þam ylcan hiwe þe we ær sædon: *omitted* f^k sædon: foresæ-
         don *L*

212   dreame: dreamum *E*

214   halig: *first* halig *preceded by* þæt ys *E*   Drihten: eart þu drihten *E*
227   *followed by* and sy þam welwillendan hælende a wuldor and lof
       butan ælcum ende on ecnysse Amen *E*

15. Memory of Saints

Manuscripts: This text is preserved in its entirety in three manuscripts, W, C, and L. In W it is on fols. 77r–82r, and the points corrector worked on it. In C it is on pp. 290–96, and in L, on fols. 114r–20v. Four further manuscripts preserve the section of the text dealing with the eight vices and their contrary virtues, lines 2.232–346, in different formats: G, R, S, and X ^{i}. The first three have been collated here, but not X ^{i}, a very late manuscript with a considerably altered version of the text.

Previously edited and translated by Skeat, vol. 1, 336–63, and edited by Leinbaugh, "The Liturgical Homilies in Ælfric's Lives of Saints." The vices and virtues section was edited and translated by Clayton, *Two Ælfric Texts.*

title   *SERMO DE MEMORIA SANCTORUM: W*; Incipit sermo de
         memoria sanctorum *L*; Sermo de memoria sanctorum quando
         uolueris *C*   Spel loca hwænne mann wille: *omitted C L*
1.1   Deus: *omitted L*   ælmihtig: *followed by* god *superscript and two*
         vertical points beneath W   þa ða: þa ðe *L*   mycelre: *C L;* my-
         celne *W*
1.2   Crist sylf: god self *C*
         lic-wurðe: *C;* gelicwurðe, *with* ge- *superscript and two vertical points*
         beneath W; gelicwurðe *L*   andsundne: *C L;* swa andsundne *W*
         swa þæt: þæt *superscript with comma beneath W*
1.3   Deum: *followed by superscript* Ðæt is ongliscre spræce; *with two*
         vertical points beneath W
         þa getacnode: getacnode þa *C*
2.3   ðam: *omitted L*
2.16   innewerdre: *C L; first* e *erased W*
2.21   cynincge: *second* -c- *superscript with comma beneath W*
2.22   cwæð þus: þus cwæð *C*
2.24   ðe: *omitted C*
2.33   unriht-wisnysse: -wis- *superscript with comma beneath W*

2.39   sona cydde God: cydde god sona *L*

2.42   eodon: eoden *with second -o -superscript above subpuncted -e- and comma beneath W*

2.46   leona: *preceded by* ðara *superscript with two vertical points beneath W*

2.58   ðam: *omitted L*

2.61   gerihtlæhte mid wordum: mid wordum gerihtlæhte *L*

2.63   wunodon: wunode *L*

2.65–67   Crist . . . swa swa: *omitted through eyeskip L*

2.67   *entire line crossed through in W*

2.70   þus: þurh þæt *C*

2.77   ðam: *omitted L*

2.88   *Latin followed by superscript* þæt is on englisc; *W*

2.94   magon: *followed by superscript* :cuman næfre *with two vertical points beneath W*

2.95   to eallum mannum: *omitted C*

2.96   *Latin followed by superscript* þæt is on englisc; *W*

2.101   untrumnysse: *followed by superscript* onlihte *with two vertical points beneath W*

2.103   untrume: *followed by superscript* menn *with two vertical points beneath W*   nean: near *L*

2.106   hælend is: is hælend *C*

2.118   becom: þa becom *C*

2.120   siþian: siðian me *L*

2.133   menn: *omitted L*

2.139   lyffetungum: lyffetunge *L*

2.141   fylian: folgian *C*

2.148   Gode andfencge: andfenge gode *L*

2.153   fægeran behate: *in reverse order with superscript signs to reader W*

2.158   heora lif: *written twice with line through first W*

2.159   wurdon: wurdon ða *C L*

2.179   drohtnunge: drohtnunge for heora drihtnes lufan *L*

2.197   ðissere: þysse *L*

2.200–201   on ðæra . . . geara: *omitted through eyeskip L*

2.206   and seo: þæt se *L*

2.209   eow: *omitted L*

2.213   se: *omitted C*   he: *omitted L*

2.218 lufu: lufe *with* v-shaped -u *over* -e *W* (*probably original scribe*)

2.226 and: *omitted L*

2.231 ðe we: we hi *C*   ne swa swa us sylfe hi lufian: ne lufian ne swa swa us sylfe *C*

2.234 þæt: þæt þæt *W*   man yt ær timan: mar ær timan et *C*

2.238 mid: *C G L R S*; for ðam, *with* for *possibly on erasure and* ðam *superscript in hand of points corrector W*   ormætum: *C G L R S*; ormæta *followed by* -n *superscript with two vertical points beneath W*   dræncum: drenceum *C*; dræncen *G*; drencum *L R S*; drænce *W*

2.239 heo: *C L R S W*; he *G*   forðan ðe: *C G L R S*; forðan *W*   oft: -t *superscript with comma beneath W*

2.241–42 se oðer leahtor is forligr and ungemetegod galnyss se is gehaten fornicatio, and he befylð: se oðer leahter is fornicatio se is gehaten forligr and ungemetegod galnyss and he befylð *C*

2.242 mannan: *L R S*; mann *followed by erasure of two letters W*; man *C*; mann *G*

2.243 lima: *with* v-shaped u *above* a *W*; lymen *G*

2.245 þridda: *followed by* leahter *superscript with two vertical points beneath W*

2.250 fulle ne beoð næfre: næfre fulle ne beoð *C*

2.251 wea-modnyss: weamodnyss oððe yrre *C*

2.252 seo: *W*; se *G L R S*   seo deð: *omitted C*   deð: *superscript with two vertical points beneath W*

2.253 *first* and: ac *G*

2.254 fifta: fifta leahter *L*

2.255 þone: *preceded by* þæt is *with two vertical points beneath and with second* -n- *superscript and two vertical points beneath W*

2.256 to: *omitted R S*

2.259 and: *omitted R S*   þæt: *followed by* is þæt se *superscript with two vertical points beneath W*

2.262 on his life nan god don: nan good don on his life *R*

2.263 him: *omitted S*   ne: *omitted C*

2.264 and: ac *C*

2.265 gecweden: gehaten *R*; *omitted G*

2.267 ðonne: *preceded by* þæt is *superscript with two vertical points beneath W*

2.269   þonne: *omitted R*

2.270   his wite: wite his *G*

2.271   se: *C G L R S*; seo *W*

2.277   ðe: *L R S*; ða *C G W*

2.278   þas: þa *S*   Drihtnes: godes *C*   fultum: fylste *G L*

2.280   þæt: *preceded by* þæt is *superscript with two vertical points beneath W*

2.284   ðonne: *followed by* swa *superscript with two vertical points beneath*
         mid gesceade his gesetnysse: hys gesetnysse mid gesceade *R*
         gesceade: sceade *preceded by* ge- *superscript with two vertical*
         points beneath W

2.285   he: heo *G*

2.286   clænnyss on Ænglisc: on englisc clænnys *C*

2.287   þæt: *preceded by superscript* þæt is *with two vertical points beneath W*

2.290   bið: *superscript with two vertical points beneath W*   swa eac: *omit-*
         ted R

2.292   þæt: *preceded by superscript* þæt is *with two vertical points beneath W*
         man: se mann *L* aspende: *preceded by* his æhta *superscript with*
         two vertical points beneath W

2.294   we: ge *C*

2.296   Drihtne: gode *G*

2.298   fordon swa: swa fordon *G*

2.299   geðyld: *G L R S*; geðyld and þolmod *followed by* -nys *added super-*
         script with two vertical points beneath W; geðyld and ðolmod *C*

2.300   þæt: *preceded by superscript* þæt is *with two vertical points beneath W*
         se mann: man *L*   ðol-mod: ðolomod *with second -o- superscript*
         and two vertical points beneath W

2.301   gewyldre: wuldre *C*

2.305   soðlice: soðlict *with superscript* -e *above* -t *with punctum and*
         comma beneath W

2.306   þæt: *omitted G*

2.307   ðonne: *preceded by* þæt is *superscript with two vertical points be-*
         neath W

2.308   demð: god demð *C*

2.309   and: þy *G*

2.311   þæt: *preceded by* þæt *superscript with two vertical points beneath W*

2.318   of: on *L*

2.323   urum: *omitted R*

2.324   mage: magon *R S*

2.325   unnyt: on unnyt *S*

2.331   þæt: ac þæt *C*

2.335   forðan se ðe: for ðam ðe se ðe *C*   wis byð: bið wis *G*   wurð: byð *G*

2.336   þeah: þeah ðe *R*

2.338   on his: on *S*

2.342   and . . . us: *all omitted C*

2.343   fylst: fultum *R*

2.344   cenlice: clænlice *L*

2.346   her: *followed by* Ðam to wuldre ðe on ecnysse rixað, ece drihten; þam sy wuldor and lof, ðe a leofað, mid fæder and mid suna and mid ðam halgan gaste on ecnysse; Amen. *added superscript with* mid ðam halgan g *superscript above the superscript marked by two vertical points beneath the line and at beginning of the phrase. The* -aste *of the word* gaste *has been cut off, presumably by binders.* W; *followed by* þærto us gefultumige se ðe leofað and rixað a buton ende. AMEN. *L*

16. On Omens

Manuscripts: This text has survived in two forms: that printed here, which is found in six manuscripts, and an augmented form, found in two (R and S). In the augmented form, which is a later but probably authentically Ælfrician version, the last four lines of the earlier text are replaced by two stories written by Ælfric, the story about Macarius found in W immediately after the *Life of Swithun* in LS 20 and printed here in that position, and a story about Saul and the witch of Endor, not found anywhere else. For the debate about who is responsible for the augmented form of LS 16, see Clayton, "Ælfric's *De auguriis*."

In W the text is on fols. 82r–85v, and the points corrector did not work on it. In C it is on pp. 231–36; in L, on fols. 197v–203r; in O, on pp. 33–40; in P, on fols. 30v–35v; and in V, on pp. 281–308. The augmented form of the text is in R, pp. 88–101, and S, pp. 347–65. All of the manuscripts have been collated for this edition.

Previously edited and translated by Skeat, vol. 1, 364–83, and edited by W. Schipper, "Ælfric's *De auguriis:* A Critical Edition with Introduction and Commentary" (PhD diss., Queen's University at Kingston, 1981). The story about Saul and the witch of Endor is edited by Pope, vol. 2, 790–96.

title   DE AUGURIIS: SERMO IN LAETANIA MAIORE: *W*; Sermo in letania maiore de epistola pauli et de auguriis *C*; Epistola Pauli *L*; Dominica .III^a. Vel quando uolueris *O*; De auguriis *P R S*; SERMO IN LETANIEM MAIORE VEL QUANDO VOLUERIS *V*

1.1   Se apostol Paulus: paulus ðe apostol *L*
       desideria: desidia *L*
       ge: *omitted C*
       gewilnað: *L O P R S V*; gewilnad *C*; gewinð *W*
       ðone gast: þam gaste *L*
       simle: æfre *L*
       færð: færð hit *R S*
       þær: þær ðær *L*
       wissigend: wisiende *C*

1.2   on: *omitted P*
       seo rihtwise: *C O P R S V*; þeo rihtwise *L*; se rihtwise *W*
       sylfum: *omitted C S*

1.3   hæðen-gild and: *C L O P R S V*; hæðengild oððe *W*
       dwollic: dollic *L*
       eow foresecge: *C L O P R S V*; fore eow secge *W*
       foresæde: *C L O P R S V*; foresecge *W*
       þa ðe: þa ða *O*
       symle: æfre *L*
       lic-hama: lichaman *L P*

1.4   non: *omitted C O R S*
       hnescan: *followed by* vel wac-mod *superscript, probably by original scribe W*
       ðe druncennyss: ða druncennesse *O*
       bið: *omitted C*
       simle: æfre *L*
       eft: *omitted C O P*

2.5   leahtras: synna *L*

2.8   symle: æfre *L*

2.10   geðyldig: and geþyldig *L O V*   *second* and *omitted C*

2.16   onbugan: abugan *R S*

2.19   and: *omitted C*

2.21   *preceded by* Sermo Sancti Augustini de auguriis *C*   sumere:
        sume *R*

2.24   ge þa: *C L O P R S V*; ge *W*

2.29   alyse: lyse *O*

2.31   untrumnysse: unrihtwisnesse *S*

2.32   galdras: aldras *C*

2.36   manega: *C L O P R S V*; *omitted W*

2.40   seo: se *V*

2.41   nan: naht *C*; na *V*

2.45   na: naht *C*

2.46   Cristen man: *L O P V*; man *C R S W*   dagum: dagen oððe be
        nihte *C*

2.47   *second* on: *omitted P*

2.49   geendunge: *omitted O*

2.51   credan: *L R S W*; his credan *C O P V*   his: *omitted R*   Dryhtne:
        drihtene *C O*; drihtne *L P R S V*; dryhten *W*

2.53   sceoccena: deofle *C*   wiglunga: *followed by* and gif he hine get
        ne cunne geleornige hine wel hraðe be ðam þe he wille godes
        bletsunge habban *V*

2.55   gedwæs-menn: sot men *C*

2.56   *second* on: *omitted P*

2.56–57 oððe on wifunge . . . bryw-lace: *omitted O*

2.57   hi man: *C L O P R S V*; man *W*   hwæs: wæs *O*

2.58   him: *omitted S*   *second* hwæt: *omitted R*

2.59   sceocca: deofol *C*

2.60   scin-cræftas: wiccecreftes *C*

2.61   leas-brædnysse: brædnysse *L*

2.62   cwyð: cwæð *O*   wiglere: leas wiglere *S*   oft secgað: secgað oft
        R

2.64   secge: secgað *R*

2.66   heo: he *R*   mannum: magen *C*

2.67   dry-cræft: wiccecreft *C L*   secað: secgæð *C*

2.68   sædon þa dry-men: þa drymenn sædan *R S*   drymen: wigele-
        res *C*

2.69   Iamnes: *C L O P R S V*; Iammes *W*

2.71   adranc: dranc *O*   sæ: *followed by* mid eallum his werode *V*

2.72   dry: wigelere *C*

2.73   Petre: sancte petre *C*

2.74   on feower tobærst: tobærst on feower *L*

2.76   Fela oðre forferdon þe folgodon dry-cræfte: fela forferden for
        oðre þe drycreft lufeden *C*

2.77   swa swa: swa *L V*   swa swa we on bocum rædað: *omitted P*   is:
        us is *C*

2.78   Cristena: cristena man *V*

2.79   ðe: *omitted V*

2.81   and: *omitted V*

2.84   stanum: *L O P R S V*; stanen *C*; stane *W*

2.85   swa swa: swa *V*   tæcað: tæcð *S*

2.87   hu: *omitted O V*   stan: *superscript with comma beneath W*

2.91   *second* mid: *omitted S*   muðe: munde *V*

2.92   gescylde: *C L O P R S V*; scylde *W*

2.94–96 *all omitted L*

2.97   ælcne: ælce *L*

2.98   bletsian: *C L O P R S V*; gebletsian *W*

2.102   wega: gewega *C*; wegum *R*; wegena *V*

2.104   hi sylfe and heora bearn: heora bearn and hi sylfe *P*

2.105   beon: beoð *O*

2.112   sumne: sume *C*   hi to: hi þe gyrnnor lufian and to *S*   habbon:
        habban sceolon *O*

2.115   and: *omitted C*   gewitleaste: gewitleastum *P*

2.118   forhogian: *second* o *altered from* e *W*

2.119   arwurðian: a wurðian *P*

2.123   sumere: sume *C*

2.128   gewissan: *C L O P R S V*; wissan *W*

2.129   mannum: nanum *R S V*

2.131   godnyss: goodnysse ful *R*

2.132   mot: *C L O P R S V*; mod *W*

2.136   þa: secan þa *O*   bote æt: bote to *C*

2.141–42 Wen is . . . on deaðe: *omitted O*

2.145   heord: flocc *O*

2.146   first *hi*: *superscript with comma beneath W*

2.148   ða: þa ferdon *V*

2.149   to: into *C*

2.150   geðafunge: *C L O P R S V*; ðafunge *W*

2.151–52 faran furðon: furþon faran *S*

2.154   þæt getimað þonne: þonne getimað þæt *O*

2.161   simle: æfre *L*   þanciað: *C L O P R V*; þancian *S*; þancige *W*

2.162   eall: *omitted V*

2.164   fandunge: fadunge *S*

2.167   for: *C L O P R S V*; fram *W*

2.169   andsæte Gode: gode andsæte *O*

2.172   deofles: deowes *C*

2.175   *first* ne: *omitted L*   deofle: deowe *C*

2.176   sceole: sceolde *R S*

2.177   swa swa: swa *P*

2.180   þæt hit is unnyt bebod: *omitted W*   ðe: þæt *C*

2.181   Declina: *C L O P R S V*; decline *W*

2.183   swa: swa swa *C*   he: man *S*

2.184   æfre: *omitted C*   sceola: sceolde *O S*

2.187   ænige: *C L O P R S V*; ænigne *W*

2.191   ælmyssum: ælmesdædum *S*   *second* on: *omitted R*

2.193   receleasan: arleasan *P*

2.194   on: *omitted O*   wadað: wændað *C*; wandiað *L*; wedað *O V*

2.197   ne: na *C*   agenne: *C L O P R S V*; agenre *W*

2.203   don sceolon: sceolon don *O*

2.206   gife and swyþe fæste: *omitted L*

2.207   oð: on *V*

2.208   mot don: do *S*

2.209   and: *omitted S*   is: *omitted S*

2.212   nu: *omitted C*

2.216   þæt: *C L O P R S V*; þæt hi *W*

2.217   on: *omitted O*   furðon: *omitted L*

2.222   ne: *added superscript with comma beneath W*   gife: fultume *W R S*

2.224   to: *omitted O*

2.226   wuldor and lof a to worulde: lof and wuldor a worulde *O*

17. KINGS

Manuscripts: There are two manuscripts of this text, W and P. In W it is on fols. 85v–91v, and the points corrector worked on it. In P it is on fols. 131v–39v.

Previously edited and translated by Skeat, vol. 1, 384–413.

2   for: for þæs *P*

3   ær: æror *P*

7   cyne-rice: rice *P*

14   ceas: *P,* geceas him, *with* ge- *and* him *superscript and two vertical points beneath each addition W*

18   ent: -n- *superscript with comma beneath W*

20   gebeote: *P;* beote *with* ge- *superscript with two vertical points beneath W*

32   wæs: wes *W by erasure (probably in error)*

36   gecwemde: *P;* cwemde *W*

40   hæðen-gild: *P;* hæðengildum *W*

46   his: hys *with* -y- *subpuncted and* -i- *above W*

47   godcundnysse: *P;* godnysse *W*

68   eft: *omitted P*

76   ar-wurðfulla: arfulla *P*

81   ðe, leof, gecyd: ðe gecydd la leof *P*

87   gedreftst: -s- *superscript with comma beneath W*

89   ic: ic na, *with* na *superscript and two vertical points beneath W*   ge-dræfde: gedrefe *P*

94   þæt: *omitted W*

96   cuman: *omitted P*

106   beworpene mid wuda: mid wuda beworpene *P*

110   se: *superscript with comma beneath W*

112   dumban: dunnan *W*

113   beworhton: *P;* bewurpon *W*

119   git: *superscript with comma beneath* W   þeah þe: þeah P

121   gewundodon: *with line through* wundodon *and* drehton *super-*
       script with two vertical points beneath W

134   under: -der *superscript with comma beneath* W

141   cucu: *omitted* P

142   astah: P; astah W, *with first* a- *superscript and two vertical points be-*
       neath

149   wolcn: -n *superscript with two vertical points beneath* W

150   unscæðþigan: unstæððigan P

165   fæt: an lytel fæt, *with* an lytel *superscript with two vertical points*
       beneath W

167   encgel: -c- *superscript with comma beneath* W

169   eft: ða P

174   forhwega: hwærhwega P

178   to: *superscript with comma beneath* W

185   ðe: P; *superscript with two vertical points beneath* W

190   neh-gebur: nehgebur *and* P

194   hetelice: hetole P

195   budon: budon him, *with* him *superscript and two vertical points be-*
       neath W

201   unrihtwisan: unrihtwisan cyninge, *with* cyninge *superscript with*
       two vertical points beneath W

204   ardlice: P; *omitted* W

207   asend: asend þa P

229   fæder: forcuða fæder, *with* forcuða *superscript and two vertical*
       points beneath W

233   het: and het P

236   God: *superscript with comma beneath* W

245   grædan: grenan P

248   man: *superscript with comma beneath* W; *omitted* P

250   forbærnde: for- *superscript with comma beneath* W   manna: *omit-*
       ted P

286   ne: *first* ne *superscript with comma beneath* W

294   fæder: *preceded by* þæt is on Englisc; *superscript (points corrector)* W

296   ac: ac he P

298   Godes: *omitted P*

300   deadne: deadne mann, *with* mann *superscript with two vertical points beneath W*

301   æfter: æfter his, *with* his *superscript and two vertical points beneath W*

303   ðæs: his *P*

310   fram: fram ðam, *with* ðam *superscript and two vertical points beneath W*

330   hwæðer: hwær *P*

331   andwyrde Hieu and cwæð unforht him to: andwyrde hieu unforht him and cwæð *P*

332   manfullan: manfulla *P*

335   Hieu him scet to: heiu him sceat to *P*; hieu hine scet, *with the* -e *of* hine *written over an erasure and* scet *followed by two erased letters W. The points corrector appears to have altered* him *to* hine *and to have erased* to.

336   tobærst: *P*; to- *superscript with two vertical points beneath W*

350   hætse: hętse *W, with* vel sceande *superscript (points corrector) W*

351   for hire gebyrdum: *omitted P*

356   to: *omitted P*   ær swa: swa ær *P*

357   on: *P*; of *W*

370   hi: *P*; hine *W*

379   gang-tun: anne gangtun *with* anne *superscript and two vertical points beneath W*

398   to: *omitted P*

409   Ælmihtiga: ælmihtiga god, *with* god *superscript and two vertical points beneath W*

411   oð: *P*; of *W*

416   awende: wende *P*

426   gehælde: gehæle *W*

433   Gode: *superscript with comma beneath W*

436   gremode: god gegremode, *with* god *and* ge- *superscript with two vertical points beneath W*; gegremode *P*

437   asende: sende *P*

454   lyfigendan: ælmihtigan *W*

455   ne: *superscript with comma beneath W*

461   awearp: wearp *P*
463   æ: æ and *P*
480   ana God: god ana *P*
481   a: *omitted W*

18. Saint Alban *and* on the Unjust

Manuscripts: This two-part text is extant as a whole only in W and in L. In W the first part, entitled *PASSIO SANCTI ALBANI MARTYRIS,* is on fols. 91v–93r, and the second, entitled *ITEM ALIA,* is on fols. 93r–94v. The points corrector worked on the second part. L, fols. 147r–51r, contains both parts, with the break between them marked by a large red capital letter. Both parts were also in f ^{k} before the Cotton fire completely destroyed them: what was fols. 226v–28v had the *Passio sancti Albanis martyris,* and fols. 228v–30r had the second part, headed *De Iniustis.* The titles and the first lines of both parts are recorded by Wanley, 208. C and P both have the second part of the text only, and there is a short extract in J, in a homily titled *In dedicatione aecclesiae.* In C this second part, lines 155–258, is on pp. 340–41. In P the same lines are on fols. 66r–67v; there is no title, but the first line is in capitals. The extract in J is on fols. 43v–44r and consists of lines 248–54, from *syllað* in line 248 to *deope* in line 254.

Previously edited and translated by Skeat, vol. 1, 414–31.

title   PASSIO SANCTI ALBANI MARTYRIS: kalendas iulii passio
         Sancti Albani martiris *L*
3   hund: hundred *L*
4   *second* and: *omitted L*
8   berypte ða unscæððigan: he rypte þa unscyldigan *L*
19   ormetre: unmætre *L*
37   hine nolde: nolde hine *L*
39   deman: demen *with -a- superscript over subpuncted second -e- by
         original scribe W*
40   eallum: e- *from* æ- *by erasure and -a- superscript with comma be-
         neath W*
42   swa: *omitted L*
45   hæðen-gilde: hæðenan gylde *L*

47	he: he on *L*
48	godum: gode *L*
56	belympð: -m- *superscript with comma beneath* W
60	*entire line omitted L*
61	to þam cwellere þus: *omitted L*
64	gebidde: gebiddan *L*
69	offrunga: *L*; godas offrunga *W*
71	medes: mede *followed by erased letter L*
81	hetelicum: hetelum *L*
82	and het: þa het he *L*
83	beheafdunge: swyrðes ecge *L*
95	hælend: -æ- *superscript by original scribe over subpuncted* -e- *W*
99	abryrd: onbrurd *L*
100	arn: and arn *L*
110	ardlice: *omitted L*
114	mihton tocnawan: mihte geseo *L*
142	wunodon: and wonuden *L*
148	horsan: hors *L*
title	ITEM ALIA: Quomodo Acitofel et multi alii laqueo se suspen-derunt *C*; *omitted L P*; De Iniustis *f*[k]
163	ðonne: þonu *with contraction mark over* u *C*
166	to: to *C L P*; on *W*
168	mid me: *omitted C*
171	hine: *C L P*; criste *W*
173	he: *omitted P* sceaðena: sceaðe *C*
179	syðað: -að *on erasure (points corrector)* W
181	wealdenda: eallwealdenda *with eall-* superscript with two vertical points beneath and final a over subpuncted *e W*; wellwillenda *L*
184	Ælmihtigan: *followed by* gode *superscript with two vertical points beneath W*
185	þe: *omitted C*
187	wealdendes: eallwealdendes *with eall-* superscript and two vertical points beneath *W*
188	þe: se þe *C*
191	þonne: þonu *with contraction mark over* u *C*
192	wel-willendan: willendan *L*

196	ræde: *followed by* acitofel gehaten *superscript with two vertical points beneath and again at beginning of superscript phrase* W
199	ongan winnan: wann *P*
201	se: *omitted P*
206	God wolde: wolde god *L*
219	heahne: heah *L* hetelicum: hetelum *L P*
221	sid-fæxede: sidfæxe *L*
224	ræd: *preceded by* un- *superscript with two vertical points beneath* W
232	hi: hine *C*
238	susle: pinunge *L*
244	riht: un *in margin with signe de renvoi before* riht *L*; unriht *P*
248	syllað eac: eac syllað *C P*; syllað heora *J*
251	to: and to *J*
252	do: doð *L*
254	he: hi *(probably* i *from* e *by erasure)* W singað: syngað *C J L P*; sincað *W*
255	mannum: manne *L*
256	þe syrwð embe us: *omitted L*

19. Saint Æthelthryth

Manuscripts: Two manuscripts have the complete text of this Life, W and L. In W it is on fols. 94v–96v, and the points corrector worked on it. In L it is on fols. 34v–36v. The text was also in f^i, on what was fols. 193–95 and fol. 136 (displaced, as Wanley, 191, notes), before the Cotton fire; of these, only what is now fol. 45 remains in part, containing from *on geleaffulum* to *mihton* (lines 61–122). The title, the first two lines, and the last five lines are recorded by Wanley, 192 and 191. The text in f^k, on what was fols. 230r–32r, was all lost in the Cotton fire. The title and the first line and a half are recorded by Wanley, 208.

Previously edited by Skeat, vol. 1, 432–41.

title	VIIII KALENDAS IULII: NATALE SANCTAE ÆÐELD-RYÐAE VIRGINIS: De Sancta æþeldryþe virgine *L*; De Sancta Æðeldriða *f^i*; IX Kalendas Iulii. Natale Sanctae Æðeld-ryðæ Virginis *f^k*

2	halgan: *followed by superscript* sancte *with two vertical points beneath* W
4	swa swa: swa *L* swuteliað: *preceded by* ge- *superscript with two vertical points beneath* W
5	hatte: *L*; hatta *W*
6	swa swa: swa *L*
9	se Ælmihtiga: *followed by* god *superscript with two vertical points beneath* W; god *L*
11	ælmihtig God: god *L* mæg eall: *with* don *superscript after* mæg *and two vertical points beneath* W; eall mæg *L*
13	þa ða hit wolde God: ða hit god wolde *L*
14	forgifen: gegifen *L*
15	ungewemmed: *omitted L*
16	swa: *second* swa *superscript with two vertical points beneath* W
17	mægðhad: *preceded by* hire *superscript with two vertical points beneath* W
18	unwemme: unwemmed *L*
20	Bedan: *omitted L*
25	se ælmihtiga God: god *L*
30	swa swa: swa *L*
33	hire: hi *L*
34	þe: *omitted L*
36	heo: *L*; heo syððan *W*
38	eft: *omitted L*
41	drohtnode: drohtnoð *L*
50	swa swa: swa *L*
52	mycel: *omitted L* þancode: *followed by* gode *superscript with two vertical points beneath* W
53	þolode: ðoloð *L*
55	swylcere: sumere *L*
65	him: *omitted* f^i gewurpan: awyrpan *L*
66	mid wuldre: *omitted L*
68	swa swa heo bæd sylf and het: *omitted L* and: and hy f^i
69	cyste: . . . te lecgan f^i
71	geendunge: *omitted L* abbudissan: *second* -b- *superscript with comma beneath* W

72	ær wæs: .æs ær f^i
75	þære: *omitted* L
80	weall standende, geworht of marm-stane: *omitted* L *apart from* weall, *which has been altered to* eall *by erasure*
83	of: on f^i
86	seo: se *with* -o *superscript and two vertical points beneath* W; ðeo L; *burn damage after* se f^i
87	ða: þære f^i
88	ealle: *omitted* f^i
92	sceawode: sceawodon L
97	þwogon: woscean L
99	bæron: legdon, *with* -g- *superscript* f^i
100	*line omitted* f^i
101	wundrunge: wuldruncge f^i
103	gemæte: gemęte W
106	gemæte: gemæte on f^i
114	*entire line appears to have been omitted* f^i gefyrn gehyrdon: ge-hyrdon gefyrn L
117	seo cyst micclum: miclum seo cyst L
119	þe: þæt f^i
124	his: L; *superscript with two vertical points beneath* W
134	Crist ure hælend: *omitted* f^i *(from Wanley's transcription)* hælend: drihten L

20. Saint Swithun *and* Saint Macarius and the Sorcerers

Manuscripts: This is a two-part text. The first part, on Swithun, is found in its entirety only in W. Parts of it are in f^d, and much of it survives in a damaged state in f^i. The second part, on Macarius and the Sorcerers, follows the first as an *Item alia* in W but is also found in R and S. The W text of the Life is on fols. 96v–103r, and the second part is on fol. 103r–v; it was worked on by the points corrector. Folios 1r–3v of f^d are binding fragments containing the text from line 19 *(and oferworht)* to line 163 *(Þa sæde se)* on fols. 1–2, and from line 379 *(hwæt)* to line 448 *(sibbe)* on fol. 3. The badly damaged f^i, on what was fols. 181v–86r, now fols. 37–42, contains the text from line 16 to line 467 (the end of the Life). Wanley, 192, records the title and the first line. R, pp. 97–98, and S, pp. 360–61, have the story of Macarius appended to their texts of *On Omens, LS* 16.

Previously edited and translated by Skeat, vol. 1, 440–73; edited by Needham, *Three English Saints,* 60–81; and edited and translated by Lapidge, *Cult of St Swithun,* 575–609. Neither Needham nor Lapidge includes the Macarius story, which was edited from R, with variants from W and S, by Pope as part of Pope, no. 29.

title	VI NONAS IULII: NATALE SANCTI SWYÐUNI EPIS-COPI: Depositio Sancti Suuithuni Mitissimi Episcopi f^i
16	Aðelwolde: *preceded by* scē *superscript with two vertical points beneath* W
21	se: $f^d f^i$; *superscript with two vertical points beneath* W
28	þurh: -h *superscript with comma beneath* W
37	to: $f^d f^i$; *added superscript with comma beneath* W
42	Eadzige nele: nele he f^d
43	him: he f^d
45	and: *omitted* f^i
54	hord: goldhord *with* gold- *superscript* W *(hand uncertain)*
62	eode: $f^d f^i$; eode swaðeah W
68	me spræc to: spræc to me, *with* me *superscript* f^d
69	eaðelice: $f^d f^i$; eaðelice up W
78	wolde hit: $f^d f^i$; hit wolde W
85	þære: þam $f^d f^i$
91	Ealmihtiga: ealmihtiga god, *with* god *superscript and two vertical points beneath* W þa: $f^d f^i$; þone W
119	swa dydon: f^d; dydon swa W *(f^i has crumbled away here)*
124	wurðfulle: -e *superscript over subpuncted* -a *(probably original scribe)* W
127	of ðam fet him: of ðam fet f^d; of his fet f^i
140	sanct: -c- *superscript with comma beneath* W
143	þurh ðone halgan: *written twice and first phrase crossed out* W
149	wurdon: wæron f^i
150	man: nan man f^d, *with* man *added in the margin*

153   ealle wurdon: wurdon ealle f^i

158   þæt: $W f^d$; *appears to be omitted* f^i

159   him: $f^d f^i$; *superscript with comma beneath* W

171   swinglum: *followed by superscript* hi *in hand probably not that of main scribe* W

180   þæt he: f^i; *superscript with comma beneath* W

181   his: *omitted* f^i

187   myslice: *omitted* f^i geuntrumode: f^i; geuntrume W

191   ealle wurdon: wurdon ealle f^i

197   gefran: f^i; befran W

218   gewislice: *omitted* f^i

221   ðone: *omitted* f^i

234   þa: *omitted* W

242–44 herian . . . nellað: *omitted* f^i

251   awæcnode: awacode f^i

252–56 and . . . bisceope: *omitted* f^i

254   hæfde: *followed by* ða *superscript with two vertical points beneath* W

280   mid ealle: f^i; *omitted* W

281   hleore: hreore *with* -l- *superscript over half-erased* -r- *and comma beneath* W

296   licgan: licgað W

305   þa: *omitted* f^i

307   witenne: f^i *appears to read* g[. . .]tanne *here*

308   plegað: plegiað *with* -i- *superscript and punctum beneath* W

315   gegaf-spræce: gegafspræcum f^i

318   ðam: *omitted* f^i; *superscript with two vertical points beneath* W

322   Ælmihtigan: *followed by* gode *superscript with two vertical points beneath* W

323   of: *followed by* his *superscript with two vertical points beneath* W

328   þa: *superscript with comma beneath* W

336   þurh: þurh sancte, *with* sancte *added at end of line by points corrector* W

354   mæsse-reafe: mæsse- *superscript with comma beneath* W

360   geðwærlæce: ge- *superscript with two vertical points beneath* W; gehwær . . . f^i

372–73 wyrigdon: *supplied by Needham,* Three English Saints, *on the basis of* the source; f^i has crumbled away at this point   and bæd . . . hine: f^i; omitted W. There is no gap in W, but the text reads: se ðe nolde wyrian þa ðe hine dydon tocwale.

374   fyond: fyond ū , with -ū inserted, possibly by points corrector W; fynd f^i

382   swa cwæde: $f^d f^i$; cwæde swa W

393   man ðe bære: man þe bære f^d; . þe bære f^i; ðe man bære W

398   hal: omitted f^i

400   ceastre: ceastre f^i, winceastre with win- superscript with two vertical points beneath W; winceastre with win- added superscript by later hand f^d

404   us: $f^d f^i$; omitted W

406   syndon: beoð f^i soðlice of Gode: of gode soðlice f^i

408   forpære: forræde f^d

414   þe: þy f^d

416   fetera: feteran f^i

420   scyttel: scyttels f^d

428   gehæftum: ge- superscript with two vertical points beneath W mannum: omitted f^d

433   sceamelum: first -e- superscript with two vertical points beneath W

439   God: f^d; crist W

440   ofslagen: acweald $f^d f^i$

443   and: þonne f^i

463   gecwemednysse: ge . . . f^i; cwemednysse W

464   þurh hi: followed by superscript barred h as a signe de renvoi, repeated at the end of line 499, where it is followed by Sy wuldor .ut sup[ra], all in hand of points corrector W

467   a: ana f^i

title   ITEM ALIA: BYSNE BE DRYMANNUM 7 BE ANUM GO-DAN MEN MACHARIUS GEHATÆN R (marginal heading by an annotating scribe named Coleman)

481   myre: an myre S

488   hi: superscript with comma beneath W

491   nis: omitted S

493   swa: geþuhð and R

494   ðæs: omitted S

498   gesawon: gesegon S

499   dry-manna: *followed by barred h as a signe de renvoi and, in margin,*
          sy wuldor vt sup[ra] *in hand of points corrector* W

21. SAINT APOLLINARIS

Manuscripts: This Life survives in its entirety only in W, fols. 103v–7v; it
was worked on by the points corrector. Two further manuscripts contain
parts of the text. The f ^{c} fragments are binding strips, torn vertically, about
twenty-five letters in width. Strip 1 of Horne 75 contains parts of lines 97–
213 (*and þam halgan were* to *forlæte þine*). Poole 10 consists of two fragments
containing parts of lines 213 (*godum*) to 253 (*ælmihtigan*). The readings from
these fragments have been taken from Collins and Clemoes, "The Common Origin." The badly-damaged f ^{k} contained the text on what was fols.
127v–31r; of this, what is now fols. 13 and 12 survive, with lines 13 (*petre*) to
80 (*byrig and se*) and lines 154 (*hæþenan*) to 225 (*ne beo þu*) remaining in part.
The title and the first line are recorded by Wanley, 207.

Previously edited and translated by Skeat, vol. 1, 472–87.

title   MARTYRIS: *omitted* f ^{k}
12   geedniwigian: *final* -i- *added superscript with punctum beneath* W
              ealdan: *followed by erasure of four to five letters* W
16   eart: -r- *superscript with comma beneath* W
24   mid his worde: *in margin (original scribe)* W   worde: wordum f ^{k}
26   and gehalgode: f ^{k}; *crossed out* W
30   þe getiþige: þæs þe tiþige f ^{k}
31   sende: *followed by* :to ðære byrig *superscript with two vertical
              points beneath* W; asende f ^{k}
33   blindne: *followed by* mann *superscript with two vertical points be-
              neath* W
36   Rauenna: *followed by* :ðære byrig *superscript with two vertical
              points beneath* W
67   se: þa se f ^{k}
74   neosunge: geneosunge *with* ge- *superscript and two vertical points
              beneath* W
77   þurh: -r- *superscript with comma beneath* W
82   mann: *followed by erasure of four to five letters* W
115   ðu: *followed by* ana *in* f ^{c}

146	se: *superscript with comma beneath* W halga: *followed by* bisceop *superscript with two vertical points beneath* W
147	on: on þone *f^c*
164	ana is: is ana *f^c*
174	ne geseah: ge ne seah *f^c*
175	naman: namen *with superscript -a- over -e- with punctum and comma beneath* W
185	þa: *superscript (original scribe)* W
187	folces: . . lce *f^c*
202	beoð ge gesunde: beoð gesund . *f^c*
203	burh-ealdor: burhge ealdor *with -ge superscript and two vertical points beneath* W
205	cwæde: *followed by* :hwæðer eart ðu *superscript with two vertical points beneath* W
226	þin: *f^c*; *superscript with two vertical points beneath* W
231	hine swa lange: swa lange hine *f^c*
242	Ælmihtigan: *followed by* :god *superscript with two vertical points beneath* W
247	wunað: leofaþ *f^c* þam: *f^c*; þære, *with* ære *on erasure and cramped* W wuldre: *crossed out and* :eadignysse *written superscript with two vertical points beneath* W

22. Saints Abdon and Sennes *and* The Letter of Christ to Abgar

Manuscripts: This is a two-part Life preserved in two manuscripts, W and L; it was once also in the badly damaged f^k, on what was fols. 131r–32v. In W the first part of the Life is found on fols. 137r–38r. It begins on a new page, following *Mary of Egypt,* a text which is not by Ælfric (for further discussion of *Mary of Egypt,* see Hugh Magennis, "St Mary of Egypt and Ælfric: Unlikely Bedfellows in Cotton Julius E. vii?" in *The Legend of Mary of Egypt in Insular Hagiography,* ed. Erich Poppe and Bianca Ross (Dublin, 1996), 99–112. The points corrector was not active on this text, but there is some correction of obvious errors and omissions by the original scribe. In L it is found on fols. 194v–95v. The title and the opening line of f^k are recorded by Wanley, 207.

The Letter of Christ to Abgar (lines 81–191) follows the account of Saints Abdon and Sennes in all three manuscripts in which it occurs. In W it is found at fols. 138r–39v, in L it is at fols. 195v–97v, and it was at 132–33v in f ^{k} but is now lost. The heading in W is *ITEM ALIA,* in L there is no heading, and in f ^{k} it is called *ALIA NARRATIO,* with Wanley noting "*sc. De Abgaro Rege.*" There is some correction by the original hand in W.

Saints Abdon and Sennes was previously edited and translated by Skeat, vol. 2, 54–59. *The Letter of Christ to Abgar* was previously edited and translated by Skeat, vol. 2, 58–67.

title	AUGUSTI *L f ^{k}*; AGUSTI *W* NATALE: PASSIO *L*
8	asende: sende *L*
23	þu: *L; added superscript with comma beneath W*
30	bugon: abugon *L*
41	nacode: *L*; nocode *W*
44	witum: þreatum *L*
52	binnan þam huse: *omitted L*
55	hi weredon hi: weredon hi *L*
56	deora: *omitted L*
60	wearð: wearð ða *L*
63	Þa þa: *L*; Þa ðe *W*
72	ar-wurðnysse: arwurdnysse *L*; awurðnysse *with* r *added superscript between* a *and* w *W*
72–75	And . . . onwrygennysse: *omitted L*
76	gehyrod: *L*; gehyrað *with* –od *added superscript with comma beneath and two puncta beneath the* –að *W* ða: þas *L*
78	forleton: aletan *L*
title	ITEM ALIA: *omitted L*; ALIA NARRATIO *f ^{k}*
82	geciged: geclypod *L*
84	se: he *L*
89	Iudeiscum: *L*; Iudescum *with second* i *added superscript with comma beneath W*
91	arærst: aræst *L W*
103	cynincge: *gap of possibly five letters' length preceding* cynincge *at top of folio W*
104–12	*Latin omitted L*

113	Þæt . . . gereorde: *omitted L*
115	witegung: *L*; witegu *with* -ng *added superscript with comma beneath W*
119	afyllan: gefyllan *L*
122	gelacnað: *L*; gelacniað *W*
123	gelyfað: *L*; gelyfð *with* a *added superscript between* f *and* ð *with comma beneath W*
124	cyninge: cyninge Abgare *L*
130	þone untrumne: þær untrume *L*
135	þam: þam ðe *L*
136	ætforan his: *L*; æt *with* foran his *added in right margin with a signe de renvoi to indicate insertion W*
137	sume: *omitted L*
139	wære soðlice: soðlice wære *L*
142	Forðan ðe: Forðan þe *L*; For ðan *with superscript* ðe *and comma beneath W*
149	gefæstnodon: gefæstnode *L*
156	he: he eac *L*
168	ferde: *omitted L*
171	mergen: morgen *L*; megen *with superscript* r *and comma beneath W*
179	Adames: Adame *L*
191	AMEN: *omitted L*

23. The Martyrdom of the Maccabees, Their Battles, *and* The Three Orders of Society

Manuscripts: The *Maccabees,* or part thereof, is found extant in eight manuscripts: C, E, L, P, R, W, f^c, and f^k. In W this Life is found on fols. 139v–53r, divided into three parts separated by an *ITEM* and an *ITEM ALIA.* The points corrector worked on this text, frequently making spelling alterations such as final *-e* to *-a,* which are not noted below. The complete Life is found also in C, pp. 341–56, where it is divided into sections, and in E, fols. 328r–42v, which is again divided into numbered sections, although the sections do not always correspond across the manuscripts. The scribe of E uses *heo* where the other manuscripts have *hi* for the nominative plural pronoun; this particular idiosyncrasy has not been noted below. In L (fols. 185r–94v) the text begins at line 320 *(here samod)*. P (fols. 58r–59v) contains *The Three Orders of Society,* with which *Maccabees* ends (line 813 to the end). R (pp. 138–39) contains the *ITEM ALIA,* with which this text ends (line 813 to the end). f^c consists of two binding strips taken from a lost manuscript and includes the opening few lines of the *passio*. See Collins and Clemoes, "The Common Origin of Ælfric Fragments." The badly damaged f^k has the opening of *Maccabees* on fol. 41 but ends at line 29 *(woldon heora)*.

Previously edited and translated by Skeat, vol. 2, 66–125, and edited online by Stuart D. Lee.

title	AUGUSTI: *C*; AGUSTUS *W*; AUGUSTUS *f^k* MACHA-BEORUM: MACHABEORUM .I. *C*
21	gebugon: ða gebugon *E*
22	þæt: *omitted C*; þa *E f^k* Godes: drihtnes *C E*
24	acwellan: *C E f^k*; cwællan *with initial* a *added superscript with two vertical points beneath, and medial* æ *altered to* e *W*
30	fylan mid: befylan mid *C*
39	ett nu: nu et *E*
54	forcuðan: forcuðostan *C*
59	and: *omitted C*
62	tocleofað: cleofað *E* cudu: *C E; preceded by superscript* heora *with two vertical points beneath W*
63	tocleofað: *C*; tocliofað *E; followed by* heora clawa *added superscript with two vertical points beneath W*
65	þæt we: *C; omitted E;* we *preceded by superscript* getacnað þæt *with two vertical points beneath W*
65–66	tocleofan . . . niwan: *C; omitted E*
66	ealdan: *C; followed by* æ *in right-hand margin W* niwan: *C; followed by superscript* gecyðnysse *with two vertical points beneath W* *It is clear that at this point W has been tampered with: the points corrector appears to have erased original text and squeezed in* þæt is on ðære ealdan æ *and on* ðære niwan *into the space provided. He has also added* gecyðnysse *superscript. MS E omits the line and a half from* þæt we . . . þa niwan.
67	and: *omitted C*

74	æ: *C E; preceded by superscript* ealdan *with two vertical points beneath W*
77	mundis: *C E; followed by* þæt is on englisc *added superscript with two vertical points beneath W*
79	ungeleafullum: *C E;* ungeleaffullan *W*
81	ða: *omitted C E* hit: t *added superscript W*
83	hit: *omitted E*
99	andsæte: *C E; followed by superscript* Gode *with two vertical points beneath W*
115	scyppendes: sceppendes *C E;* scyppendes Drihtnes *W*
124	"God sylf . . .": God self *C E; preceded by* and hi cwædon þus *added superscript with a comma beneath and two vertical points at the start of the addition W*
125	þæt: *C E; followed by* is þæt *added superscript with two vertical points beneath W*
128	behamelod wurde: wurde behamelod *C;* wurðe behamolod *E*
131	cwæð to: cwæð þa to *E*
139	gesetnyssum: *E;* gesetnessum *C;* gesetnysse *W*
141	mid him: him mid *C*
148	mid: mid ðam *E*
152	swa swa ðu: *E;* swa swa þu *C;* swa swa *followed by superscript* ðu *with comma beneath W*
155	þe: *omitted E* teartlice on witum: *omitted E*
160	beo: sy *E*
161	sona: *omitted C E*
168	nu: *omitted C*
175	abeah: beseah *E*
176–77	ic . . . heofonum: *omitted E*
182	ac: and *C*
184	þus: *omitted C E*
185	ge: *omitted E*
193	he do: do he *C*
195	oðre þa: oþre þe *C E* acwealde: cwealde *E*
title	ITEM: II *C E;* DE PUGNA MACHABEORUM *f^k*
206	awritan: *C E;* vel asecgan *added superscript W*

221 for: fram *E*

222 eallra: *omitted E*

232 fleah ða: *C E*; fleah *followed by superscript* ða *and two vertical points beneath W*

238 Mathathian: *E*; Mathathiam *C*; Mathian *with* tha *added superscript after first* a *with two vertical points beneath W*

243 strængðe: strengðe *C*; strægðe *E*; strænðe *with* g *added superscript with a comma beneath W*

245 adræfde: todræfde *C E*

249 mycel is: is mycel *E*

252 gemyndige nu: nu gemyndige *E*

260 ge: *omitted E*

263 tomergen: *C*; tomergan *E*; tomegen *with* r *added superscript with comma beneath W*

264 geðoht: goda þoht *E*

266 for: *omitted E*

273 wæs: wearð *E*

275 Hwæt: III Hwæt *C E*

280 gescrydde: gescylde *C*

282 fynd: feondum *C*; his feondum *E*; his *added in right margin following* wiþ *W*

282–83 mid . . . gelic: *omitted C*

287 se: *C E*; seo *with the* o *added superscript with two vertical points beneath W*

288 geblissode his: geblessode þa his *E*

289 þa: *omitted E* lande: *C E*; lande *altered to* landum *with superscript* um *over subpuncted* e *W*

302 þe: þa *E*

305 þa him: him ða *E*

306 mage: magon *E*

307 nu . . . mete-leaste: *omitted E*

313 syndon: synde *C*; synd *E*; ðonne we *added superscript with two vertical points following* syndon *W*

317 ge: *omitted E*

323 ða asprang: asprang ða *L*

325 þeoda: þa þeoda *E*

327 gewinnum: *C E*; winnum *preceded by* ge *added superscript with comma beneath W*

329 Hwæt: IIII Hwæt *C E*; III Hwæt *L*

330 on mode: on his mode *E*

332 to: *C E L*; on *W*

339 healdan: *C E L*; *preceded by superscript* ge *with two vertical points beneath W*

342 stiðan: stiðum *C L*; *omitted E*

349 ðe: *omitted C E L*

353 lytlum: micclum *E*

354 ða: *omitted C*   wolde: wolden *E*; woldon *L*

357 todræfde: dræfde *C E*; todrefde *L*

358 ofslagene: ða ofslagene *L*   þusend: þusenda *C E L*

359 ða: *omitted E*   fram: fram þære *L*   þa ða he fram fyrde gecyrde: *C*; þa he fram fyrde gecyrde *E*; þa ða he fram þære fyrde gecyrde *L*; *in margin with signe de renvoi W*

362 ða: *omitted L*

363 Eft: IIII. Eft *L*

366 micclum: mid mycclum *C*

368 þusend: þusenda *L*

370 ælmihtig: *omitted L*

374 hi: þa *E*   lufigendra: lifigendra God *E*

377 þær: *omitted E*

385 lac: *C E*; *preceded by superscript* heora *with two vertical points beneath W*

386 Iudas: *V.* Iudas *C E*   ða hine: hine ða *E*

389 forbernde: bærnde *L*   bysmore: *E*; bismære *C*; bymore *with* s *added superscript with comma beneath W*   tawode: tucode *E L*

390 Efne: Æfre *C*; .*V.* Efne *L*

392–93 hi . . . hæfdon: *omitted C*

403 afligenne: flegenne *E*

404 gesette: *omitted L*

409 aflymde: flemde *E*

413 gewylde: gefelde *E*

417 ontende: onælde *L*

420 to feohtenne fæstlice: þa to feohtanne færlice *E*

423 feohtes: folces *L*

428 ðusend: þusenda *C E*

429 hæðenan: hæðenes *L*

430 hæðenan: hæðenan folces *E*

435 oferferdon: oferferde *C*

439 manfullan: *E W*; manfullum *C L*

440 gewendon: gewende *E L*

441 an mycel burh: mycel burh an *C*

442 næs: *omitted C* naþre: nanre *E*

449 abrecan: tobrecan *C E L*

450 ofslogon ealle: ealle *omitted C E L*

451 wendon: awændon *C*

453 lifigendan: ælmihtigan *L*

458 ða: þær *C E L*

461 beswicene: besmitene *E*

464 ðær: þa *C*

465 feoh: facn *C E L*

469 gegaderode ða: ða gegaderode *L*

482 Hit: VI Hit *C E L*

483 ær: her *E*

485 mid: mid his *C*

496 sceotende: *C E L*; i *added superscript between* t *and* e *with two vertical points beneath* W

498 hund: *C E L*; hund *with* -red *added superscript with long ligature of* r *extending down to the line* W

502 hi: *C E L*; *second* hi *added superscript with two vertical points beneath* W

507 foroft: oft for *C*

510 gerædedum: *C E L*; gerædum *with* de *added superscript with two vertical points beneath* W

511–12 secgað gehwær ða halgan Godes bec: secgað þa halgan Godes bec gehwar *L*

514 swilce: hwilan *E* her: ær *C E*

515 ða dyreste: dyriste þa *C*; dyreste ða *E L*

519 of menniscum: on menniscum *C L* of þam Iudeiscum cynne: *omitted E*

520 Marian: sancta *added in right margin following* of *W*

523   man-cynne: *C E*; manncynne *L*; cynne *W*

524   ge on: ge *omitted E*   ealdan: *omitted E*

527   þe: *omitted E*   wunian: wuniað *E*

528   swaðeah: þeah *C*

531   Betwux: VII Betwux *C E L*

539   þam fylðum: yflum *C*

548   æl-fremede: *L*; æfremedum *C E*; ælfremedom *W*   ecum: *E L*
        ecan *W*

550   ongebroht: on ongebroht *C*; gebroht *E*

551   þe: þa *E*

552   þa on: on *C E L*

553   wiðsocon siðþan: siððan wiðsocon siðþan *C*; siððan wiðsocan *E*;
        syððan wiðsocon *L*

554   eac swa: *C E L; followed by* hine *added superscript with two vertical
        points beneath W*

556   nean: near *C L*

558   twentig: XXX *E*

563   wera: *C E L*; manna *W*

564   mid cræfte: *C E L; omitted W*

573   nytena: *erasure between this word and* mæst *of a word's length W*

581   geferena: gefera *E*

584   atogenum: anum *E*

587   ða: hine *added right-hand margin W*   hi: *omitted E*

593   here-lafe: here *E*

595   hæfde: he hæfde *L*

597   Hwæt: VIII Hwæt *C E L*

598   leasungum: leasunge *C*; leasungea *E*; læasunge *L*

601   hi: hi mid *C L*; mid *E*

604   gefeohte: *C E L; added superscript with comma beneath W*

608   and nolde: and *omitted C E L*

610   ða: *omitted E*

613   þa sceawode: *large space between the two words, possible erasure W*

617   awæg: onweg *E*

623   com: *C E L; added superscript with two vertical points beneath W*

625   scinende: *W*; scinendan *C E L*

626   ða: þe *C*

629 hundteontig þusenda: *C*; *omitted E*; hun[d]tweontig ðusenda *L*;
   an hund þusenda manna *written over an erasure with a large space*
   remaining at the end stroked through, probably by the points correc-
   tor W

632 mid: *omitted E*

637 hi: him *C E L*

638 an ne belaf: nan ne behalf *E*

643 Wunodon: Hi wunedon *L*

648 Hit: VIIII Hit *C E*; IX *L* gecydd: þa gecyd *C*

649 eall his folc: his folc eal *C*; his folc eall *E L*

651 funde: fulde *C E*

652 mid: and mid *E*

658 werod: *omitted C*

662 earhlicum: eardlicum *C*

666 gefylcum: gehwilcum *C*

667 þa: *omitted E L*

668 ðyder: þider þider *C*

675 on: hine on *L* on: *followed by* ðære byrig *added in right margin,*
   probably by the points corrector W

679 gefremode: *C E L*; fremode *with* ge *added superscript with comma*
   beneath W

681 Menigfealde: *followed by erasure of a word W*

684 Ælmihtigan: *followed by* Godes *added superscript, probably by the*
   points corrector W

685 to alecgenne his fynd: his feond to alecgenne *L*

690 and het: and *omitted E L*

698 beoð: beo *C E L*

702 ealde folc: *C E L*; ealde Godes folc *W* wæpnum: þam wæpnum *C*

706 synd: *C E L*; synd *with* on *added superscript with two vertical points*
   beneath W feower: feower .X. *L*

709 reðan: *omitted L*

710 oðre: heora *E*

712 gefeoht þe: gefeoht is *C E L*; is *added superscript with two vertical*
   points beneath following gefeoht *W* cymð: becymð *C E L*

714 And: *omitted E* gefeoht: gefeoht is *C*

716   Israhela: X. Israhela *C E L*

717–19   he . . . And: *omitted L*

719   ealle: *omitted C*

721   wiþ: wið ða *E*

722   þusend: *C E L; followed by superscript* manna *with two vertical points beneath W*

737   dæge: life *C E L*

740   and: *omitted E*

742   Iohannes: XI Iohannes *L*

745   and: *omitted E*

746   We: XI We *E*

747   secgan: awritan *C*; writan *E L*

754   of: for *E*

755   lacum: lace *C*

758   geciged: geclypod *L*

759–60   to handa . . . cyninge: *omitted L*

766   widewena: wydewan *L*   wan-hafolra: walhafolra *C*   manna: *omitted C E L; added superscript apparently by the original scribe W*

771   wundor: wuldor *E*

776   swa: swa swa *C E L*

777   heah-engel: engel *C*

783   dumb swa: swa dumb *C E L*

786–88   on þære . . . Gode: *omitted E*

788   ælmihtigan: ælmihtig *L*

791   sceolde: scoldon *E*

797   beon moste: moste beon *L*

802   mage: magon *E*

806   gescynt: gescylt *C L*

808   wiþer-sacen: wiðerwinnan *C E L*

812   we: and we *E*

title   DE TRIBUS ORDINIBUS SAECULI: *R; omitted C E L P W;* QUI SINT ORATORES, LABORATORES, BELLATORES *C E*; XII *E*; ITEM ALIA *W*

813   Is: Is nu *P*; Git iss *R*   swaðeah: *omitted R*

816   *Laboratores:* þæt *E*   þa: *omitted P*

824 forþy: *C L R*; forðig *P*; *added superscript with comma beneath following* nu *W*

827 gesewenlice: *C P R*; gesenlice *E*; *omitted L W*

829 þeowan: þiowas *E*; þeowas *L R*

835 gecampe: gewæpne *E*

836 eac: þæt eac *C*   gebringan: belucan *R*

837 Egiptisca: *C E L P R*; Egiptisc *W*

839 to þam cweart-erne: *omitted L*

840 heofonlicum: heofonlican *E*

845 þa halgan þa: þa þa halgan *C*; þam halgum *P*

846 eft: *omitted R*

848 þa: *omitted E*

849 he: *omitted R*

851 asloh: sloh *E*   godnysse: godcundnysse *E P*

852 se munuc: secge we *R*

853 woruld-ðingc: þing *L*

855 þa: *omitted C*

860 arleasra: eallra *R*

863 hi furþon: hi forbæron and furðon *R*

Notes to the Translation

11. SHROVE SUNDAY

This is a composite sermon in a mixture of ordinary and alliterative prose. Section 2.8–11 and section 4 were taken from a text on penance found as part of a series of texts following CH II in Cambridge University Library Gg.3.28, edited and translated by B. Thorpe, *The Homilies of the Anglo-Saxon Church: The First Part, Containing the "Sermones catholici," or Homilies of Ælfric,* 2 vols. (London, 1844–1846; reprinted Hildesheim, 1983), vol. 2, 602–6. The two sections excerpted for LS 11 follow each other directly in *De penitentia,* but in LS 11 Ælfric inserted a story from Jerome's Letter 1 to Innocent between them (*Sancti Eusebii Hieronymi Epistulae,* ed. I. Hilberg, CSEL 54 [Vienna, 1910; 2nd ed. 1996], 1–9). Ælfric may have composed sections 1 and 5 specifically for their place in this set, recycled 2.8–11 and 4, and incorporated 3. The text is not sourced in *Fontes Anglo-Saxonici.*

title   There was ambiguity in this period regarding the beginning of Lent: Ash Wednesday or Shrove Sunday. The manuscripts transmitting LS 11 do not agree on the day for which it was intended.

1.1   In F the text is prefaced by this unique paragraph printed in Ker, 52–53; it incorporates the concluding note, section 6, which is otherwise missing from F's text:

>   *We willað eow areccan gyt ane lytle tihtinge embe ure gemænan sawle þearfe. and eow is micel þearf þæt ge hyt mid micelre gymene understandon þæt we eow secgan willað; we hyt nagon to forsuwigenne þæt we folce heora þearfe ne secgan. understande se ðe wille; þis spel þe ic eow secgan wille. gebyrað nu on Wodnesdæg on þyssere wucan. ac we hyt wyllað nu eow asecgan. for ðan þingon þe her beoð*

399

nu todæg manna ma þonne on Wodnesdæg beon; Nu secg ic eow þæt æghwilcum men gebyrað mid rihte þæt he beo gescrifen on þissere wucan. oððe huruþinga on ðære oðere;

(We still wish to utter to you one little exhortation concerning the common need of our souls, and it is very necessary for you that you understand with great care what we wish to say to you. We must not refrain from telling the people what they need to know, let him understand it who will. This sermon that I intend to address to you belongs now on Wednesday of this week, but we intend to say it to you now because there are more people here today than there may be on Wednesday. Now I say to you that it is rightly fitting for every person to be confessed during this week or at least in the next.)

1.11–14   *Now forty days will not be completed . . . only now*: Ælfric, as B. Bedingfield, *The Dramatic Liturgy of Anglo-Saxon England* (Woodbridge, 2002), 80, has pointed out, is not entirely consistent about the number of fast days in Lent or when Lent begins. Here he perhaps registers an unease at his own inconsistency by saying: *swa swa hit gefyrn geset wæs, þeah ðe we hit eow nu secgan* (as it was decreed long ago, although we are telling you this only now).

1.22–25   Genesis 3:17–20.

2.2   *Ælfstan*: Abbot of the Old Minster, Winchester, who became bishop of Ramsbury in 970.

spoke shamelessly: The verb *wealian,* here "to speak shamelessly, insolently," is related to *wealh,* "foreigner."

2.8   *Decline from evil, and do good*: Psalms 36:27.

2.9   *If the wicked . . . he committed*: Ezekiel 18:21–22.

3.4   *already mentioned*: The young man has actually not been mentioned before now. This section may originally have been part of some other text.

3.67–73   2 Samuel 1:10 and 1:15–16.

4   *Unless you forgive . . . your sins*: Matthew 6:14.

5.22   *Glory be to him in eternity. Amen*: This original ending in W, which was followed by the note (section 6), was considerably changed by the points corrector, who produced an ending that incorporates the note about Ash Wednesday into the main text and reads: *We sædon nu þis spel, for ðan þe her bið læs manna on Wodnesdæg ðonne nu todæg beoð and eow gebyrað þæt ge beon gescrifene on ðissere wucan, oððe huru on ðære oðre. Sy him a wuldor ðe leofað and rixað on ecnysse, ece Drihten. Amen.* (We have delivered this sermon now, because there will be fewer people here on Wednesday than there are today and it is fitting for you to be confessed during this week, or at least during the next one. Glory be to him always who lives and reigns in eternity, eternal Lord. Amen.) C, M, and O read (quoted from M): *Si him a wuldor on ecnysse Amen. We sædon nu þis spell, for þam þe her bið læs manna on Wodnes-dæg and eow gebyrað þæt ge beon gescrifene on þysre wucan oððe huru on þære oðre.* F has *Si him a wuldor on ecnysse Amen* and ends here with no following note; it incorporated the note into its introductory paragraph.

12. ON THE PRAYER OF MOSES FOR MID-LENT SUNDAY

This sermon, much discussed in the context of Ælfric's response to the Vikings and contemporary problems, has been described by Godden, "Apocalypse and Invasion," 135, as one in which he "attempts to place the Viking attacks in terms of the divine will and the end of the world. This is one of the most politically charged of all Ælfric's writings, though much of the charge is just below the surface and the implications are at times puzzling and at times naïve." The principal source is the Bible. Lines 116 to 127 are based on *De duodecim abusivis,* a seventh-century Hiberno-Latin text. This text is not sourced in *Fontes Anglo-Saxonici.*

1–29	Exodus 17:8–13.
94	*in the universally observed Lent*: That is, in the liturgical season of Lent. Old English *lencten* could be used to denote a period of fasting other than the forty days before Easter.
116–27	This gnomic passage is based on the seventh-century Hiberno-Latin text *De duodecim abusivis;* Ælfric also produced an Old English adaptation of this text. See Clayton, *Two Ælfric Texts.*
147–55	The allusion here is to the reign of King Edgar (959–975), noted for his support of Benedictine monasticism, and to the after-

math of his death, when there was a reaction against reformed monasticism. The plague and famine may allude to the great pestilence among cattle that the *Anglo-Saxon Chronicle* records as first occurring in England in 986. The Viking attacks of this period began with sporadic incursions in the 980s but became very serious in the 990s, leading eventually to the Danish conquest of England by Cnut in 1016.

156–74   Leviticus 26:3–36, much abbreviated.

185–89   Genesis 6–7.

190–215   Genesis 18:20–19:28.

221–29   Numbers 16:1–34. Ælfric also deals with this episode, in similar terms, in Pope, no. 20, *De populo Israhel,* lines 249–54.

230   *grumbled*: The verb *ceorian* means "to murmur, to complain, to grumble"; murmuring is a sin in both Old and New Testaments. It is also a major theme in Pope, no. 20, *De populo Israhel,* written ca. 1000 (Pope, vol. 2, 639), which deals with a number of occasions on which the Israelites angered God by complaining and were punished for it. Ælfric stresses the contemporary relevance in lines 287–88.

237–38   Matthew 12:25, Mark 3:24, Luke 11:17.

240–67   2 Samuel 24 and 1 Chronicles 21. David's great sin is to take a census of his people. As Godden, "Apocalypse and Invasion," 136, points out, at a time when the English people were, as this text makes clear, suffering famine and heathen attacks, "the political bite of this text is striking," suggesting, as it does, that God punished David's people because of the king's sin.

272   *And the souls of those who were killed there were saved*: We have not been able to find a source for this statement. It may well be Ælfric's own addition.

273–81   A brief summary of the book of Jonah.

280   *to the almighty God*: As Skeat, vol. 1, 542, points out, the "reading in F restores the true text"; Skeat does not include *to ðam ælmihtigan Gode* in his text, but it is attested by T as well as by F, and its inclusion gives two normal Ælfrician lines rather than one abnormally long one, as in Skeat's edition. From this point on, the line numbers differ by one from Skeat.

13. SAINT GEORGE

There is no historical evidence for Saint George, who was said to have been born in Cappadocia and martyred in Lydda in the early fourth century. The early legends, written in Greek, date from the early fifth century and spread rapidly; there are two main families of Latin legends, in the first of which George's enemy is the Persian emperor Datianus. This is the family known in Anglo-Saxon England. The version of the *Passio Georgii* used by Ælfric is one that combines features of BHL 3373 and 3374. John E. Matzke, "Contributions to the History of the Legend of St. George," *Proceedings of the Modern Language Association* 17 (1902): 464–535, and 18 (1903): 99–171, discusses the legends and prints a text, which he calls *Za,* that is close to what served as Ælfric's source. Zettel, 223–24, points out that this text is in two copies of the Cotton-Corpus legendary, BL, Cotton Nero E. i, part 1, fols. 203v–5v, and Salisbury Cathedral Library 221, fols. 218v–21r. See Whatley, "Acta Sanctorum," 229–31. The text is sourced in *Fontes Anglo-Saxonici.*

title   George's feast day is on April 23.

1–2   *Heretics have written . . . called George*: The source for this statement is probably the *Decretum Gelasianum,* a sixth-century work, part of which lists books forbidden to Christians. See *Das Decretum Gelasianum de libris recipiendis et non recipiendis,* ed. Ernst von Dobschütz, Texte und Untersuchungen zur Geschichte der Altchristlichen Literatur 38, part 4 (Lepizig, 1912).

6   *Datianus*: There was no emperor of that name, although he features as an emperor in the hagiography of Saints George and Alexandria. See B. de Gaiffier, "Sub Daciano Praeside: Étude

de quelques Passions espagnoles," *Analecta Bollandiana* 72 (1954): 378–96.

Cappadocia: The region of Cappadocia in central Anatolia, now in Turkey.

17–19 Psalms 95:5. Compare LS 2, lines 38–40.

90 Psalms 69:2.

14. Saint Mark *and* The Four Evangelists

The source for the first part of this two-part text is the anonymous *Passio Marci,* BHL 5276, and Ott, *Über die Quellen,* showed that the version closest to the Old English is that in AS, April, vol. 3, 347–49. See Frederick M. Biggs, *Sources of Anglo-Saxon Literary Culture: The Apocrypha,* Instrumenta Anglistica Mediaevalia 1 (Kalamazoo, 2007), 48–49. Copies of this text are found in BL, Cotton Nero E. i, part 1, fols. 205v–6v, and Salisbury Cathedral Library 221, fols. 221r–23r, which Zettel, 224–25, notes are even closer to Ælfric's version than the AS text. The text is sourced in *Fontes Anglo-Saxonici.*

title Mark's feast day is on April 25.

13 *Alexandria*: The city of Alexandria in Egypt, still called by the same name.

27 *Anianus*: As Zettel, 224, showed, the variant in the Cotton-Corpus legendary, like the AS version, preserves the same form of the shoemaker's name as Ælfric has.

80–87 Psalms 30:6.

106–18 Although Ælfric might appear to be mentioning here the preface to Jerome's translation to the gospels, Jerome does not talk about the evangelists there. The preface in which he does speak of them is the preface to his *Commentary on Matthew,* as Ott, *Über die Quellen,* 41, pointed out; see *Commentariorum in Matheum libri IV,* ed. D. Hurst and M. Adriaen, Corpus Christianorum Series Latina 77 (Turnhout, 1969).

116–18 Ezekiel 13:3 and 13:6. The quotation is from Jerome's preface to his *Commentary on Matthew.*

120–22 Matthew 7:15.

131, 154 *gospel passages*: These lines have an unusual use of the plural, *þa god-spel,* where we would expect the singular. Godden, CH III, gives "gospel passage" as one of the meanings of the word, however, and this seems to be how Ælfric is using it here.

156   *the land of Achaea:* A province in the south of Greece.

159   *John, the son of Christ's mother's sister:* See Pope, vol. 1, 217–20, on this: "That the mother of James and John, the sons of Zebedee, was the Virgin Mary's sister is a notion that recurs several times in Ælfric's writings, always, so far as I have observed, without warrant from whatever Latin author Ælfric is following for the surrounding details" (217).

176–77   *just as the four rivers that run from paradise together water all this orb:* The *Fontes* database records Isidore of Seville's *In libros veteris ac novi testamenti proemia* (PL 83, col. 175) as the source for these lines. As Frederick M. Biggs, "Ælfric's Mark, Other Things, and Apostolic Authority," *Studies in Philology* 104 (2007): 227–49, at 246, notes, Ælfric may also be drawing on Jerome's Preface to his Commentary on Matthew here.

179–84   Ezekiel 1:5, 1:10. Compare Apocalypse of Saint John 4:7.

190–91   Mark 1:3.

193–94   Luke 1:5.

200   *the divine writer:* This is the only place in Ælfric where the word *driht-wurða* occurs; otherwise it is attested only twice in a hymn, where it is also applied to John the Evangelist. It glosses *theologe* in the hymn, and, as the DOE says, it is an epithet for John the Divine. W and f^k preserve it correctly, but E and L do not, no doubt because of its unfamiliarity.

213–15   Revelation 4:8.

15. Memory of Saints

Clemoes, "Chronology," 222, argued that this text, which "places the passions of martyrs in a historical perspective and relates them to the reader's struggle against sin" was intended to open the LS collection. No direct source has yet been discovered for the first part of the text (1 and 2.1–210); it draws repeatedly on the Bible (see below), but we do not know whether Ælfric composed it independently. It provides a framework for the LS collection in its discussion of the different types of saints whose Lives are included. The second half of the text, from 2.211 onward, is also found as the first half of a composite text, *De octo vitiis et de duodecim abusivis,* and it is based principally on Alcuin's *De virtutibus et vitiis* (PL 101, cols. 613–38) and on Cassian's *Conlationes* and his *De institutis coenobiorum;* see *Iohannis Cassiani opera: Conlationes XXIIII,* ed. M. Petschenig, CSEL 13 (Vienna, 1886), and *Iohannis Cassiani opera: De institutis coenobiorum,* ed. M. Petschenig, CSEL 17 (Vienna, 1888). There are also significant parallels to penitential literature. For a detailed discussion of the sources of the second section of this text, see Clayton, *Two Ælfric Texts,* 71–107. The text is not sourced in *Fontes Anglo-Saxonici.*

title The note following the title states that this text can be read at any time, rather than being assigned to a particular feast day. The placing of the text in W suggests a date in May, as it is placed between Mark (April 25) and Rogationtide, the three days before Ascension Thursday. There is some early evidence for a feast of all the martyrs or all the saints in May. Insofar as Anglo-Saxon calendars record the feast of May 13, however, they note it only as the feast of the dedication of Saint Mary's church.

1.1–3 As Pope, vol. 1, 116n4, points out, lines 1–35 (that is, 1.1–3 in this edition) of this text are "too loosely metrical for assurance."

1.1 *I am Alpha and Omega . . . Almighty*: Revelation 1:8.

1.2 *just*: Christ calls Abel just in Matthew 23:35.

  the seventh man from Adam: Jude 1:14 mentions Enoch, the seventh from Adam.

2.2–3 Job 1:8 and 2:3.

2.23–24 Acts of the Apostles 13:22 and 1 Samuel 13:14. Compare LS 17.28–31.

2.25–26 2 Kings 2.

2.27 *like Enoch*: Genesis 5:24 describes how Enoch was seen no more because he was taken by God, and Hebrews 11:5 says that Enoch was taken without dying because of his faith.

2.34 *fiery chariot*: The fiery chariot is in 2 Kings 2:11.

2.36–42 Daniel 3.

2.67   *like a boundary between Moses and us*: In his *Sermo* 293, Augustine calls John a boundary between the Old and New Testaments (PL 38, col. 1328).

2.69–70   Matthew 11:11.

2.88–91   Matthew 11:29.

2.95–98   Matthew 4:17.

2.99–101   Matthew 4:23.

2.102–5   Matthew 4:24.

2.106–8   *healed . . . savior . . . heal . . . savior's*: There is a pun on *hælend* and *hælan* here in the Old English, because *hælend*, "savior," also means "healer." "Heal" and "healer" would be more literal translations.

2.107–9   Luke 9:1, and see Matthew 10:8.

2.110   *as Christ himself did*: The gospel accounts of Christ cleansing the leper are Matthew 8:2–3, Mark 1:40–42, and Luke 5:12–14.

2.112–14   Luke 10:1.

2.119–44   Luke 9:57–62, and compare Matthew 8:19–20.

2.171   *Arius*: The originator of the heresy that denied the true divinity of Christ. Arius lived from ca. 250 to ca. 336.

2.177   See 1 Timothy 3:2, Titus 1:8.

2.207   See Matthew 24:22, Mark 13:20.

2.111–12   See 1 Corinthians 13:13.

2.224–26   Matthew 22:37–39, Mark 12:30–31, and Luke 10:27.

2.227   Matthew 5:44, Luke 6:27.

2.241   *fornication*: Old English *forligr* covers both fornication and adultery.

2.243   1 Corinthians 6:15.

2.246   1 Timothy 6:10.

2.258–59   See 2 Corinthians 7:10.

2.303–5   Luke 21:19.

2.306–7   Ecclesiastes 7:10.

2.316–17   Philippians 3:20.

2.346   This text seems to have ended without a concluding doxology, as it still does in C. However, the points corrector in W, obviously dissatisfied with this, added another conclusion superscript and in the margin: *Ðam to wuldre ðe on ecnysse rixað, ece*

407

Drihten; þam sy wuldor and lof, ðe a leofað, mid Fæder and mid Suna and mid ðam Halgan Gaste on ecnysse. Amen. (To his glory who reigns in eternity, the eternal Lord; to whom be glory and praise, who lives forever, with the Father and with the Son and with the Holy Spirit in eternity. Amen.) In L, a different ending has been added, but this time integrated into the writing of the homily rather than as a later addition: *Þærto us gefultumige se ðe leofað and rixað a buton ende. Amen.* (May he who lives and reigns forever without end help us to go there. Amen.)

16. ON OMENS

Both in content and in form, this sermon falls into two parts, aptly summarized in the title in C: *Sermo in letania maiore de epistola Pauli et de auguriis* (A sermon for Rogationtide on the letter of Paul and on omens). The principal sources for the first part are the letters of Paul, with quotations from Galatians, 1 Timothy, and 1 Corinthians; this section also contains a passage similar to some lines in LS 1. The principal source for the second part is Caesarius of Arles's *Sermo* 54, as Max Förster, "Altenglische Predigtquellen I," *Archiv für das Studium der neueren Sprachen und Literaturen* 116 (1906): 301–14, pointed out. There are also parallels with the so-called *Pseudo-Egbert Penitential,* now called the *Old English Penitential;* see *Die altenglische Version des Halitgar'schen Bussbuches,* ed. Josef Raith (Hamburg, 1933; reprinted Darmstadt, 1964), also edited on Allen Frantzen's Penitentials website: http://www.anglo-saxon.net/penance/. The text is sourced in *Fontes Anglo-Saxonici.*

title W names this text *De auguriis* in its table of contents but then notes only the occasion at the start of the text itself: *Sermo in laetania maiore.* The manuscripts vary greatly in what they call the text, C's title being the most comprehensive. The sermon is assigned to Rogationtide, the three days before Ascension Thursday, an important time of fasting, prayer, and processions. Ælfric wrote homilies for all three days of Rogationtide in both CH I and II. Ascension Thursday can fall between April 30 and June 3, depending on the date of Easter.

1.1 *the teacher of all peoples*: In 1 Timothy 2:7, Paul terms himself *doctor Gentium* (the doctor [i.e., teacher] of the Gentiles).

Brethren . . . the lusts of the flesh: Galatians 5:16–17.

the flesh desires what is contrary to the spirit . . . to the flesh: Here Ælfric is translating *Caro enim concupiscit adversus spiritum, spiritus autem adversus carnem* (Galatians 5:17). See Alexander, "W. W. Skeat and Ælfric," 43–44. W's *gewinð* is an error, and the other manuscripts all preserve the correct reading.

But the soul . . . subject to its commands: This is very similar to LS 1.20. As Godden points out: "The Lives 1 passage is itself based on Ælfric's Boulogne sermon which is in turn based here on Alcuin's *De Animae Ratione*." See Malcolm R. Godden, "The Sources of Lives 17 (On Auguries) (Cameron B.1.3.18)," *Fontes Anglo-Saxonici: World Wide Web Register* (First published 2002; updated 2007). http://fontes.english.ox.ac.uk/.

1.2   *If you are led . . . under the law*: Galatians 5:18.

The law is not . . . guilty: 1 Timothy 1:9.

1.3   *The works of the flesh . . . God's kingdom*: Galatians 5:19–21.

1.4   *Brethren . . . the kingdom of God*: 1 Corinthians 6:9–10. As Rhonda L. McDaniel, "Hnescnys," 87, points out, Ælfric omits Paul's *masculorum concubitores* (those who lie with men) in addition to translating *molles* (which in the Latin means "soft, effeminate") as *hnescan* (those who are morally soft/weak; DOE, under *hnesce,* adj.), and he then specifies in the next clause precisely what he means by this term. See McDaniel, "Hnescnys: Weakness of Mind in the Works of Ælfric," in *Intertexts: Studies in Anglo-Saxon Culture Presented to Paul E. Szarmach,* ed. Virginia Blanton and Helene Scheck, Medieval and Renaissance Texts and Studies 334, Arizona Studies in the Middle Ages and the Renaissance 24 (Tempe, 2008), 79–90.

This is what you were . . . our God: 1 Corinthians 6:11.

2.6–17   *The fruits of the Spirit . . . evil desires*: Galatians 5:22–24.

2.58   *when a child is born to them:* For this meaning for *hwæt*, see DOE, under *hwæt,* III.A.1.c.

2.62   *one sorcerer*: The corresponding passage in Caesarius has an unspecified someone say this, not a *wiglere*.

2.68–71   The source for these lines is the pseudo-Marcellus *Passio sanctorum apostolorum Petri et Pauli,* in *Acta Apostolorum Apocrypha,* ed. R. A. Lipsius and M. Bonnet (Leipzig, 1891), vol. 1, 119–77.

2.139–43   Matthew 10:29–31.

2.144–53   Matthew 8:28–34, Mark 5:2–13.

2.171–72   1 Corinthians 10:21.

2.173–75   Matthew 6:24.

2.176–220 This passage is drawn from the Old English translation of Bo-
            ethius's *Consolation of Philosophy;* see Godden and Irvine, *The
            Old English Boethius,* vol. 1, B 41. On Ælfric's use of the *Old Eng-
            lish Boethius* in this text, see Malcolm R. Godden, "Ælfric and
            the Alfredian Precedents," in Magennis and Swan, *A Compan-
            ion to Ælfric,* 151–54.

2.179–82   Psalms 36:27.

2.183   See 2 Corinthians 9:6, 1 Corinthians 3:8.

17. KINGS

The sources of this text are the four biblical books of Kings. Ælfric gives
a selective abbreviation, concentrating on good and bad kings and how
they relate to the prophets as representatives of the church. The relevant
biblical passages are noted below. The text is not sourced in *Fontes Anglo-
Saxonici.*

title   No occasion is mentioned for the reading of this text, but Kings
            was read in the monastic office from the second Sunday af-
            ter Pentecost until the first Sunday in August; Christopher A.
            Jones, ed., *Ælfric's Letter to the Monks of Eynsham,* Cambridge
            Studies in Anglo-Saxon England 24 (Cambridge, 1999), 147 and
            222. As Pentecost is fifty days after Easter, this usually gives a
            date in May to begin Kings, and here it comes between LS 16,
            assigned to Rogationtide, and the feast of Saint Alban, on June
            22.

1–7   These lines summarize 1 Samuel 8–10.

1   *Saul:* Saul was the first king of a united kingdom of Israel and
            Judah. His reign is traditionally dated to the late eleventh cen-
            tury BCE.

1–11   As Pope, vol. 1, 116n4, says, lines 1–11 are "too loosely metrical
            for assurance," but they gradually become regular.

8–9   1 Samuel 13 and 15.

10–11   1 Samuel 16:14, 1 Samuel 18:10.

12   1 Samuel 15.

14   1 Samuel 16. David, who probably died ca. 970 BCE, was, according to the Old Testament, the first king of the Judaean dynasty, and he succeeded Saul as king of the united kingdom of Israel and Judah.

15–27   1 Samuel 17.

19   *Goliath*: A giant Philistine warrior.

28–31   Acts of the Apostles 13:22, 1 Samuel 13:14.

32–36   David's reign is recounted in 2 Samuel 2–24, 1 Kings 1–2, and 1 Chronicles 11–19.

45–49   1 Kings 16:29–32.

45   *Ahab*: King of Israel in the ninth century BCE.

46   *Baal*: The word means "lord" or "owner," and it is used in the Old Testament of the Semitic deities associated with fertility of the land and of animals.

48   *a fierce devil, found by means of heresy*: This line is difficult to translate. The translation offered here is guided by Ælfric's use of *afundene* in Pope, no. 21, line 155: *Manega oþre godas wæron mislice afundene, and eac swilce gydenan, on swiðlicum wurðmynte geond ealne middaneard, manncynne to forwyrde* . . . (Many other gods, and likewise goddesses, were variously to be found in great honor throughout the world, to the ruin of mankind . . .).

50   *Jezebel*: Jezebel, wife of Ahab and notorious for promoting pagan cults.

53   *Elijah*: Elijah, traditionally the greatest prophet of Israel, who lived in the ninth century BCE.

53–153 1 Kings 17–18.

75   *Obadiah*: Obadiah managed Ahab's household.

154–70 1 Kings 19:1–8.

171–214 1 Kings 21:1–23.

214–26 1 Kings 22:1–38.

214–15 *Ahab the king advanced . . . great army*: In the Vulgate (1 Kings 22), Ahab decides to retake Ramoth Gilead from the king of Syria.

227–68 1 Kings 22:51–52, and 2 Kings 1.

228   *Ahaziah*: A king of Israel in the ninth century BCE.

268   *Jehoram*: A king of Israel in the ninth century BCE.

269   2 Kings 3:1–2 (this gives the reign as twelve years).

270–72   Compare 2 Kings 9:22.

273–97   2 Kings 2:1–13.

276   *Elisha*: A prophet in the ninth century BCE, the disciple of and successor to Elijah.

300–301a 2 Kings 4.

301b–8   2 Kings 13:20–21.

309–12   2 Kings 5.

315–56   2 Kings 9.

317   *Jehu*: A king of Israel in the ninth century BCE.

357–85   2 Kings 10.

368   *Samaria*: A city in Israel.

388–433 2 Kings 18–20, and 2 Chronicles 29–32.

389   *Hezekiah*: King of Judah who reigned at the end of the eighth century and the beginning of the seventh century BCE.

396   *Sennacherib*: King of the Assyrians from 705 to 681 BCE.

412   *Isaiah*: A prophet in the eighth century BCE.

434–51   2 Kings 21:1–17, and 2 Chronicles 33.

434   *Manasseh*: A king of Judah in the seventh century BCE.

438   *the Chaldean people*: A Semitic people who ruled Babylon for a period.

439   *Babylon*: A city on the Euphrates River.

452   *Amon*: A king of Judah in the seventh century BCE.

452–57   2 Kings 21:19–24, and 2 Chronicles 33:21–25.

458   *Josiah*: A king of Judah in the seventh century BCE.

458–72   2 Kings 22 and 23:1–29, and 2 Chronicles 34–35.

18. SAINT ALBAN *AND* ON THE UNJUST

Alban was a Christian martyr in Roman Britain who probably died in the reign of Diocletian, ca. 303 in the Roman town of Verulamium, now St. Albans. The source for the first part of this text is Bede's *HE,* Book 1, chapters 6–8, which Ælfric followed closely. The second part, headed *De iniustis* in f ^{k}, appears to be a freely composed piece by Ælfric; in it he uses biblical passages (Luke 23, 2 Samuel 15–18, Matthew 27) to make a series of points. Clemoes, "Chronology," 221, suggested that this part reads "like an extract from a letter" and said that it seems to have little to do with the first part of the text. It certainly reads like a response to contemporary conditions and problems that disturbed Ælfric in the unsettled times of the Scandinavian invasion (Godden, "Ælfric's Saints' Lives and the Problem of Miracles," 296–97). See Whatley, "Acta Sanctorum," 62–64. The text is sourced in *Fontes Anglo-Saxonici.*

title   L gives the date of Alban's feast, June 22. It is unusual for W not to record the date, but it is also missing from f^k.

1   *Diocletian*: Roman emperor from 284 CE to 305 CE. The Diocletianic Persecution was the most severe of the Roman persecutions of Christians.

3–4   *two hundred years and eighty-six after Christ's incarnation*: Bede gives this date for Diocletian's accession.

17   *came to England*: What was later to become England was, of course, called Britain and part of the Roman Empire in this period.

133   *Aaron and Julius*: Bede calls them *Legionum urbis cives,* citizens of the City of Legions, which is possibly Caerleon-on-Usk. Gildas was the first to mention them, in *De excidio Britonum (On the Ruin of Britain).*

148   *Hengest and Horsa*: Traditionally, the leaders of the first wave of Germanic invasions of Britain in the fifth century.

150   *Augustine*: A Roman monk who was chosen by Pope Gregory to lead a mission to convert the English to Christianity. He arrived in Kent in 597 and became the first archbishop of Canterbury.

151   *Gregory*: Pope Gregory the Great (ca. 540–604).

164–68   Luke 23:32–43.

196–223   2 Samuel 15–18.

225–27   Matthew 27:3–5.

241–43   *as books tell us . . . crookedness*: There are many biblical condemnations of judges accepting bribes, but the closest formulation appears to be Deuteronomy 16:19.

248–54   See Frank Barlow, *The English Church 1000–1066,* 2nd ed. (London and New York, 1979), 183–208, on private ownership of churches in England; he notes that "the lord's church tended to be treated like his mill and oven and other seigneurial monopolies" (186).

19. Saint Æthelthryth

Æthelthryth was an East Anglian princess who became queen in Northumbria and then abbess of Ely; she died in 679. Married twice, she is reputed to have remained a virgin. The principal source for this Life is Bede's *HE,* Book 4, chapter 19; the text is sourced in *Fontes Anglo-Saxonici* and discussed in detail by Gretsch, *Ælfric and the Cult of Saints,* 215–31. Ælfric restructured the narrative radically, as Gretsch demonstrates. The story narrated in lines 123–30 is based on Rufinus, *Historia monachorum* (see Schulz-Flügel, *Tyrannius Rufinus, Historia monachorum,* 16.50–112). It is discussed by Peter Jackson, "Ælfric and the Purpose of Christian Marriage: A Reconsideration of the *Life of Æthelthryth,* Lines 120–30," *Anglo-Saxon England* 29 (2000): 235–60, and by Gretsch, *Ælfric and the Cult of Saints,* 218–21.

title   Æthelthryth's feast day is on June 23.

5   *Anna*: King of the East Angles from ca. 636 to ca. 654.

8   *a ruler*: Æthelthryth's first husband, whom she married ca. 652, is named as Tondberht by Bede. Bede describes him as a *princeps,* and the Old English calls him an *ealdorman.* We have translated with "ruler" here, as Tondberht was ruler of the small kingdom of the South Gyrwe in the fens of East Anglia; an *ealdorman* when Ælfric was writing was someone holding an office conferred by the king.

14   *Ecgfrith*: King of the Northumbrians from 670 to 685. Æthelthryth married him ca. 660.

19   *Wilfrid*: Wilfrid (ca. 634–709) was bishop of Northumbria for most of the period from 664 to 709 and a controversial figure. His Life was written by a contemporary, Stephen of Ripon, sometimes known as Eddius Stephanus; available in translation in J. F. Webb and and D. H. Farmer, trans., *The Age of Bede* (rev. ed. Harmondsworth, 1998), 105–84.

20   *Bede*: Bede (ca. 673–735), a monk of Wearmouth-Jarrow, was
       the most learned and prolific Latin writer of Anglo-Saxon Eng-
       land.

38   *Ely*: The double monastery of women and men founded by
       Æthelthryth, who was also its first abbess (ca. 672).

70   *Seaxburg*: Anna's eldest daughter, married to Eorcenberht, king
       of Kent (r. 640–664), before becoming abbess of Ely after
       Æthelthryth. She died ca. 700.

78   *Grantchester*: A village near Cambridge. It had been a small Ro-
       man settlement, so the sarcophagus was almost certainly Ro-
       man.

80   *standing by the wall*: It is explicitly the city walls in Bede.

123   *one nobleman*: He is a merchant in Rufinus, *Historia monachorum.*

20. SAINT SWITHUN *AND* SAINT MACARIUS
AND THE SORCERERS

Swithun was bishop of Winchester from 852 to 863. Very little is known of
his life, but he became a major saint of the Benedictine Reform in England
after his remains were translated into a shrine in the Old Minster in Winchester in 971. Gretsch's conclusion in *Ælfric and the Cult of Saints,* 191–92,
is "that Ælfric did not entirely approve of important aspects of the cult
of St Swithun: a saint without a biography, who applied his miraculous
and intercessory powers indiscriminately on behalf of innocent and guilty
persons alike, and who had made a habit of appearing to people in their
dreams. And yet, he was a paramount saint of Winchester, culted especially at the Old Minster, Ælfric's intellectual and spiritual home." The
sources for this text are Lantfred's *Translatio et miracula S. Swithuni,* probably written ca. 972/73 (Lapidge, *Cult of St Swithun,* 217–333), and the *Epitome translationis et miraculorum S. Swithuni* (Lapidge, *Cult of St Swithun,*
553–73). The *Epitome* must have been written after 984, probably by Ælfric,
(Lapidge, *Cult of St Swithun,* 558). Lapidge, in his edition, notes the source
for each section of Ælfric's Life; the use of sources in this text is also discussed in detail by Gretsch, *Ælfric and the Cult of Saints,* 174–92. It is not
sourced in *Fontes Anglo-Saxonici.*

In W, a short account of how Saint Macarius dispelled an illusion of the devil by which a young woman appeared as a mare is appended to the *Life of Swithun,* with the heading *Item alia* (Another in the Same Manner). The Macarius story appears in two other manuscripts, R and S, as part of a conclusion to *On Omens* (LS 16). The Macarius story reinforces the warnings about false dreams included in the Swithun text. Its source, as Pope, vol. 2, 789, points out, is Rufinus's *Historia Monachorum* (see Schulz-Flügel, *Tyrannius Rufinus,* 28.3).

title   Ælfric's text is for the feast of Swithun's deposition on July 2 (the anniversary of his death), not for what is now known as Saint Swithun's Day, the feast of his translation on July 15.

1   *Edgar*: King of the Mercians and Northumbrians from 957 to 959, and king of the English from 959 to 975. Edgar's support of the Benedictine Reform in England was crucial to its success.

14   *Winchester*: This city, sixty-one miles southwest of London, was the center of the Benedictine Reform movement, which began in the middle of the tenth century. The cult of Saint Swithun was central to the reform movement.

16   *Æthelwold*: Æthelwold, born between 904 and 909, studied under Dunstan at Glastonbury, was abbot of Abingdon (ca. 954–963), and then bishop of Winchester (963–984). He was one of the leading figures in the Benedictine Reform movement and had much influence with King Edgar.

19   *a structure*: See Lapidge, *Cult of St Swithun,* 268, for a short discussion of the type of structure built over Swithun's tomb.

21–23   *the saint was brought . . . new building*: This refers to the translation of Swithun from his tomb outside Winchester Cathedral to a shrine inside, in a lavish ceremony held on July 15, 971.

26–27   *the priest who is called Eadsige . . . their vices*: The allusion here is to the expulsion, on Æthelwold's orders and with the support of King Edgar, of the secular clergy from the Old Minster, Winchester, in 963. Eadsige was one of the secular canons expelled, but he later returned to the Old Minster and became the sacrist responsible for the shrine of Saint Swithun. The Old Minster was constructed in 648 by King Cenwalh of Wessex and was a cathedral from the 660s onward.

33 *Winchcombe*: A town in the Cotswolds, about eighty-five miles north of Winchester.

44 *one ring*: The rings are iron rings set into the lid of Swithun's tomb.

85 *his having caused their expulsion*: That is, Eadsige blamed Æthelwold for the expulsion of the secular clergy.

91–92 See Matthew 23:12, and Luke 14:11 and 18:14.

115 *New Minster*: New Minster, Winchester, founded in 901.

116 *Judoc*: A Breton saint who died ca. 668. Winchester acquired his relics ca. 901 and observed his feast.

141 *Saint Peter's house*: The Old Minster, Winchester.

167 *a very small offense*: Here and in line 416, Ælfric stresses that people were being severely punished for very little; Gretsch, *Ælfric and the Cult of Saints*, 186–87, points out that miracles performed on prisoners are much more frequent in Lantfred (eight as opposed to Ælfric's two) and that Ælfric adopts only those where the prisoner's offense was trivial.

267–68 *in accordance with the sentence ... cut off his ears*: Mutilation is a feature of late Anglo-Saxon law. See Katherine O'Brien O'Keeffe, "Body and Law in Late Anglo-Saxon England," *Anglo-Saxon England* 27 (1998): 209–32.

290–306 This story is not in Lantfred or in the *Epitome*; Gretsch, *Ælfric and the Cult of Saints*, 187, says that it is almost certain that Ælfric did not invent it, but that "this story probably lets us glimpse the oral tradition which the cult of Swithun will have fostered in the decades after 971."

307–17 Another section without a source in Lantfred or the *Epitome*.

323 *nobleman*: A *þegn* in the Old English, this person is an ealdorman in Ælfric's source for this passage, Lantfred's *Translatio et Miracula S. Swithuni*. It appears that he was Ælfhere of Mercia (d. 983), the most powerful ealdorman of his day, Lapidge, *Cult of St Swithun*, 533n787.

372–73 Because Skeat did not know of the eyeskip from one *hine* (him) to the next in W, the numbering of this edition deviates by one line from Skeat from this point.

373 Compare Luke 23:34.

374 Compare Matthew 5:44, and Luke 6:28.

375–77 Romans 12:20.

400 *to the city*: Skeat, and Lapidge, *Cult of St Swithun,* 584, read *Winceastre* here, but *win* is a superscript addition with the two vertical points beneath that are characteristic of the points corrector. It is clear from the context that Winchester is meant, as it has been mentioned in line 385.

403 *Lantfred*: Lantfred was a priest and monk, probably from Francia (Lapidge, *Cult of St Swithun,* 219), who wrote the *Translatio et Miracula S. Swithuni* while a monk in the Old Minster in Winchester.

413 Jeremiah 29:8–9.

444–64 These lines are not paralleled in the sources.

449 *naval force*: This refers to the Viking ships that were attacking England when Ælfric was writing LS.

453 *eight kings*: The D, E, and F versions of the *Anglo-Saxon Chronicle* record Edgar meeting with six other kings at Chester in 972 (properly 973), and other almost contemporary sources also mention the meeting. Post-Conquest accounts agree with Ælfric in having eight kings. See David Thornton, "Edgar and the Eight Kings, AD 973: Textus et Dramatis Personae," *Early Medieval Europe* 10 (2001): 49–79.

470 *wizards*: The word *wischeras* is unique; Skeat translates it as "diviners," while BT Supplement suggests "wizards." Pope, vol. 2, 797, suggests a link with Old English *wisc* or *wysc* (wish) and points to the Old Norse cognate, *ósk,* as having associations with the gods.

21. Saint Apollinaris

Apollinaris is thought to have been the first bishop of Ravenna in the second century; from the fifth century he was regarded as a martyr, although his martyrdom is not certain. The *Passio Apollinari* (BHL 623) is probably a seventh-century text. Ælfric's Life is closest to the Latin version published in AS, July, vol. 5, 344–50. The Latin text is in two manuscripts of the Cotton-Corpus legendary, BL Cotton Nero E. i, part 2, fols. 49r–52r, and Salisbury Cathedral Library 222, fols. 27v–33v, and Zettel points out that they share readings with Ælfric's source. Ælfric radically changes the emphasis of the Latin in this abbreviated adaptation of the source. See Whatley, "Acta Sanctorum," 87–88. The text is sourced in *Fontes Anglo-Saxonici.*

title   Apollinaris's feast day is on July 23.

1   *Claudius*: Roman emperor from 41 CE to 54 CE.

2   *Antioch*: Now the city of Antakya, Turkey. According to tradition, Saint Peter was the first bishop of Antioch.

19   *Ravenna*: A city in northeastern Italy.

38   *a high-ranking officer*: A military tribune in the source.

72   *nobleman*: Boniface is a *nobilissimus vir* in the Latin.

98   *protector*: the Latin describes Rufus as a *patricius et consul* (patrician and consul). Ælfric uses *mund-bora* (protector) five times otherwise, all in religious contexts, and the use of *mund-bora* here seems unusual for him. We have not emended, as W and f᪰ᶜ are in agreement, but Ælfric gives *ræd-boran* (counselors, consuls) as the Old English for *consulas* in his version of the Old Testament Judges (*The Old English Heptateuch and Ælfric's Libellus de Veteri Testamento et Novo, Vol. I.*, ed. Richard Marsden, EETS o.s. 330 [London, 2008], 198, lines 267–69), and *ræd-bora* would add to the alliterative pattern of the line.

223   *hidden*: There is something odd about this line, as the centurion is clearly not hidden from Demosthenes, but fᶜ, insofar as it survives, agrees with W here. The Latin reads *qui et ipse iam Christianus erat occulte* (who was himself already secretly a Christian), translated in the next line of the Old English, but has nothing that corresponds to *bediglod* (hidden). It is possible that the scribe was influenced by *digellice* (secretly) in the following line and that there was a different past participle here originally.

249   *the wall*: The city wall. In the Latin he is buried outside the walls.

22. Saints Abdon and Sennes *and* The Letter of Christ to Abgar

Although Abdon and Sennes may be unfamiliar to a modern audience, there is a significant body of evidence pointing to knowledge of these two Persian kings, whose story circulated as part of the legend of Saint Lawrence from as early as the sixth century (Whatley, "Acta Sanctorum," 39). There is little historical evidence to confirm the date or precise circumstances of their martyrdom, however. The *Passio sanctorum Abdonis et Sennetis* (BHL 6) appears as part of a composite text in two manuscripts of the Cotton-Corpus legendary: BL, Cotton Nero E. i, part 2, fols. 67r–73r, and Oxford, Bodleian Library MS Fell 1, fols. 57r–67r (see Jackson and Lapidge, 139; Zettel, 23 and 48). As Zettel notes, these copies derive from a textual tradition that differs slightly from that available to Ælfric (Zettel, 227–28). The feast of Abdon and Sennes is marked in the *Old English Martyrology* for July 30 (Christine Rauer, ed. and trans., *The Old English Martyrology: Edition, Translation and Commentary* [Woodbridge, 2013], 148–49), and in Bede's *Martyrology* (Whatley, "Acta Sanctorum," 39–40).

For the apocryphal *Letter of Christ to Abgar,* Ælfric drew on Rufinus's translation of Eusebius's *Ecclesiastical History.* Latin versions of the *Letter* from Anglo-Saxon England are preserved in BL, Cotton Galba A. xiv, and BL, Royal 2. A. xx, where the apotropaic qualities of the text are made explicit (see Christopher M. Cain, "The Apocryphal Legend of Abgar in Ælfric's *Lives of Saints*," *Philological Quarterly* 89 [2010]: 303–402). Although these two Lives (*Abdon and Sennes* and the *Letter of Christ to Abgar*) are designated as a single text in all three manuscripts in which they are preserved, as Skeat points out, "it is not clear why this Letter is introduced at this place, as it belongs rather to the *Life of Saint Thomas*" (Skeat, vol. 2, 448). Cain, "The Apocryphal Legend of Abgar," argues that the condemnation of the *Letter* by the *Decretum Pseudo-Gelasianum* and its widespread use as an amuletic text "likely conditioned Ælfric's reception of the text" (386) and that he "did not choose the patently obvious arrangement suggested by his Latin sources" (396) in an attempt to distance the *Letter* physically and intellectually from the controversy surrounding the *Life of Thomas,* to which Ælfric alludes in the Latin preface to that Life. Both parts of the text are sourced in *Fontes Anglo-Saxonici.*

title   Saints Abdon and Sennes (also known as Sennen) are commemorated on July 30.

1   *Decius*: Decius (249–251 CE) became emperor in 249, and in 250 he issued an edict that everyone in the Roman Empire should offer a sacrifice to the Roman gods and on behalf of the well-

being of the emperor. He appears also in CH I 29 (the *Passion of Saint Lawrence*) and CH II 27.188, 195 (the *Passion of Saint James* and *Seven Sleepers*).

31   *Valerian*: The imperial prefect under the emperor Decius (see CH I 29, the *Passion of Saint Lawrence*).

title   The heading "Letter of Christ to Abgar" is not attested in any manuscript but is used to aid the differentiation between and discussion of the two parts of the text. "*ITEM ALIA*" ("another in the same manner") is the title preserved in W.

104–6   *Blessed are you . . . believe and live*: These lines echo John 20:29 where Jesus addresses Thomas, who had doubted the truth of the resurrection and demanded to see Christ's wounds for himself, and serve as a reminder of the original context of this Letter as part of the passion of Thomas.

108   *first I have to fulfill that for which I was sent:* There is a possible echo of Luke 4:43 here; the Letter as a whole draws on biblical Latin, even if the Bible is never directly quoted.

128   *Thaddeus:* Thaddeus of Edessa was, according to Eusebius, sent by Thomas to preach and evangelize in Edessa and throughout Syria, Mesopotamia, and Persia. He is sometimes identified with Judas Thaddeus the apostle, and Ælfric alludes to this when he notes that he was "also called Judas by his other name" (134).

163   *a severe foot disease*: This appears to be gout.

23. THE MARTYRDOM OF THE MACCABEES, THEIR BATTLES, *AND* THE THREE ORDERS OF SOCIETY

This text falls into three parts, a *passio*—which includes some explanation by Ælfric of the Jewish food laws described in the book of Leviticus—followed by an account of the Maccabees' battles as described in the deuterocanonical Jewish books 1 Maccabees and 2 Maccabees, greatly condensed. Finally, it ends with a section on the three orders of society, including a discussion of the importance of spiritual warfare to the monastic life and to the community as a whole. For discussion of the place of the three orders of society in Anglo-Saxon political thinking and, more specifically, in

the writings of Alfred and Ælfric, see Timothy Powell, "The 'Three Orders' of Society in Anglo-Saxon England," *Anglo-Saxon England* 23 (1994):
103–32. The text is sourced in *Fontes Anglo-Saxonici.*

title   The feast day of the Maccabeean martyrs is commemorated on
         August 1, as indicated within the text (lines 201–2).
1   *Alexander*: Alexander the Great (356–323 BCE) conquered Judea
         as part of his massive empire-building enterprise. The story of
         the Maccabees, which draws in this section from 1 Maccabees
         1:1–67, albeit in a form that has been significantly condensed
         in Ælfric's account, tells how the Greek ruler Antiochus at-
         tempted to suppress Jewish practices and Jewish law but was
         met by a revolt.
7   *Antiochus*: Antiochus IV Epiphanes (175–164 BCE) was a Greek
         king of the Seleucid Empire.
20   *the old law*: Ælfric uses the term *seo ealde æ* (the old law) to refer
         to the Old Testament and, more specifically within this text, to
         the food laws as described in the book of Leviticus. He fre-
         quently sets it in opposition to the New Testament or the Gos-
         pels established by Christ, as at lines 58–59: *þa ealdan gecyðnysse
         and Cristes gesetnysse, þæt is seo ealde æ and seo niwe gecyðnyss* (the
         old testament and Christ's command, that is to say the old law
         and the new testament). See Andrew P. Scheil, "Anti-Judaism in
         Ælfric's *Lives of Saints,*" *Anglo-Saxon England* 28 (1999): 65–86.
32–36   The story of Eleazar is drawn from 2 Maccabees 6, but Ælfric
         uses the material of 1 Maccabees 1:65 (*Et multi de populo Israhel
         definierunt apud se ut non manducarent inmunda, et elegerunt magis
         mori quam cibis coinquinari inmundis,* "And many of the people of
         Israel determined with themselves that they would not eat un-
         clean things, and they chose rather to die than to be defiled
         with unclean meats") to unite the story with the previous de-
         scription of the Jewish subjection under Antiochus.
32   *scribe*: Eleazar is described in 2 Maccabees 6:18 as one of the
         leading scribes *(unus de primoribus scribarum),* indicating that he
         was one of the most learned scholars of Mosaic law at the time.
37–85   This digression or exposition of the biblical material is drawn

from Leviticus 11. C. Grant Loomis, "Further Sources of Ælfric's Saints' Lives," *Harvard Studies and Notes in Philology and Literature* 13 (1931): 1–8, suggests that the Old English lines may also indicate knowledge by Ælfric of Bede's *In Pentateuchum Leviticum* (PL 91, cols. 345–46).

65   *that we should divide our hooves in those two testaments*: This passage clearly caused some difficulty for the scribe of E and has been expanded on by the points corrector in W. Ælfric seems to be admonishing his audience to divide their attention and their observances between the two covenants, the Old and the New Testaments.

77   *All things are clean to the clean*: Titus 1:15. The theme is also found in Romans 14:20, as Stuart Lee notes in the commentary to his edition.

80   *it has claws*: Leviticus 11:4 and 11:26 make it clear that ungulate animals whose hooves are not divided (11:26, *omne animal quod habet quidem ungulam sed non dividet*) are unclean; Leviticus 11:6 is more specific and names the hare: *lepus quoque nam et ipse ruminat sed ungulam non dividit* (the hare also for it chews the cud but does not divide the claw). It is possible that there is some corruption in the Old English text at this point, for in all three surviving manuscripts it states that the hare is *clifer-fete*, literally, "claw-footed," but does not stipulate that the hoof or claw is undivided. One would expect something in keeping with line 62 and the description of those animals deemed unclean, *þe ne tocleofað heora clawa þeah ðe hi cudu ceowan* (that do not divide the hooves though they chew the cud). Since all three manuscripts are unanimous in their reading, however, it is also possible that Ælfric expected an Anglo-Saxon reader to know that the claws of the hare were not cloven and felt no need to expand on it.

109–200   The story of the seven brothers is found at 2 Maccabees 7.

115   *our creator's law*: The Latin refers to the *Dei leges* ("laws of God," 2 Maccabees 7:2).

125   *the fifth book*: Deuteronomy. Compare Deuteronomy 32, a canticle sung by Moses for the remembrance of the law.

God will comfort his servants: In the Old English Ælfric states that God will comfort his servants, but in the Latin of the Vulgate, however, God finds comfort or pleasure in his servants: *Et in servis suis consolabitur* ("And in his servants he will take pleasure," 2 Maccabees 7:6).

139 *his commandments*: Compare *Dei leges* ("laws of God," 2 Maccabees 7:11).

201 *Lammas day*: Lammas day (*Hlaf-mæssan dæg*, "bread-Mass day") was a celebration to mark the wheat harvest.

title W separates this section with the simple heading *ITEM* (in the same manner), which is included in the Old English section of the text in this volume; on the facing translation page, however, the title recorded in Wanley's transcription of f^k is also used.

209–74 1 Maccabees 2:1–70.

217 *Mathathias*: The Old English describes Mathathias as *ðam fore-sædan ðegene* (literally, "the aforementioned servant"), having described him above as *sum heah Godes þægn* (a high-ranking servant of God). The term *þegn* can be difficult to translate: within an Anglo-Saxon context it referred to the rank of nobility below the ealdorman, but the force of the term within an Old Testament context is difficult to ascertain. The circumlocution makes it clear Ælfric is referring to Mathathias.

254 *and that justified him*: The Vulgate here reads *et reputatum est ei ad iustitiam* ("and it was reputed to him unto justice," 1 Maccabees 2:52), an echo of Genesis 15:6, *Credidit Abram Deo et reputatum est illi ad iustitiam* (Abram believed God and it was reputed him unto justice).

259 *valiantly*: Vulgate *viriliter* (1 Maccabees 2:64).

271 *and observe God's law with good practices*: The Latin reads *intendite in praeceptum legis* ("take heed to the precepts of the law," 1 Maccabees 2:68). For a similar use of *godum biggengum*, see the *Prayer of Moses* (LS 12), line 114: *and mid godum biggencgum Gode gecweme* (and pleasing God with good practices).

275–385 1 Maccabees 3:1–4:54.

288 *his people, who were called Jacob*: After wrestling with the angel, Jacob was given the name Israel (Genesis 32:28).

289   *the furthest land*: Compare *ad novissimum terrae* ("to the utmost part of the earth," 1 Maccabees 3:9).

334   *seven thousand heavily armed*: According to the Vulgate, the seven thousand soldiers were on horseback: *quadraginta milia virorum et septem milia equitum* ("forty thousand men and seven thousand horsemen," 1 Maccabees 3:39).

345   *our sanctuary*: *Sancta nostra* (1 Maccabees 3:59).

360   *purple cloth*: A sign of influence and prestige in the Roman world.

374   *Overthrow them with the swords of those who love you*: 1 Maccabees 4:33 reads, *Deice eos gladio diligentium te* (Cast them down with the sword of them that love thee).

386–459   1 Maccabees 5:1–68.

400   *a troop*: The Old English *fultum*, "help" or "support," can also have the sense of "military support, a troop, or an army."

460–81   2 Maccabees 12:39–46.

482–508   2 Maccabees 10:24–38.

531–96   1 Maccabees 6:1–7:4.

549   *Eupator:* Antiochus V Eupator succeeded his father, Antiochus IV, as ruler of the Greek Seleucid Empire (163–161 BCE).

595   *Demetrius:* Demetrius I Soter (185–150 BCE) ruled from 161 to 150 BCE.

597–647   1 Maccabees 7:4–8:17.

597   *Alcimus:* Alcimus was a high priest of Israel (162–159 BCE) and a supporter of the Syrians.

648–78   1 Maccabees 9:1–22.

651   *Bacchides*: A Hellenistic Greek general sent by Demetrius to establish Alcimus as high priest in Jerusalem.

716–28   1 Maccabees 9:28–56.

729–33   1 Maccabees 12:23.

734–41   1 Maccabees 14:4 and 16:19.

742–45   1 Maccabees 16:21–24.

746–806   2 Maccabees 3:1–40.

751   *Seleucus:* Seleucus IV Philopater, son of Antiochus III, ruled from 187 to 175 BCE as the predecessor to Antiochus IV.

title   "On the Three Orders of Society" is a translation of R's heading, *DE TRIBUS ORDINIBUS SAECULI*. W reads *ITEM ALIA* (another in the same manner), and C and E read *QUI SINT ORATORES, LABORATORES, BELLATORES* (those who pray, work, and fight).

834   *Julian:* Julian the Apostate was Roman emperor from 361 to 363 CE.

844   *those dearest to him*: There is ambiguity in the Old English here as to whether *his leofestan menn* (his dearest people/men) are the centurion's household or his soldiers.